Civil Procedure in Nigeria

Civil Procedure in Nigeria

Caroline Omochavwe Oba

This book was originally published as a monograph in the International Encyclopaedia of Laws/Civil Procedure.

Founding Editor: Roger Blanpain
General Editor: Frank Hendrickx
Volume Editor: Wannes Vandenbussche

Wolters Kluwer

Published by:
Kluwer Law International B.V.
PO Box 316
2400 AH Alphen aan den Rijn
The Netherlands
E-mail: lrs-sales@wolterskluwer.com
Website: www.wolterskluwer.com/en/solutions/kluwerlawinternational

Sold and distributed by:
Wolters Kluwer Legal & Regulatory U.S.
7201 McKinney Circle
Frederick, MD 21704
United States of America
E-mail: customer.service@wolterskluwer.com

ISBN 978-94-035-4621-6

e-Book: ISBN 978-94-035-4382-6
web-PDF: ISBN 978-94-035-4812-8

The Author

Dr Caroline Omochavwe Oba holds a Doctoral Degree in Law from the University of Jos, Nigeria. She is currently the Deputy Director General and Head of Nigerian Law School Yenagoa Campus. She has taught Civil Litigation at the Nigerian Law School for over sixteen years. She has written on a wide range of topics in civil procedural law in both national and international journals and book chapters. She is one of the editors of the *Civil Litigation Practice Handbook* published by the Council of Legal Education in Nigeria. She was admitted to the Nigerian Bar in 2000 and has considerable experience as an attorney. She is a member of the Nigerian Bar Association and the National Association of Law Teachers in Nigeria. She is married with children.

The Author

Table of Contents

Table of Contents

List of Abbreviations

1999 Nigerian Constn	1999 Constitution of the Federal Republic of Nigeria as amended
ACA	Arbitration and Conciliation Act
AG	Attorney General
AGF	Attorney General of the Federation
AFWLR	All Federation Weekly Law Report
AMDC	Abuja Multi-Door Courthouse
ANOR	Another
ANLR	All Nigerian Law Report
Art.	Article
CA	Court of Appeal of Nigeria
Cap	Chapter
CBN	Central Bank of Nigeria
CPD	Continuing Professional Development
FED	Federal
FUT	Federal University of Technology
HC	High Court
HCCPR	High Court Civil Procedure Rules
HCCPR Abuja	High Court Civil Procedure Rules of the Federal Capital Territory Abuja 2018
HCCPR Lagos	High Court Civil Procedure Rules of Lagos State 2019
JUSUN	Judicial Staff Union of Nigeria
LAC	Legal Aid Council
LFN	Laws of the Federation of Nigeria
LMDC	Lagos Multi-Door Courthouse
LPA	Legal Practitioners Act
LPDC	Legal Practitioners Disciplinary Committee
LPELR	Law Pavilion Electronic Law Report
NBA	Nigerian Bar Association
NCR	Nigerian Criminal Reports

List of Abbreviations

NIN	National Identification Number
NJC	National Judicial Council
NMLR	Nigerian Monthly Law Report
NWLR	Nigerian Weekly Law Report
NSCC	Nigerian Supreme Court Cases
ORS	Others
Pt	Part
RPC	Rules of Professional Conduct
SC	Supreme Court of Nigeria
SCNJ	Supreme Court of Nigeria Judgment
SCNLR	Supreme Court of Nigeria Law Report
SCPA	Sheriff and Civil Process Act

Preface

This monograph on civil procedure in Nigeria is designed to provide students, academics, lawyers and other interested persons with accessible, clear and needful information on the laws regulating civil litigation in Nigeria. The increasing need internationally for information enabling comparative studies of procedural laws of different countries has made this work imperative.

Nigeria, a former colony of Britain, has had her legal system greatly influenced by English rules of practice and procedure. Nonetheless, Nigeria has over the years since her independence developed unique laws and rules that guide civil proceedings in Nigerian courts. Nigeria practises a federal system of government, and by that, the laws and rules of states courts are within the legislative preserve of the relevant authorities in each of the thirty-six states of the Federation. The extant laws/rules regulating civil proceedings in these state courts and in the Federal Capital Territory, Abuja, are however similar in substance. The constraint of the written material permitted for this work has meant that the laws/rules of civil proceedings in state courts in the thirty-six states cannot all be mentioned, but the ones analysed sufficiently represent the others. As such, this work will give readers the necessary insights into the practice and procedure of civil litigation in Nigeria.

The work is divided into eleven parts with each part addressing specific areas of procedure in civil proceedings in Nigeria both at trial and on appeal. The work also provides information on alternative means of resolving disputes in Nigeria other than litigation. In addition, vital information on the various actors that drive the administration of justice in civil proceedings ranging from Judges, Magistrates and Registrars to legal practitioners are also provided.

This monograph is a product of in-depth research drawn from close to two decades of teaching civil procedure at the Nigerian Law School and practice of law, and it is hoped that the reader finds this particular monograph both beneficial and enlightening.

I would like to express my gratitude to Prof. Isa Hayatu Chiroma SAN, the Director-General of the Nigerian Law School, for encouraging intellectual pursuits among the academic faculty of the institution. My appreciation goes to the Head of Academics at the Nigerian Law School Abuja Campus, Mr S.A. Osamolu, Mrs M.O. Egbe and Mr P.C. Okorie for their support and encouragement.

To my husband Hon Justice Christopher Oba and God's heritage in our custody Isaac and Awesome, I say thank you for your love and support.

As an author, I have endeavoured to minimize the errors in this work. However, I take responsibility for any errors discovered by readers.

General Introduction

§1. General Background

I. Geographical Background

1. Nigeria, which is officially known as the Federal Republic of Nigeria, is located in West Africa and is bounded in the west by the Republic of Benin, in the east by Chad and Cameroon, in the north and north-east by Niger and Lake Chad respectively and in the south by the Gulf of Guinea. Its total compact area is estimated at about 923,768 square kilometres.[1]

2. As of 2019, Nigeria's population is estimated at over 200.96 million people.[2] It is the most populous country in West Africa and the seventh in the world. It is reputed to be the most populous black nation on earth. The country has about 250 different languages and ethnic nationalities with three major ethnic groups, namely the Yorubas, the Igbos and the Hausas.

3. Geographically, and for political convenience, the country is divided into six geo-political zones namely: the south-south, the south-west, the south-east, the north-central, the north-west and the north-east.

II. Historical Background

4. Based on archaeological evidence, parts of Nigeria have been inhabited by man as far back as the Stone Age which is the period between 500,000 and 9,000 B.C.[3] The findings suggest that the people who occupied the territory now known as Nigeria during this age bear the same physical and cultural semblance with the people of present-day Nigeria.

5. Nigeria is a former colony of Britain, which became one entity as now known in 1914, following the amalgamation of the Northern and Southern Protectorate. The name Nigeria is said to have been derived from the River Niger, which runs

---

1. *See* http://worldpopulationreview.com/countries/nigeria-population/, accessed 4:46 pm on 20 Oct. 2019.
2. *Ibid.*
3. *See* http://www.nigeria.gov.ng/index.php/2016-04-06-08-38-30/history-of-nigeria, accessed 4:50 pm on 20 Oct. 2019.

through the whole country.[4] The River Niger is one of the longest rivers in Africa. The predominant group in the north of Nigeria is the Hausa.

6. Nigeria attained independence from British rule in 1960 and became a Republic on 1 October 1963. Given its colonial background, the lingua franca in Nigeria is the English language. The country is a secular state and has Christianity and Islamic religion as the two major religions.

7. On the international sphere, Nigeria is a member of the Economic Community of West African States, one of the founding members of the African Union, and is a member of the United Nations.

III. Legal System

8. Nigeria practised a federal system of government even before its independence by the Nigerian (Constitution) Order in Council 1960 No. 1652. This gave birth to the Federal Constitution of 1960 under a parliamentary system where each of the regions (three in number namely the Northern, Western and Eastern Regions) had its own constitution. The Republican Constitution of 1963 retained the same political structure but the regions increased to four, with the creation of the Midwestern Region. The military took over power in 1966 and practised expectedly a unitary system of government because of the command structure of the military. The military was in control of the affairs of the country from then to 1979 when a President was elected under a federal system of government. There was another incursion by the military from 1983 to 1999. However, on 29 May 1999, the military handed power back to a democratically elected government, and the country is currently under democratic rule.

9. This checkered political history has also impacted the legal system of the country. When the military was in power, the provisions of the Constitution of the country (which is the ground norm) were suspended, and the Nigerian State was governed by decrees. When Nigeria operated a regional system of government, the three regions operated autonomously. The parliament of the three regions made laws for the governance of the regions. In 1971, the regional system was changed, and twelve states were created out of the entity called Nigeria. This was further increased to nineteen states and the Federal Capital Territory in 1976, and further to thirty-six states and the Federal Capital Territory in 1999. Nigeria currently operates the 1999 Constitution as amended (1999 Nigerian Constn).

10. The 1999 Nigerian Constn creates three tiers of public powers both at the federal and state levels, namely the executive, legislative and judicial powers. The executive power is exerted by the President of the Federal Republic of Nigeria (the

4. The British journalist Flora Shaw who later became the wife of Frederick Lugard, the British administrator who is credited with the amalgamation of the Northern and Southern Protectorate.

President also exercises this power in the main through the ministers, heads of ministries, departments and agencies) at the federal level and by the Governors of the thirty-six states (the Governors also exercises their powers through commissioners, heads of ministries, department and agencies) at the state level. The President and the Governors are elected by Nigerians into the office for a term of four years and can be re-elected for another term of four years.

11. The legislative powers are exercised by the legislature made up of members of the National Assembly at the federal level and of the State Houses of Assembly at the state level. The National Assembly is made up of the Senate (109 senators in all) and the House of Representatives (made up of 365 members). The number of legislators at each State House of Assembly is dependent on the delineation of the state into constituencies, which is a function of population. The legislators are elected by Nigerians for a term of four years and can be re-elected as many times as possible. The President and the Governors also exercise some form of legislative power, as their assent is required for bills passed by the National or State Houses respectively to become laws. This power of the President and the Governors comes up at the last stage of the legislative procedure. In the main, the President gives his assent to most bills passed but has withheld assent to a number of bills. In instances where the President or the Governors withhold their assent to a bill, the relevant legislature can veto their powers. In practice, this is a very difficult task for the legislators to undertake and is hardly ever done. When a bill has been passed into law, it is published in the appropriate official gazette in English, which is Nigeria's official language.

12. The judiciary made up of federal and state courts of different hierarchies exercises judicial powers in Nigeria. For discussion on the hierarchy of courts in Nigeria, *see* below paragraphs 22–23 and 80. The courts in Nigeria are not categorized into ordinary courts or constitutional courts or the likes. The same court that hears ordinary matters can hear constitutional matters. All the superior courts of record established under the 1999 Nigerian Constn can entertain constitutional cases alongside any other kind of action for which jurisdiction has been conferred on them. The courts in Nigeria apply federal or state laws whichever are applicable, regional instruments that Nigeria has domesticated and treatises to which Nigeria is a signatory.

13. Under Part 1 of the Second Schedule to the 1999 Nigerian Constn, the federal legislature solely makes laws for the federation on matters listed under the exclusive legislative list. With respect to matters under the concurrent list in Part 1 of the Second Schedule to the 1999 Nigerian Constn, the National Assembly makes laws for the federation including laws applicable in federal courts and in the courts in the Federal Capital Territory. Both the National Assembly and the various State Houses of Assembly can legislate on matters listed in the concurrent legislative list.

14. A state in the federation is at liberty to adopt a law made by the federal legislature as state law. Where there is a conflict between the provisions of federal law and state law with regard to matters under the concurrent list, the position of the law is that the law made by the National Assembly shall prevail, and the state law will be void to the extent of the inconsistency.[5] However, where a State House of Assembly legislates on an area where the National Assembly had legislated on for the Federation, the state law will be inoperative while the federal law exists. In situations like this, the courts have held that the federal law will be said to have covered the field with respect to the issue legislated upon and the particular provision of the state law will be inoperative during the lifespan of the federal law.[6] Matters provided for in the residual list of Part 1 of the Second Schedule to the 1999 Constn are strictly under the purview of the state legislature to legislate on.

15. As a former colony of Britain, Nigeria is a common law country, and English law has greatly influenced its legal jurisprudence. As such there are many English law principles embedded in Nigerian legal architecture including civil procedure.

§2. Delimitation of the Subject Matter

I. Definition of the Term 'Civil Procedure'

16. Civil procedure refers to the body of rules that guide the conduct of civil proceedings in court. It covers issues such as the courts having jurisdiction over civil proceedings, how civil actions are commenced and prosecuted, how decisions are given by the court, how these decisions are enforced by the court, how such decisions are appealed against and the conduct of the appeal. As a body of laws, it assists the court in its task of adjudication of issues in contention before it.

17. Civil procedure forms part of adjectival law like criminal procedure as opposed to substantive law. The nexus between the two types of law is that while substantive law defines the rights and obligations of parties in an action, adjective law like the civil procedure is the means by which these rights and obligations are enforced.

II. Distinction Between Civil Procedure and Other Types of Procedure

A. Civil Procedure and Administrative Procedure

18. The purpose of administrative procedure is to review an agency or body decision. This could either be to grant or deny a permit or licence or an approval or rule. At the end of the hearing, a recommendation is made to the agency or body concerned for it to take the final action whereas a civil procedure is aimed at determining whether one party is liable to the other. Another distinction lies in the fact that the sanctions or decisions made through a civil procedure are carried out by the courts while that of an administrative procedure is by a non-judicial body.

---

5. Section 4(5) of the 1999 Nigerian Constn.
6. *EDOSACA v. Osakue* (2018) 16 NWLR (Pt) 1645 199 (CA).

B. Civil Procedure and Disciplinary Procedure

19. The purpose of a disciplinary procedure is to find out whether an individual's behaviour is in violation of the rules of conduct of a particular profession. For example, proceedings before the Legal Practitioners Disciplinary Committee (LPDC) are to ascertain whether the conduct of a legal practitioner is in violation of the rules of professional conduct (RPC) for lawyers in Nigeria. The LPDC is a non-judicial body. This is not the case with civil proceedings.

C. Civil Procedure and Criminal Procedure

20. Every proceeding in a court in Nigeria is either a civil case or a criminal one. However, whereas civil procedure regulates proceedings relating to the enforcement of private rights that is commenced by individuals or juristic persons in their names, criminal procedure regulates proceedings relating to the enforcement of public rights usually commenced by or on behalf of public authorities like a state in Nigeria or the Federal Government of Nigeria.

III. Separate Court Systems and Rules of Procedure in Nigeria

21. In Nigeria, we have superior and inferior courts of records. The superior courts of records are courts created under the Nigerian Constn. The inferior courts of records are created by the laws of the various states based on the power given to the states under the Constn.

22. At the top of the ladder of superior courts of record is the Supreme Court of Nigeria (hereafter 'SC'). There is only one Supreme Court in Nigeria, and it is situated in the nation's capital Abuja. Next is the Court of Appeal of Nigeria. There is one Court of Appeal of Nigeria, but it sits in different divisions with each division having a presiding justice. There are currently sixteen divisions of the Court of Appeal in Nigeria. Following this court is the Federal HC. On the same hierarchy with the Federal HC is the HC of the Federal Capital Territory, Abuja, the HC of states, the National Industrial Court, the Sharia Court of Appeal, and the Customary Court of Appeal. These are all courts of co-ordinate jurisdiction. This means in the hierarchy of courts, these courts are on the same level. However, the Constn and any statute establishing them confer each with specific areas of jurisdiction.

23. The inferior courts of records are the courts not expressly created by the Constn but are established under state laws. They are the Magistrates'\District Courts, Upper Area Court, Area Courts, Customary Courts, Area Customary Courts, Sharia Courts and Mobile Courts. The Magistrates' Courts in the northern part of Nigeria are referred to as District Courts when exercising their civil jurisdiction. When the court is exercising its criminal jurisdiction, the same presiding officer is referred to as a Magistrate but called a District Judge when presiding over civil claims. The Customary Court including the Customary Court of Appeal is mainly found in the southern part of the country while the Area and Sharia courts are found in the north. But some states in the north like Plateau State have Customary Courts in addition to Area and Sharia Courts. For a detailed discussion on the various courts *see* paragraphs 82–95. Different courts have their civil proceedings regulated by distinct rules of court. These rules are made by the heads of the various courts based on the powers conferred on them by the Constn. For example, the Chief Justice of Nigeria makes the SC Rules;[7] the President of the Court of Appeal makes the Court of Appeal Rules;[8] the Chief Judge of the various states and that of the Federal Capital Territory, Abuja, make the Civil Procedure Rules for the HC and the inferior courts of record in their respective jurisdictions.

24. The HCs in the various states of the Federation and the Federal Capital Territory have their own Civil Procedure Rules. It is impracticable within the confines of the volume of this work to refer to the High Court Civil Procedure Rules (HCCPR) of the thirty-six states and the Federal Capital Territory. The work will only refer to the HCCPR of Lagos State and the HC of the Federal Capital Territory, Abuja for practicability and ease of reference. The choice of these two jurisdictions is due to the strategic position they occupied as the legal hobnob of Nigeria and the capital city respectively, and the two jurisdictions represent the southern and northern parts of the country. Moreover, the HCCPR of the various states are similar in content, and reference to the HCCPR of Lagos and Abuja substantially represents the procedure in civil proceedings in any HC in Nigeria.

§3. Sources of Civil Procedure

I. Brief Historical Perspective of Sources of Civil Procedure in Nigeria

25. There are various sources of civil procedure law in Nigeria. The chief of them is the Rules of court. Each court in Nigeria has its own Rules of court or as it is mostly called civil procedure rules. In addition, apart from the federal courts, which have the same Rules of court applied throughout the federation, the relevant authorities in the various states make rules for courts created by states. As such, each state has its own Rules of court regulating civil proceedings in different courts. Rules of court have been a source of civil procedure in Nigeria for a long time. From the 1963 Nigerian Republican Constitution down to the extant Constn, which is the 1999 Nigerian Constn as amended, there are provisions empowering the heads of courts,[9] the Parliament,[10] the National Assembly[11] or the House of Assembly of a state[12] to make rules for the practice and procedure of the various courts.

7. Section 236 of the 1999 Nigerian Constn.
8. Section 248 of the 1999 Nigerian Constn.
9. Section 122(2) of the 1963 Nigerian Constitution, ss 216 and 227 of the 1979 Nigerian Constitution, ss 236 and 248 of the 1999 Nigerian Constn.
10. Section 122(3) of the 1963 Constn.
11. Section 233 of the 1979 Constn.
12. Sections 239 and 244 of the 1979 Constn.

26. An attempt was made in 1987 to have uniform civil procedure rules for the HCs throughout the country, but this did not succeed. The thirty-six states of the federation of Nigeria and the Federal Capital Territory, Abuja, all have their own HCCPR. The same applies to the inferior courts of record like the Magistrates' Court, Customary Court, District Court and Sharia Court.

A. *Rules of Court*

27. Procedural regulations guiding civil proceedings are contained in the rules of the various courts in Nigeria. Rules of court regulate how civil claims are commenced, conducted and determined, judgments are enforced and appeals against decisions are made in civil litigation to ensure the smooth running of the judicial process. They are the main source of civil procedure in Nigeria.

28. Rules of court are to be observed and obeyed in such a way as to achieve a just, effective and expeditious dispensation of justice. In the order of precedence of legislations, statutes take precedence over Rules of court. However, the courts have held that where a Rule of court is made through powers conferred on the enacting authority by the 1999 Nigerian Constn, then such Rules take precedence over statutes.[13] In that light, where there is a conflict between provisions in such Rules and a statute, the provisions in such Rules will prevail.

29. The different levels of courts in Nigeria have different Rules of courts regulating civil proceedings. In addition, the thirty-six states in Nigeria and the Federal Capital Territory all have their different HCCPR. Examples of Rules of court include the Magistrates' Court Civil Procedure Rules of various states (such as Magistrate Court Civil Procedure Rules of Lagos State 2009), District Court Rules of the various states in the north and the Federal Capital Territory, Abuja (such as the District Court Rules of the Federal Capital Territory, Abuja),[14] the HCCPR of various states (such as the High Court Civil Procedure Rules of Lagos State 2019 (HCCPR Lagos) and the High Court Civil Procedure Rules of the Federal Capital Territory, Abuja 2018 (HCCPR Abuja)), National Industrial Court (Civil Procedure) Rules 2016, Customary Court of Appeal Rules of the various states in the south and the Federal Capital Territory, Abuja, the Sharia Court of Appeal Rules of the various states in the north and the Federal Capital Territory, Abuja, the Federal HCCPR 2019, the Court of Appeal of Nigeria Rules 2016 and the Supreme Court Rules 1985 as amended. The heads of these courts make these rules as empowered by the Constn or the laws setting them up.

30. Where there is a lacuna in the Rules, the courts adopt such procedure that will in its view do substantial justice between the parties concerned.[15]

---

13. *Abia State University v. Ayaibe* (1996) 3 NWLR (Pt 439) 646 at 661 (CA).
14. Cap 495 Laws of the Federation of Nigeria (Abuja) 1990.
15. Section 2 HCCPR Abuja 2018 and Order 1 Rule 1(3) HCCPR of Lagos State 2012.

B. *Statutes Creating Courts*

31. Some statutes creating some court provide for the procedure in some aspect of the civil litigation in such court. Some examples are the Court of Appeal Act that provides for time within which to appeal against the decision of an HC to the Court of Appeal[16] and the Magistrates' Court Law of Lagos State 2009 that provides that counsel should write a demand letter before commencing an action.[17]

C. *The 1999 Nigerian Constitution as Amended*

32. The Nigerian Constitution contains some provisions regulating the procedure in civil cases. For example, it provides for when an appeal can come to the Court of Appeal from the Federal HC / HC of states / HC of the Federal Capital Territory, Abuja as of right or with leave of court.[18]

D. *Decisions of Courts*

33. Some decisions of the superior courts of records, especially the SC, have provided for the procedure to be followed in certain circumstances in a civil trial. This usually happens when the relevant statutes or Rules of court do not make provision for such issues. For example, in the case of *Marian A Craig v. Victor Craig*,[19] the SC laid down the procedure to be adopted before a trial court can make an order of non-suit, which is that the court should invite the parties or their counsel to address it on the propriety or otherwise of making the order. It is subsequent to this decision that some HC rules incorporated this procedure in their rules.[20]

E. *Practice Directions*

34. This is a direction given by the appropriate authority (usually the head of the particular court) on how particular provisions in the Rules of court should be complied with. In *University of Lagos v. Aigoro*,[21] it was held that Practice Directions provide useful insights as to how to carry out provisions in Rules of court. In recent times, the heads of some of the superior courts of record have been using Practice Directions to make far-reaching provisions for the practice and procedure of the courts that they preside over. Ideally, these provisions ought to be contained in the Rules of court and not in a Practice Direction. A good example is the HCCPR

---

16. Section 24(2)(b) of the Court of Appeal Act Cap C 36 Laws of the Federation of Nigeria (LFN) 2004.
17. Section 38(2) Magistrate Court Law of Lagos State 2009.
18. Section 241(1)(2) of the 1999 Nigerian Constn.
19. (1966) 1 ANLR 173 (SC).
20. Order 38 of the HCCPR Lagos and Abuja.
21. (1984) 11 SC 152.

Lagos, which came with two Practice Directions[22] containing extensive procedural steps with respect to some of the provisions in the Rules. Where there is a conflict between a Practice Direction and the Rules, the provisions of the Rules prevail.

F. *Special Statutes on Procedure*

35. There are some statutes that regulate specific aspects of a civil trial or specific proceedings. These include the Sheriff and Civil Process Act[23] (SCPA) which makes provisions for service of court processes outside the jurisdiction and enforcement of all types of judgment in Nigeria, Foreign Judgment (Reciprocal Enforcement) Act which regulates enforcement of foreign judgments, Company Winding up Rules which deals with winding-up proceedings of a company, the Matrimonial Causes Act which deals with matrimonial proceedings, Fundamental Rights Enforcement Procedure Rules which provides for how a person can enforce their rights as contained in the Constn and other legal instruments.

§4. General Features of the Administration of Justice in Civil Matters

I. Characteristics of the Procedure

36. The administration of justice in civil procedure in Nigeria has some distinct characteristics, which are discussed below.

A. *Adversary Procedure*

37. Civil procedure like the adjudicatory system in Nigeria generally is adversarial. An adversarial system of justice is one that involves parties putting forward their respective cases before an impartial arbiter who decides in favour of one party based on the strength of the party's case. An adversarial system has been defined as, one involving active and unhindered parties contesting with each other to put forth a case before an independent decision-maker.[24] The parties are allowed to conduct their cases in the ways they deem fit. They can do so in person or through a counsel of their choice. At the end of every civil suit in court, the arbiter hands down a decision, which favours one of the parties, as against the other. This is opposed to an inquisitorial system of adjudication where the judge is in charge of the trial proceedings and is the one who determines which questions should be asked and generally defines the scope of the inquiry.

22. High Court of Lagos State Expeditious Disposal of Civil Cases Practice Direction No. 1 of 2019 Backlog Elimination Programme and High Court of Lagos State (Expeditious Disposal of Civil Cases) Practice Direction No. 2 of 2019 Pre-action Protocol.
23. Cap S6 LFN 2004.
24. B.A. Garner (ed.), *Black's Law Dictionary* 58 (8th ed., West 2004).

B. Role of the Judge and of the Parties

38. The major feature of the adversary system of adjudication practised in Nigeria is the passive and inactive role of the judge in the presentation of cases in court. This position has been given judicial acknowledgement in the case of *Osude v. Azodo*[25] where the SC stated that: 'the role of the judge in a case is at best that of an attentive listener to all that is said by both sides … and the judge speaks mainly to deliver judgment'.[26] The judge in an adversary system is regarded as an impartial umpire. Though judges are in charge of the courts that they preside over, the judges are not allowed to take over the conduct of the case from the parties. The judge must not be seen to be descending into the arena of conflict. The impartiality of the judge is so important that it is enshrined in the 1999 Nigerian Constn.[27] The judge is to dispassionately look at all the facts and evidence before it, evaluate them, apply the law and then put them on an imaginary scale. The party, in whose favour the scale tilts, then gets a judgment in his favour.

39. Since parties win or lose based on the strength of their respective cases, it is their duty to put before the court all evidence that will help establish their case and sway the mind of the judge in their favour. They must put before the court the facts, evidence and laws that support their case. Also, they are required to bring to the attention of the court laws or decisions of superior courts that are not in their favour. In such a case, the party putting forward an adverse position could distinguish it from the current case before the court and give the court reasons why such a position should not be applied by the court. The claimant must prove his case on the balance of probabilities and cannot rely on the defendant's failure to get their claims granted by the court.

40. The impartial disposition of the judge does not take away the responsibility of the court on its motion raise issues, which the parties did not address in their submissions. However, upon raising such issues, the judge is under obligation to call on the parties to address the court on those issues. Besides, when evaluating the evidence admitted before it in the course of writing its ruling or judgment, a judge is duty-bound to apply the applicable laws irrespective of whether the parties had referred the court to such laws or not. This is because a court of law is obliged to take judicial notice of all laws or enactments and subsidiary enactments made under them in force or previously in force in Nigeria.[28]

C. Oral and Written Procedure

41. In civil proceedings, some aspects of the proceedings adopt the written procedure while others involve the oral procedure. At the inception of the case, the

25. (2017) 15 NWLR (Pt 1588) 293 (SC).
26. *Supra* at p. 319.
27. Section 36(1) of the 1999 Nigerian Constn.
28. Section 122 of the Evidence Act 2011.

claimant and the defendant are required to file their claims and defences respectively in court in a written form. This is done for example by the claimant filing a writ of summons together with the supporting documents and the defendant filing in response, a statement of defence and the supporting documents.

42. Pretrial proceedings are also in written form. Where there is a need to make interlocutory applications, the parties file their motions in written form and move the court orally to grant their application.

43. However, during the trial, in the examination of witnesses and the parties, a major part of the proceedings is by oral testimony. This will generally apply to proceedings initiated by writ of summons or petitions in the HCs or claims in the Magistrates' Courts.

44. There are, however, some proceedings that generally do not admit oral testimony. Actions commenced by originating summons and origination motions do not normally require examination of witnesses. The court determines the issues between the parties on the basis of the affidavit evidence before the court, the exhibits and the written addresses. Oral testimony will only be required in such proceedings when there are conflicts in the affidavit evidence.

45. The mode adopted in commencing an action is determined by the nature of the claim of the claimant and the requirement of the law. For example, the Rules of court require the use of a writ of summons for contentious matters while matters that are not likely to be contentious such as interpretation of a statute or written instrument can be commenced by an originating summons.[29]

II. Fundamental Guarantees

46. There are fundamental guarantees that assure litigants of justice in the litigation process. The 1999 Nigerian Constn provides for some guarantees, others are contained under international treaties and reciprocal arrangements and others evolved by general principles of law and practice. Some of these fundamental guarantees are provided for in the 1999 Nigerian Constitution and others form part of the general principle of law.

A. *Constitutional Guarantees*

1. Establishment of Courts by the Constitution or Law

47. The 1999 Nigerian Constn as amended provides for the establishment of superior courts of records and permits the National Assembly or State Houses of

29. Order 2 Rules 2 and 3 HCCPR Abuja and Order 5 Rules 1 and 4 HCCPR Lagos.

Assembly to establish inferior courts of record in Nigeria.[30] By this provision, judicial powers of the federation are vested with the federal courts while judicial powers of a state are vested with the state courts. The judicial powers vested on courts in Nigeria extend to all inherent powers and sanctions of a court of law notwithstanding anything to the contrary in the 1999 Nigerian Constn. It also extends to all matters among persons or between government or any person in Nigeria, to all actions and proceedings for the determination of the civil rights and obligations of such person.

48. The judicial powers of the courts in Nigeria does not however extend to any issue or question as to whether any act or omission by any authority or person or as to whether any law or any judicial decision is in conformity with the Fundamental Objectives and Directive Principles of State Policy set out in Chapter 11 of the 1999 Nigerian Constn, and the power of the court shall not extend to entertaining matters relating to any existing law made on or after 15 January 1966 as to the competence of any authority or person to make such law.[31]

2. Independence and Impartiality of the Courts

49. The 1999 Nigerian Constn provides that a court of law should be constituted in such a manner to secure its independence and impartiality.[32] This provision is basic and makes forum shopping unacceptable. Where a judge or any of the justices in a judicial panel has any connection with any of the litigants, they shall excuse themselves from presiding over the case. There must not be any appearance of interference with the impartiality of a judge in the exercise of the judge's duties. Also where a judge had handled a matter as a legal practitioner before being appointed as a judge, such a judge must be excused in the event that the same matter comes before the judge's court. This is because 'justice must not only be done it must also be seen to be done'.

3. Publicity of Trials

50. The 1999 Nigerian Constn provides that proceedings of a court or tribunal in the determination of a person's civil rights and obligations including any question or determination by or against any government or authority from commencement to the announcement of the decision of the court or tribunal shall be held in public.[33]

---

30. Section 6 of the 1999 Nigerian Constn as amended by s. 2 of the Constitution of the Federal Republic of Nigeria (Third Alteration) Act 2010.
31. Section 6(6)(c–d) of the 1999 Nigerian Constn.
32. Section 36(1) of the 1999 Nigerian Constn.
33. Section 36(3) of the 1999 Nigerian Constn.

51. A proceeding is held in public where the venue for the court sitting is open to members of the public including the press. However, the guarantee is not an absolute one. A court can exclude from its proceedings persons other than the parties in the action and their legal practitioners in any of the following circumstances:[34]

(a) in the interest of defence;
(b) for reasons of public safety;
(c) for reasons of public order;
(d) for reasons of public morality;
(e) regarding issues of the welfare of persons who have not attained the age of 18;
(f) for reasons of protection of the private lives of the parties; and
(g) to such extent as the court may consider necessary by reasons of special circumstances in which publicity would be contrary to the interest of justice.

52. The limitation on this guarantee of publicity of trials allows a Minister of the Federal Government of Nigeria or a Commissioner in the Government of a state to apply to the court that it is not in the public interest for a proceeding to be held in public. Where the court is satisfied that the application has merit, it will make arrangements for evidence relating to the matter to be heard in private and shall take such other action as may be necessary or expedient to prevent the disclosure of the matter.

53. The HCCPR provides that subject to the provisions of the 1999 Nigerian Constn, a judge may for special reasons hear a particular cause or matter in the presence only of the parties, with their legal practitioners, if any, and the officers of the court.[35] Due to the COVID-19 pandemic, the NJC has approved remote hearings for all courts in Nigeria through platforms like Skype, Zoom, Microsoft Team, etc.[36] Flowing from these guidelines, some courts have come up with Practice Directions to regulate remote hearings of certain proceedings such as matters that are decided on the basis of affidavit evidence, urgent interlocutory applications, fundamental rights enforcement matters, adoption of final written addresses and delivery of judgment.[37] Whether remote hearing of cases can be accommodated within the confines of the 1999 Nigerian Constn requirement for the public hearing has been pronounced upon by the SC in the cases of *Attorney General of Lagos State v. Attorney General of the Federation & Anor*[38] and *Attorney General of Ekiti State v. Attorney*

34. Section 33(4) of the I999 Nigerian Constn. This exception relate to criminal trials. There is no reason while it should not apply to civil trials given that the origin of the principle behind the need for public trials relates mainly to criminal trials.
35. Order 49 Rule 2 HCCPR Lagos; Order 52 Rule 2 Abuja.
36. This was done through the National Judicial Council Guidelines for Court Sittings And Related Matters in the COVID-19 Period made in April 2020.
37. These include the Lagos State Judiciary Remote Hearing of Cases COVID-19 Pandemic Period Practice Direction May 2020, the HC of the Federal Capital Territory, Abuja Practice Direction May 2020 and the Federal HC of Nigeria Practice Directions 2020 for the COVID-19 period May 2020.
38. (2020)12 NWLR (Pt 1738) 345.

Generation of the Federation.[39] The SC held in these cases that virtual court sittings are not unconstitutional. It should be noted that the cases were not heard on the merits as the court considered the issues brought by the plaintiffs as being speculative.

4. Fair Hearing

54. There is a guarantee of a fair trial to every person in the determination of his civil rights and obligations including a determination by and against any government or authority. This guarantee is hinged on the twin principle of natural justice namely the principle of *audi alteram partem* and *nemo judex in causa sua*. This principle has constitutional backing[40] and is supported by the general principle of law. The Court of Appeal of Nigeria has held that for a proceeding to qualify as one in which there has been fair hearing, it must meet certain conditions namely:[41]

(1) the panel seized of the matter must be constituted in such a manner as to secure its independence and impartiality; and
(2) the party against whom an allegation has been made must be afforded ample opportunity to make his defence and must be given the opportunity to be heard in his defence.

55. The principle *audi alteram partem* means every party in a dispute should be heard before a decision is reached. By this principle, generally, a court will not give a decision in a matter without having heard from all parties concerned. Decisions affecting a person's rights and obligations should not be given behind the person's back.

56. There are, however, exceptions to this guarantee. One exception is where the decision given will not affect the interest of the party who was not given an opportunity to be heard. A good example is an application for substituted service of the originating processes in a suit on a defendant. It is brought by way of an ex parte application where the defendant is not put on notice and even where the defendant happens to be in court when the application is taken, the defendant would not be heard. The rationale behind this exception is that granting such an application does not affect the interests of the defendant. The application seeks to bring to the attention of the defendant the fact of a suit filed against such defendant.

57. Another exception is where extreme urgency is an issue. The rules require at least two clear days between the filing of an application and the hearing of it.[42] Where a situation demands extreme urgency in the grant of an application, putting the other party on notice will likely defeat the essence of the application as it may

39. (2020) 12 NWLR (Pt 1738) 349.
40. Section 36(1) of the 1999 Nigerian Constn.
41. *Okogi v. Okoh* (2010) 9 NWLR (Pt 1199) 311 at 325 (CA).
42. Order 43 Rule 4 HCCPR Lagos; Order 43 Rule 6 HCCPR Abuja.

present a situation where the decision of the court will be rendered nugatory. Examples include hearing of an application for an interim injunction or one for an Anton pillar order. However, the orders based on such ex parte application are usually given for a definite short period. For example, under the Abuja and Lagos HCCPR, an order of interim injunction is given for seven days from the date of the order and may be extended for another seven days. In addition, an application for interim injunction is heard on the condition that an application on notice must also have been filed and should be served on the other party.[43]

58. Another situation where a court may give a decision without hearing the other side is when a law or rule of court requires that an application be brought ex parte. An example is an application for third-party proceedings where a defendant in a suit is asking the court for leave to issue and serve third-party notice on a party who is not a party to the pending suit. The application is made on the ground that the party to be joined as a third party may bear eventual liability either in whole or in part in the event that the claimant's case succeeds. The court upon an ex parte application by the defendant may grant leave to issue and serve a third-party notice.[44]

59. The second principle of fair hearing, which is *nemo judex in causa sua*, connotes that no person shall be a judge in his own cause. This means that a person having an interest in a case cannot be the arbiter over such a case. This principle prevents judicial officers from presiding over cases where their impartiality will be in doubt. The practice is that where a case is assigned to a particular judge and the judge has an interest in the case or the court's impartiality will be in doubt given the relationship of the judge with any of the parties or the issues in the case, the judge will decline jurisdiction and make an order for the reassigning of the case to another judge. The legal cliché that 'justice must not only be done it must also be seen to be done' comes to bear in such situations.

5. Trial Within a Reasonable Time

60. This is another guarantee that has both constitutional and statutory backing. The 1999 Nigerian Constn guarantees a fair trial within a reasonable time.[45] It is trite that justice delayed is justice denied. The Rules of court prescribes the time period within which various steps in the litigation process should be taken. Also, several innovations have been introduced by the Rules of court to ensure that trials are concluded within a reasonable time. One such is the frontloading system that requires a claimant, at the time of filing of the action, to attach to the originating process the statement of claim, written statements on oath of the witnesses in the case and copies of documents sought to be relied upon during trial. The same

43. Order 43 Rule 3 HCCPR Abuja; Order 43 Rule 3(3–4) HCCPR Lagos.
44. Order 13 Rule 21 HCCPR Abuja; Order 13 Rule 19 HCCPR Lagos.
45. Section 36(1) of the 1999 Nigerian Constn.

requirements are expected of the defendant when filing the defence in the case. Second, the Case Management Conference / Pretrial Conference helps to streamline a case for trial by ensuring that all possible pretrial issues are dealt with expeditiously and the case file is handed to a trial judge.

61. Besides these, there are special procedures for specific kinds of claims that have fixed time periods for their adjudication. For example, an election petition arising from an election into the position of President of Nigeria, Governor of a state in Nigeria, Senator of the Federal Republic or member of the House of Representatives, Member of State House of Assembly must be disposed of within one hundred and eighty days of filing of the petition and any appeal consequent upon within sixty days.[46]

62. Matters brought under the Fast Track Procedure have about fifty-one days from commencement of trial to judgment[47] or a period not exceeding nine months from the commencement of the action till the final judgment.[48]

63. There are also proceedings at the Small Claims Courts where the entire period of proceedings from filing till judgment does not exceed sixty days.[49]

64. There is also the Pre-action Protocol applicable in Lagos State HCs that when properly implemented will ensure matters are concluded within a reasonable time. At the HC in Lagos State, claimants are required at the point of filing their originating process, to include among other documents, a Pre-action Protocol Form 01 with necessary documents (in HC of Lagos State (Expeditious Disposal of Civil Cases) Practice Direction No. 2 of 2019 on Pre-action Protocol, the accompanying documents is captioned Pre-action Protocol Bundle).[50] To give directions as to how this provision in the HCCPR is to be carried out, the Chief Judge of Lagos State made the HC of Lagos State (Expeditious Disposal of Civil Cases) Practice Direction No. 2 of 2019 on Pre-action Protocol. Essentially, by this Practice Direction, the Pre-action Protocol requires that a person wishing to commence an action in court must before doing so ensure that the following steps are taken:

(a) The person wishing to commence an action (claimant) shall prepare and deliver to the other party a memorandum of claim which sets outs the concise details of the claim including the basis upon which the claim is made, a summary of the facts, reliefs and remedies sought, exhibit in support of the claims as well as a proposal for the settlement of the dispute through the use of alternative dispute resolution (ADR) mechanisms.

46. Section 285(6)(7) *ibid.*
47. Order 37 Rule 12 HCCPR Abuja.
48. Order 56 Rule 1 HCCPR Lagos.
49. Article 12(2) of the Practice Direction for Small Claims Courts in Lagos State.
50. Order 5 Rule 1(2) and Order 5 Rule 5(3) of the HCCPR Lagos.

(b) The party against whom the claim is made (respondent) shall within seven days of service of the memorandum of claim and the accompanying documents serve the party making the claim with his response to the memorandum of claim as well as the proposal for settlement.
(c) Where the respondent fails to file his response to the memorandum within the stipulated seven days, the claimant shall send a reminder to the respondent giving additional seven days to respond failing which, the claimant shall file an affidavit of the respondent's failure to participate in settlement talks.
(d) In the event that the respondent responds to the memorandum of claim, the claimant being able to take an objective view of the dispute vis-à-vis the interest of both the claimant and the respondent should attempt to have the dispute settled out of court.
(e) Where the parties are unable to settle the dispute, evidence of attempt to settle must be adduced.
(f) Where the parties proceed to litigation, they are to deliver an agreed list of issues for the determination of the court.
(g) Even after the commencement of litigation, parties must continue to explore the possibility of reaching a settlement.
(h) All the correspondence and documents filed in furtherance of the requirement under this Practice Direction form the documents to be contained in the Pre-action Protocol Bundle that is filed along with the Pre-action Protocol Form 01.

65. However, where a matter cannot go on because a party is for a cogent reason unable to go on with the case on a date it is fixed for hearing, it will amount to the denial of fair hearing for the court to go on with the matter in the absence of the party. As such a party can apply for an adjournment of a matter listed for hearing and the court may in its discretion grant it. This does not detract from the fact that the matter would be decided within a reasonable time. The SC has held that for the court to become seized and take cognizance of a letter of adjournment, the letter must be filed with the registry of the court and prescribed fees paid.[51]

6. Appeals

66. The right to appeal is a constitutional right for every litigant. A party in an action who is not satisfied with the decision of the trial court can appeal against it. The appellate court is empowered to review the decision of the lower court and either affirms, alters or overturns the decision of the lower court. Where a litigant is not satisfied with the decision of the appellate court, the matter may be further appealed against depending on the provision of the law.

67. Generally, appeals in a matter can be made as far as to the SC, which is the highest court in Nigeria and is situated in the Federal Capital Territory, Abuja.

---

51. *Registered Trustees of the Presbyterian Church of Nigeria v. John Asuquo Etim* (2017) 13 NWLR (Pt 1581) 1 (SC).

68. However, by constitutional provision some appeals cannot be made up to the SC. For example, appeals from the National Assembly and State Houses of Assembly Election Tribunals[52] and appeals from the National Industrial Court[53] end at the Court of Appeal and the parties cannot appeal further to the SC. However, any appeal that goes to the SC is a final appeal as it is the apex court in Nigeria, and there can be no appeal from its decision. This constitutional guarantee of the right to appeal can be exercised as of right or with the leave of court.[54] This means that though a party has a right to appeal, depending on factors such as the subject matter of the appeal, the nature of the appeal, the party can exercise this right with or without recourse to the court for consent to exercise the right.

69. There are however cases where a person has no right to appeal. This also is provided for in the 1999 Nigerian Constn. By section 241(2)(a) of the 1999 Nigerian Constn, there is no right to appeal against the decision of a Federal HC or an HC granting unconditional leave to defend to a defendant in an action commenced under the summary judgment procedure. Also by section 241(2)(b) of the 1999 Nigerian Constn there is no right to appeal against an order of decree absolute for the dissolution or nullity of marriage where the party seeking to appeal has had time and opportunity to appeal against the decree nisi from which the order absolute was founded and had not appealed.

B. General Principles Governing the Proper Administration of Justice

1. Guarantee of Putting Opposing Party on Notice as to a Party's Case

70. There is a guarantee in civil proceedings that a party is not allowed to spring surprises on the other party. As such a party is expected to plead in the party's statement whatever the party seeks to lead evidence on during the trial. The principle is that both the court and the parties are bound by the pleadings of the parties and a party shall not be allowed to lead evidence in support of a fact that is not pleaded. Evidence given in support of facts not pleaded goes to no issue. Where a party is faced with a situation where the party had failed to plead a vital fact and need to lead evidence on it or has already led evidence in support of it, an amendment of the party's statement must be made with the leave of the court with the other party put on notice. Where leave is granted for such amendment, it allows the party to lead evidence in support of such facts that have been introduced by reason of the amendment or allow the evidence already given in the case to align with the facts pleaded as the case may be. The other party is necessarily allowed consequential amendments.

52. Section 246(3) of the 1999 Nigerian Constn as amended by s. 8 of the Constitution of the Federal Republic of Nigeria (Second Alteration) Act 2010 Act No. 2.
53. Section 243(4) of the 1999 Nigerian Constn as amended by s. 5 of the Constitution of the Federal Republic of Nigeria (Third Alteration) Act 2010 Act No. 3.
54. Sections 241 and 242 of the 1999 Nigerian Constn.

2. Privileged Communications

71. There is the guarantee that communications between parties that are marked privileged cannot be used against the parties during civil proceedings. This includes statements in any document marked 'without prejudice' made in the course of negotiation for a settlement of a dispute out of court.[55] This allows parties to be free during out-of-court attempts to settle a dispute.

3. Substantiation of Decisions

72. The decisions of a court of law in Nigeria must be backed up by the reasons for the decisions. Decisions of the court must be substantiated by the reasons for it flowing from the law. As a result of this, litigants are guaranteed that the justice that will be dispensed by a court is not based on the personal idiosyncrasy of a judge but by the established law of the state. This allows for reliability of the law by the citizenry such that if the set of facts are brought before another judge the decision is expected to be the same.

55. Section 196 of the Evidence Act 2011.

Part I. Judicial Organization

Chapter 1. The Courts and Their Members

73. This chapter takes a look at courts in Nigeria, x-raying its structure and administration, the appointments and discipline of its members and issues surrounding incompatibilities with their functions.

§1. COURT

I. Structure of the Court System in Nigeria

74. The organization of the court system in Nigeria is both a federal and state matter. Section 6(6) of the 1999 Nigerian Constn creates superior courts of record while the Houses of Assembly of the various states are empowered to create inferior courts of record in the states. The notion of judiciary refers to the courts and the officers that work in the judiciary. Judicial functions are exercised by the various courts on the basis of the jurisdiction conferred on them either by the 1999 Nigerian Constn or by the statute creating the court. Nigeria does not have courts tagged as constitutional courts or administrative courts. Recently, there have been calls for the creation of specialized courts like constitutional courts, election petition courts and courts to handle corruption cases but they have not yet materialized.

75. The courts in Nigeria are a creation of the 1999 Nigerian Constn or the statutes setting up the particular court. There are several categorizations of courts in Nigeria, which shall be discussed here. However, the discussions are centred on courts having civil jurisdiction. First is the categorization of courts as superior courts of record and inferior courts of record. Superior courts of record are the courts created under the 1999 Nigerian Constn. They are namely: the SC; the Court of Appeal; the Federal HC; the National Industrial Court; the HC of the Federal Capital Territory, Abuja; an HC of a state; the Sharia Court of Appeal of the Federal Capital Territory, Abuja: a Sharia Court of Appeal of a state; the Customary Court of Appeal of the Federal Capital Territory, Abuja; and a Customary Court of Appeal of a state.

76. The inferior courts of record consist of courts existing in Nigeria but not specifically created under the 1999 Nigerian Constn. They are a creation of state laws made by the various Houses of Assembly of the thirty-six states of the Federation of Nigeria or an Act of the National Assembly of Nigeria with respect to the Federal Capital Territory, Abuja. Examples of courts created by state laws are Magistrates' Courts, Customary Courts, District Courts, Area Courts and Sharia Courts of the various states of the Federation of Nigeria, etc. The District Courts,[56] the Area Courts[57] and the Sharia Courts[58] of the Federal Capital Territory, Abuja are examples of inferior courts created by an Act of the National Assembly of Nigeria. This is because it is the National Assembly that legislates for the Federal Capital Territory, Abuja.

77. There is also the categorization of courts into state courts and federal courts. The thirty-six states in the country are empowered by the 1999 Nigerian Constn to establish courts to administer justice in the states. State courts include the HC of a state, a Customary Court of Appeal of a state, a Sharia Court of Appeal of a state, Magistrates' Courts, Customary Courts, Area Courts, Sharia Courts, Mobile Courts, in a state, etc. The federal courts are courts established by the Federal Government of Nigeria as empowered by the 1999 Nigerian Constn. They include the SC, the Court of Appeal of Nigeria, the Federal HC, the HC of the Federal Capital Territory, Abuja, the National Industrial Court, the Sharia Court of Appeal of the Federal Capital Territory and the Customary Court of Appeal of the Federal Capital Territory. In the same vein, the Magistrates' Court in the Federal Capital Territory, the Area Courts in the Federal Capital Territory, the Customary Courts in the Federal Capital Territory, the Sharia Courts of the Federal Capital Territory are also considered as federal courts due to the fact that they were established by acts of the federal parliament which is the legislative body empowered to make laws for the Federal Capital Territory, Abuja.

78. Courts can also be categorized as courts of original, appellate or supervisory jurisdiction. Some courts can only exercise original jurisdiction such as the District Courts, Area Courts, Customary Courts and Sharia Courts. Some courts have only appellate and supervisory jurisdiction such as the Sharia Court of Appeal and the Customary Court of Appeal. Others have original, supervisory and appellate jurisdiction such as the SC, Court of Appeal, Federal HC and HC of states including the HC of the Federal Capital Territory, Abuja.

79. The Magistrates' Courts in the southern part of Nigeria have both original and appellate jurisdiction. It must be noted that it is only in the southern part of Nigeria that Magistrates' Court exercises appellate jurisdiction over appeals from the Customary Courts.[59] The inferior courts of records[60] generally are trial courts but the Magistrates' Courts in the southern part of Nigeria have jurisdiction to hear

56. Section 4 District Court Act 1960 Cap 495 LFN (Abuja) 1990.
57. Federal Capital Territory, Abuja Area Courts (Repeal and Enactment) Act 2010.
58. Federal Capital Territory, Abuja Sharia Court Act.
59. Section 28(1)(e) Magistrates' Court Law of Lagos State 2009.
60. These are courts not expressly listed in the 1999 Nigerian Constn.

appeals from Customary Courts. In the same light, the Upper Area Courts in the northern part of Nigeria hear appeals from the Area Court in the northern part of the country.

80. Below is the hierarchical structure of the court system in Nigeria except that in Southern Nigeria, the customary court is below the Magistrates' Court in the hierarchy and civil appeals from the Customary Court goes to the Magistrates' Court:

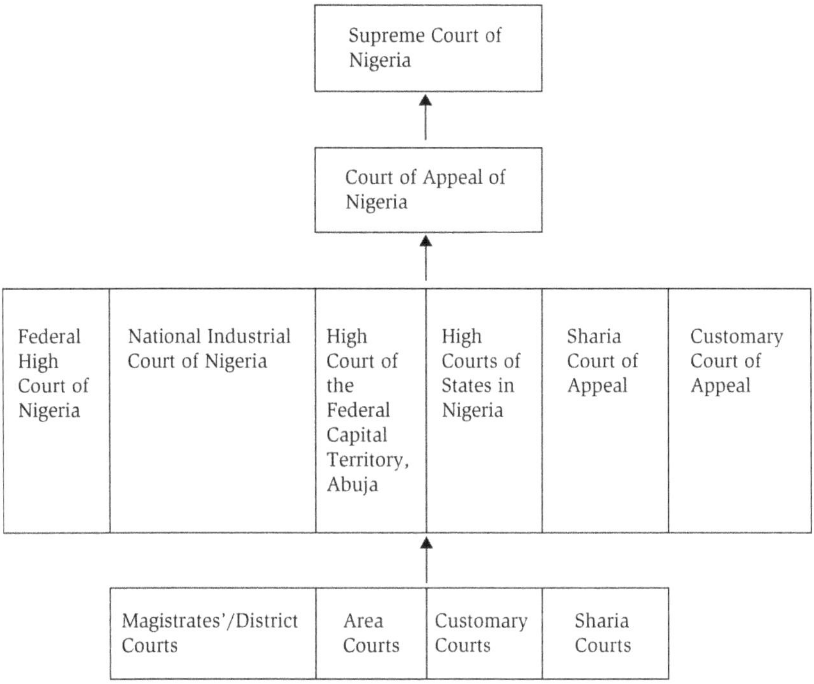

81. By the principle of *stare decisis* the courts below a particular court are bound to follow the principles laid down by that court. It is considered an act of judicial rascality where a court refuses to follow the decision of a court superior to it. However, a court can distinguish the facts and circumstances of a case before it from the principle as laid down by a higher court and as such may not follow the principle laid down by the higher court.

82. The composition of each court is as laid down by the 1999 Nigerian Constn or a statute. The SC is made up of the Chief Justice of Nigeria (who is the head of the court) and such number of Justices of the SC not exceeding twenty-one.[61] The court is properly constituted in exercising any jurisdiction conferred on it by the

61. *See* s. 230(2) of the 1999 Nigerian Constn.

Constn if it consists of not less than five justices of the court. However, where the SC is sitting in its original jurisdiction, hearing appeals on the interpretation of the 1999 Nigerian Constn or on whether any provisions of Chapter IV of the 1999 Nigerian Constn (which are the fundamental rights provisions) has been, is being or is likely to be contravened, it shall be properly constituted with seven justices of the court.[62] This is usually referred to as a full court of the SC.

83. The Court of Appeal of Nigeria is made up of the President of the Court of Appeal (who is the head of the court) and such number of justices of the court not less than forty-nine of which at least not less than three shall be learned in Islamic law and not less than three shall be learned in customary law.[63] The 1999 Nigerian Constn empowers the National Assembly of Nigeria to increase the number of justices of the court. Based on this power, the number of Justices of the Court of Appeal has been increased to ninety.[64] For the purpose of exercising any jurisdiction conferred on it by the Constn or any other law, the Court of Appeal is properly constituted if it consists of not less than three Justices of the Court of Appeal and in the case of appeals from the Sharia Court of Appeal or Customary Court of Appeal, the Court of Appeal shall be duly constituted if it consists of not less than three Justices of the Court of Appeal learned in Islamic Personal Law or Customary Law respectively.[65]

84. The Federal HC is made up of the Chief Judge of the Federal HC (who is the head of the Court) and such number of judges of the court, as may be prescribed by an Act of the National Assembly of Nigeria.[66] The Federal HC is properly constituted if it consists of at least one judge of the Court.[67]

85. The National Industrial Court of Nigeria is made of the President of the Court and such number of judges as the National Assembly may prescribe. The Court is properly constituted if it consists of a single judge, or not more than three judges as the President of the National Industrial Court may direct.[68]

86. The HC of the Federal Capital Territory, Abuja, consists of the Chief Judge of the Court and such number of Judges of the HC as may be prescribed by an Act of the National Assembly.[69] The HC of the Federal Capital Territory is duly constituted if it consists of at least one judge of the Court.[70]

---

62. Section 234 *ibid.*
63. Section 237(2) of the 1999 Nigerian Constn.
64. Court of Appeal Act No. 15, 2005 as amended by s. 2 of the Court of Appeal (Amendment) Act 2013.
65. Section 247(1) of the 1999 Nigerian Constn.
66. Section 249(2) *ibid.*
67. Section 253 *ibid.*
68. Section 254E(1) of the 1999 Nigerian Constn as amended by s. 6 of the Constitution (Third Alteration) Act 2010.
69. Section 255 of the 1999 Nigerian Constn.
70. Section 258 *ibid.*

87. The Sharia Court of Appeal of the Federal Capital Territory, Abuja, consists of the Grand Kadi of the Sharia Court of Appeal and such number of Kadis of the Sharia Court of Appeal as may be prescribed by an Act of the National Assembly.[71] The Sharia Court of Appeal is properly constituted if it consists of at least three Kadis of the Court.[72] Each of the states of the Federal Republic of Nigeria that requires it is entitled to a Sharia Court of Appeal which shall consist of a Grand Kadi and such number of Kadis as may be prescribed by a law of the House of Assembly of the state.[73]

88. The Customary Court of Appeal of the Federal Capital Territory, Abuja, is made up of the President of the Customary Court of Appeal and such number of judges as may be prescribed by an Act of the National Assembly.[74] For the purpose of exercising any jurisdiction conferred on it by the 1999 Constn or any other law, the Customary Court of Appeal is properly constituted when it consists of at least three judges of the court.[75] Each of the states of the Federal Republic of Nigeria that requires it is entitled to a Customary Court of Appeal which shall consist of a President of the Customary Court of Appeal and such number of judges as may be prescribed by a law of the State House of Assembly.[76] Both the Sharia Court of Appeal of a state and the Customary Court of Appeal of a state have the same constitution as their counterpart in the Federal Capital Territory, Abuja.[77]

89. Each of the thirty-six states of the Federation have an HC which consists of the Chief Judge of the state and such number of judges as may be prescribed by a law of the House of Assembly of the state.[78] For the purpose of exercising the jurisdiction conferred on it by the 1999 Nigerian Constn or any other law, the HC of a state is duly constituted with at least one judge of the court.[79]

90. For the inferior courts of record, only the courts in Lagos and Abuja will be mentioned as the Magistrates' Courts in both jurisdictions largely represents the positions in the Magistrates' Courts in the southern and northern part of Nigeria respectively. The Magistrates' Court in Lagos is duly constituted with a single Magistrate sitting alone.[80] The District Court in the Federal Capital Territory, Abuja, is duly constituted with one District Judge.[81] The Customary Court in Lagos is duly

71. Section 260(2) *ibid.*
72. Section 263 *ibid.*
73. Section 275 *ibid.*
74. Section 265(2) *ibid.*
75. Section 268 *ibid.*
76. Section 280(2) *ibid.*
77. Sections 278 and 283 of the 1999 Nigerian Constn respectively.
78. Section 270(2) *ibid.*
79. Section 273 *ibid.*
80. Section 48 of the Magistrates' Court Law of Lagos State 2009.
81. Section 47 District Court Act 1960 Cap 495 LFN (Abuja) 1990.

constituted with a President and at least two or four members as the case may be.[82] The Area Court in the Federal Capital Territory, Abuja is duly constituted with an Area Court Judge sitting alone.[83]

91. Besides the regular courts discussed above, there are Tribunals set up to adjudicate over special proceedings and are dissolved after the completion of such proceedings. Examples of such are Election Tribunals, which preside over petitions arising from elections in Nigeria.

92. The National and State Houses of Assembly Election Tribunals preside over election petitions arising from elections into the office of a Senator of the Federal Republic of Nigeria, a member of the House of Representatives of the Federal Republic of Nigeria or a member of a State House of Assembly. This Tribunal consists of a Chairman who shall be a Judge of the HC and two members who shall be appointed from among Judges of the HC, Kadis of a Sharia Court of Appeal, Judges of a Customary Court of Appeal or other members of the judiciary not below the rank of a Chief Magistrate.[84] The quorum for the Tribunal to be properly constituted is the chairman and one member.[85]

93. The Governorship Election Tribunal hears election petitions arising from governorship elections. It is duly constituted with a chairman (who shall be an HC Judge) and two members (who shall be appointed from among Judges of the HC, Kadis of a Sharia Court of Appeal, Judges of a Customary Court of Appeal or other members of the judiciary not below the rank of a Chief Magistrate).[86] The quorum for the Tribunal to be properly constituted is the chairman and one member.[87]

94. The Local Government Elections Tribunal hears election petitions emanating from local government elections. Each of the states in the Federation is empowered to set up a local government Elections Tribunal to adjudicate over petitions arising from local government elections conducted by states under laws established by the states. However, the Area Council Elections Tribunal for the Federal Capital Territory, Abuja (as they are referred to) is established under the Electoral Act.[88] The Area Council Elections Tribunal is duly constituted with a Chairman and two members.[89] The Chairman shall be a Chief Magistrate and the two other members shall

82. Section 2 Customary Courts Law of Lagos State Cap C19 Laws of Lagos State 2004.
83. Section 2(1) of the Federal Capital Territory, Abuja Area Court Act 2010.
84. Sixth Schedule to the 1999 Nigerian Constn as amended by s. 30 of the Nigerian Constitution (First Alteration) Act 2010 and s. 10 the Nigerian Constitution (Second Alteration) Act 2010.
85. Section 285(4) of the 1999 Nigerian Constn as amended by s. 9 of the Constitution (Second Alteration) Act 2010.
86. Sixth Schedule to the 1999 Nigerian Constn as amended by s. 30 of the Nigerian Constitution (First Alteration) Act 2010 and s. 10 the Nigerian Constitution (Second Alteration) Act 2010.
87. Section 285(4) of the 1999 Nigerian Constn as amended by s. 9 of the Nigerian Constitution (Second Alteration) Act 2010.
88. Section 135(1) of the Electoral Act 2010 as amended.
89. Section 135(2) *ibid.*

be appointed from among Magistrates of the Judiciary of the Federal Capital Territory, Abuja, and legal practitioners of at least ten years post-call experience, non-legal practitioners of unquestionable integrity or other members of the Federal Capital Territory Judiciary not below the rank of a Magistrate.[90] Appeals from this Tribunal go to the Area Council Election Appeal Tribunal whose decision is final.[91]

95. The chairman of the Area Council Election Appeal Tribunal shall be a Judge of the HC, and the two members shall be appointed from among the Judges of the HC of the Federal Capital Territory, Abuja, Kadis of the Sharia Court of Appeal of the Federal Capital Territory, Abuja, Judges of the Customary Court of Appeal of the Federal Capital Territory, Abuja, or other members of the judiciary of the Federal Capital Territory, Abuja, not below the rank of Chief Magistrate. The composition of the Area Council Election Appeal Tribunal is a Chairman and two members. The quorum of the Area Council Tribunal is the chairman and one member.[92]

II. Administration of the Court

96. The Chief Justice of Nigeria is the head of the judiciary in Nigeria and also the head of the SC. However, the various courts have their administrative heads. The President of the Court of Appeal is the head of the administration of the Court of Appeal. Aside from that, the various Court of Appeal divisions in the country are presided over by one of the Justices of that Court of Appeal division. There are currently sixteen divisions of the Court of Appeal in Nigeria.

97. The Chief Judge of the Federal HC heads the Federal HC of Nigeria. The court sits in various divisions across the country, and each such division will have the most senior judge as the administrative judge.

98. The Chief Judges of states and of the Federal Capital Territory, Abuja are the administrative heads of the HCs in the states and the Federal Capital Territory, Abuja respectively. They are also the administrative heads of the inferior courts of records in the various states and the Federal Capital Territory, Abuja. The role of an administrative judge includes assigning cases filed in a particular division to the different judges in that division, seeing to the general day-to-day running of the activities of the courts in that division.

99. With regard to assigning of cases filed in the HC of each state and the Federal Capital Territory, Abuja, the Chief Judges delegate this task to the Administrative Judges in each of the judicial divisions in the states and the Federal Capital Territory, Abuja. The most senior judge in a judicial division who is the Administrative Judge assigns cases filed in that division to the judges sitting in that division.

90. Section 135(3) *ibid.*
91. Section 136(1) *ibid.*
92. Section 136(3) *ibid.*

100. There is no regulation or law that determines how cases are assigned to judges. However, in Lagos where the court is divided into criminal divisions, civil divisions, probate division, family division, fast tract division and so on, the cases are assigned to different judges based on the division the judge is serving in at the material time vis-à-vis the nature of the case. In Abuja, some judges preside mostly over particular kind of cases, like corruption cases, criminal matters, family matter, but there are no clear specialized divisions as is found in Lagos. Cases can also be assigned to judges based on the current caseload of each court.

101. In the administration and organization of the courts, the judges are assisted by the Chief Registrar of the court who is the sheriff of the court and other officers in the registry such as the various court registrars and clerks who play a very vital role in the filing, registration, service of court processes, preparation of enrolment orders of the courts, compilation of records of appeal, execution of court judgments and so on.

102. The sittings of the HC are held every day except public holidays; during the week beginning with Easter Monday; during the period beginning on Christmas eve and ending on 2 January next following; during the week designated as settlement week; and during the annual vacation effective from the last week of July and ending on a date not more than six weeks later as the Chief Judge may declare by notification in the Gazette or by any other means that the Chief Judge deems appropriate. (In Lagos, it is not later than forty-two working days. The HC of the other thirty-five states of the federation also has similar provisions.)[93] Nonetheless, a matter may be heard by a judge during the period when the courts are not expected to sit where such a matter is urgent or a judge at the request of all the parties in a matter agrees to hear such a matter. An application for an urgent hearing is made by motion ex parte and the decision of the judge on the application is final.[94] When the HC is on a long vacation, the time for filing and serving pleadings shall not run unless otherwise directed by the judge.[95]

III. Bench and Ministere Public / Public Prosecutor

103. The bench in Nigeria is made up of judges of both the superior courts of record and the inferior courts of records. In Nigeria, we do not have the Ministere Public. However, the Federal Ministry of Justice and the various States Ministries of Justice, which is headed by the Attorney General of the Federation (AGF) and the Attorney General (AG) of states respectively, operate the department of Civil Litigation and Public Law. This department provides services such as legal representation for the Federal and State Government and their agencies in court and arbitration tribunals in matters involving breach of contracts, enforcement of

93. Order 49 Rule 4 HCCPR Lagos; Order 52 Rule 4 HCCPR Abuja.
94. Order 49 Rule 5 HCCPR Lagos; Order 52 Rule 5 HCCPR Abuja.
95. Order 49 Rule 6 HCCPR Lagos; Order 52 Rule 6 HCCPR Abuja.

fundamental rights, cancellation of oil prospecting licences, taxation matters, property matters, initiation of actions to assert public rights and interest, etc. Some Ministries of Justice also specifically operate the Office of the Public Defender, which deals with both civil and criminal matters. In Lagos State, the Office of the Public Defender handles matters such as matrimonial causes, employer and employee matters, breach of contract, landlord and tenant matters, etc. where services such as legal aid and advice, deployment of ADR mechanisms to settle disputes are rendered to members of the public.[96] Public officers head these departments, and they are appointed the same way public servants are appointed into the Public Service in Nigeria except for the AGF or AG of states who are political appointees.

IV. Appointment of Judges

104. In Nigeria, it is only the appointment of judges to the superior courts of record that has a somewhat uniform procedure, as there are bodies and authorities set up by the 1999 Nigerian Constn responsible for this. The appointment into the offices of judges of inferior courts of records differs from state to state, and for the most part, there is no defined procedure for it. In the light of this, the discussions on the appointment of judges are largely on appointment to the superior courts of record. Mention will be made of how Magistrates in Lagos State and the Federal Capital Territory, Abuja are appointed.

105. It is important to outline the bodies and authorities responsible for the appointment of judges into the superior courts of record, their powers and functions before undertaking a discussion of the procedure for appointment.

A. *Bodies and Authorities Responsible for Appointment of Judges into the Superior Courts of Records*

1. The National Judicial Council

106. The National Judicial Council (NJC) is a creation of the 1999 Nigerian Constn[97] and is the highest regulatory body of the judiciary in Nigeria. The NJC is made up of the following members:[98]

(a) the Chief Justice of Nigeria who shall be the Chairman;
(b) the next most senior Justice of the SC who shall be the Deputy Chairman;
(c) the President of the Court of Appeal;
(d) five retired justices selected by the Chief Justice of Nigeria from the SC or Court of Appeal;
(e) the Chief Judge of the Federal HC;

96. *See* section 2(1) of the Office of Public Defender Laws of Lagos State 2011.
97. Paragraph 20 of Part 1 of the Third Schedule to the 1999 Nigerian Constn.
98. *Ibid.*

(f) the President of the National Industrial Court;
(g) five Chief Judges of states to be appointed by the Chief Justice of Nigeria from among the Chief Judges of the states and of the HC of the Federal Capital Territory, Abuja in rotation to serve for two years;
(h) one Grand Kadi to be appointed by the Chief Justice of Nigeria from among the Grand Kadis of the Sharia Courts of Appeal to serve in rotation for two years;
(i) one President of the Customary Court of Appeal to be appointed by the Chief Justice of Nigeria from among the Presidents of the Customary Courts of Appeal to serve in rotation for two years;
(j) five members of the Nigerian Bar Association (NBA) who have qualified to practise for a period of not less than fifteen years, and one of whom shall be a Senior Advocate of Nigeria, appointed by the Chief Justice of Nigeria on the recommendation of the National Executive Committee of the NBA to serve for two years and subject to reappointment; however, these five members of the NBA shall sit in the NJC only for the purposes of considering the names of persons for the appointment to the superior courts of record; and
(k) two persons not being legal practitioners who in the opinion of the Chief Justice of Nigeria are of unquestionable integrity.

107. The secretary of the NJC who must be a legal practitioner is appointed by the NJC on the recommendation of the Federal Judicial Service Commission.[99]

108. With regard to the appointment of judges of the superior courts of record, the NJC is empowered by the 1999 Nigerian Constn to carry out certain functions.[100] First, the NJC is empowered to recommend to the President of the Federal Republic of Nigeria from among the list of persons submitted to it by the Federal Judicial Service Commission for appointment to the offices of the Chief Justice of Nigeria, Justices of the SC, the President and Justices of the Court of Appeal, the Chief Judge and the Judges of the Federal HC, the President and Judges of the National Industrial Court and the Judicial Service Committee of the Federal Capital Territory, Abuja, persons for appointment to the offices of the Chief Judge and Judges of the HC of the Federal Capital Territory, Abuja, the Grand Kadi and Kadi of the Sharia Court of Appeal of the Federal Capital Territory, Abuja, and the President and Judges of the Customary Court of Appeal of the Federal Capital Territory, Abuja.

109. Second, the NJC is empowered to recommend to the Governors of the thirty-six states in Nigeria from among the list of persons submitted to it by the State Judicial Service Commissions, persons for appointment to the offices of the Chief Judges of states and Judges of the HC of states, the Grand Kadi and Kadi of the Sharia Court of Appeal of states, Abuja, and the President and Judges of the Customary Court of Appeal of states.

---

99. Paragraph 22 of Part 1 of the Third Schedule to the 1999 Nigerian Constn.
100. Paragraph 21 *ibid.*

110. Third, the NJC advises the President and Governors on any matter pertaining to the judiciary, as may be referred to the NJC by the President or the Governors.

2. The Federal Judicial Service Commission

111. The Federal Judicial Service Commission is also a creation of the 1999 Nigerian Constn and is comprised of the following members:[101]

(a) the Chief Justice of Nigeria, who shall be the Chairman;
(b) the President of the Court of Appeal;
(c) the AGF;
(d) the Chief Judge of the Federal HC;
(e) the President of the National Industrial Court;
(f) two persons each of whom has been qualified to practise as a legal practitioner in Nigeria for a period not less than fifteen years drawn from a list of four persons so qualified recommended by the NBA; and
(g) two other persons not being legal practitioners who in the opinion of the President of the Federal Republic of Nigeria are of unquestionable integrity.

112. The Federal Judicial Service Commission with regard to the appointment of judges to courts set up by the Federal Government is empowered to advise the NJC in nominating persons for appointment to the office of the Chief Justice of Nigeria, a Justice of the SC, the President of the Court of Appeal, a Justice of the Court of Appeal, the Chief Judge of the Federal HC, a Judge of the Federal HC, the President of the National Industrial Court, a Judge of the National Industrial Court and the Chairman and members of the Code of Conduct Tribunal.[102]

3. State Judicial Service Commission

113. This body established under the Constitution is made up of: the Chief Judge of the state, who shall the Chairman; the AG of the state; the Grand Kadi of the Sharia Court of Appeal of the state if there is any; the President of the Customary Court of Appeal of the state if there is any; two members who are legal practitioners and have been qualified to practise as legal practitioners in Nigeria for not less than ten years; and two other persons not being legal practitioners, who in the opinion of the Governor of the state are persons of unquestionable integrity.[103]

114. The State Judicial Service Commission in regards to the appointment of judicial officers is empowered to advise the NJC on suitable persons for nomination to the office of the Chief Judge of the state, the Grand Kadi of the Sharia Court of

---

101. Paragraph 12 *ibid.*
102. Paragraph 13 *ibid.*
103. Paragraph 5 of Part 11 of the Third Schedule to the 1999 Nigerian Constn.

Appeal of the state if any, the President of the Customary Court of Appeal of the state if any, Judges of the HC of the state, Judges of the Sharia Court of Appeal of the state if any and Judges of the Customary Court of Appeal of the state if any.[104]

4. Judicial Service Committee of the Federal Capital Territory Abuja

115. This body set up under Part 111 of the Third Schedule to the 1999 Constn, comprise of the Chief Judge of the Federal Capital Territory, Abuja who shall be the Chairman; the Attorney General of the Federation; the Grand Kadi of the Sharia Court of Appeal of the Federal Capital Territory, Abuja; the President of the Customary Court of Appeal of the Federal Capital Territory, Abuja; one person who is a legal practitioner and has been qualified to practise law in Nigeria for a period of not less than twelve years; and one other person not being a legal practitioner, who in the opinion of the President of the Federal Republic of Nigeria is of unquestionable integrity.[105] The Judicial Service Committee of the Federal Capital Territory, Abuja in relation to the appointment of judicial officers is empowered to recommend to the NJC suitable persons for nomination for appointment to the office of Chief Judge of the Federal Capital Territory, Abuja; a Judge of the HC of the Federal Capital Territory, Abuja; the Grand Kadi of the Sharia Court of Appeal of the Federal Capital Territory, Abuja; the President of the Customary Court of Appeal of the Federal Capital Territory, Abuja; a Kadi of the Sharia Court of Appeal of the Federal Capital Territory, Abuja; and a Judge of the Customary Court of Appeal of the Federal Capital Territory, Abuja.

5. The President of the Federal Republic of Nigeria

116. The President is the appointing authority for all judges of the superior courts of record in all federal courts including the superior courts of records of the Federal Capital Territory, Abuja. The President of the Federal Republic of Nigeria appoints persons to the office of Chief Justice of Nigeria, Justice of the SC, President Court of Appeal of Nigeria, Justice of the Court of Appeal, Chief Judge of the Federal HC, Judges of the Federal HC, President of the National Industrial Court, Judges of the National Industrial Court, Chief Judge of the Federal Capital Territory, Abuja, Judges of the HC of the Federal Capital Territory, Abuja, Grand Kadi of the Sharia Court of Appeal of the Federal Capital Territory, Abuja, Kadis of the Sharia Court of Appeal of the Federal Capital Territory, Abuja, President of the Customary Court of Appeal of the Federal Capital Territory, Abuja, and Judges of the Customary Court of Appeal of the Federal Capital Territory, Abuja.

117. The President of Nigeria does the appointment on the recommendation of the NJC. However, for the Chief Justice of Nigeria, Justices of the SC, President Court of Appeal of Nigeria, Chief Judge of the Federal HC, President of the

104. Paragraph 6 *ibid.*
105. Paragraph 1 of Part 111 of the Third Schedule to the 1999 Nigerian Constn.

National Industrial Court, Chief Judge of the Federal Capital Territory, Abuja, Grand Kadi of the Sharia Court of Appeal of the Federal Capital Territory, Abuja, and President of the Customary Court of Appeal of the Federal Capital Territory, Abuja, their appointments are in addition subject to the confirmation of the Senate of the Federal Republic of Nigeria.

118. Worthy of mention is the fact that the President is under obligation to appoint from the list of nominees for appointment recommended by the NJC. The President cannot go aside this list. Where the President is not satisfied with the list of nominees, it can ask the NJC to recommend other persons. But the President may choose to appoint only some persons out of the list sent and decline appointing the other names on the list.

6. Governor of a State

119. The Governor of a state is the appointing authority for the judges of the superior courts of record in the state. These are the Chief Judges of states, HC Judges in the states, Grand Kadis and Kadis of the Sharia Court of Appeal in states that established the Sharia Court of Appeal, the President and Judges of the Customary Court of Appeal in states that established the Customary Court of Appeal. A governor appoints these judges on the recommendation of the NJC. For the appointment of the Chief Judges of states, President Customary Court of Appeal and the Grand Kadi of the Sharia Court of Appeal, their appointment are in addition subject to the confirmation of the State House of Assembly.

120. It must be noted that the Governor is under an obligation to appoint from the list of nominees for the appointment recommended by the NJC. The Governor cannot go aside this list. Where the Governor is not satisfied with the list of nominees, he can ask the NJC to recommend other persons. But the Governor may choose to appoint only some persons out of the list sent and decline appointing the other names on the list.

B. Procedure for Appointment of Judges of the Superior Courts of Record in Nigeria

121. The appointment of judges of the superior courts of record in Nigeria is regulated by the NJC Revised Guidelines and Procedural Rules 2014 that came into force on 3 November 2014. The NJC made these rules based on powers conferred on it by the 1999 Constn.[106]

---

106. Paragraph 21(a)(i) of Part 1 of the Third Schedule to the 1999 Nigerian Constn.

122. The process of appointment of a judicial officer to a superior court of record starts with the head of the particular court that wants to appoint notifying the appropriate authority of this fact. In the case of appointment to the superior court of record in the thirty-six states in Nigeria, the head of the State Judicial Service Commission (who is the Chief Judge of the state) will send a notice stating the number of judicial officers to be appointed to the Governor of the state concerned.[107] A copy of the notice and the Governor's response to it is then served on each member of the Judicial Service Commission/Committee of the state concerned.

123. With regard to the Federal Capital Territory, Abuja, the chairman of the Judicial Service Committee of the Federal Capital Territory, Abuja (who is the Chief Judge of the Federal Capital Territory, Abuja) shall give notice of such intended appointment to the Chief Justice of Nigeria who is the chairman of the NJC.[108]

124. In the case of a federal court other than the HC of the Federal Capital Territory, the head of the court shall give notice of the number of judicial officers to be appointed to the Chief Justice of Nigeria who is the chairman of the Federal Judicial Service Commission.[109] A copy of the notice sent to the Governor of a state or the Chief Justice of Nigeria as the case may be is sent to the Secretary of the NJC at the same time.[110]

125. On receipt of the notice the Secretary of the NJC advises the Chief Justice of Nigeria as the Chairman of the NJC on the number of judicial officers that can be appointed in furtherance of the request made in the notice. The Secretary to the NJC gives this advice based on the relevant budgetary provision of the NJC for that particular year.

126. It is pertinent to add that the NJC is the body constitutionally empowered to collect, control and disburse all moneys, capital and recurrent, for the judiciary in Nigeria.[111] The Chairman of the NJC having considered the advice given by the Secretary would decide on the notice of intended appointment. The chairman of the relevant State Judicial Service Commission/Committee or the relevant head of court, as the case may be, would be notified of the decision of the Chairman of the NJC. The notification would be to the effect that the appointment of judicial officers may be proceeded either with respect to the original number of judicial officers intended to be appointed or with a specified reduction in the number proposed to be appointed. This decision of the Chairman of the NJC shall be final unless the relevant chairman of a State Judicial Service Commission/Committee or the relevant

---

107. Rule 2(1) of the NJC Revised Guidelines and Procedural Rules 2014.
108. Rule 2(2)(b) *ibid.*
109. Rule 2(2)(a) *ibid.*
110. Rule 2(3) *ibid.*
111. Paragraph 21 of Part 1 of the Third Schedule to the 1999 Nigerian Constn.

head of court, as the case may be, shows grounds to the satisfaction of the chairman of the NJC why the number of judicial officers to be appointed should be reviewed.[112]

127. On receipt of the decision of the chairman of the NJC, the chairman of the relevant State Judicial Service Commission/Committee or head of court, as the case may be, shall do the following:[113]

(a) Call for expression of interest by suitable candidates by a public notice placed on the website of the Judicial Service Commission/Committee concerned, on notice boards of courts and notice boards of NBA branches. The notice shall specify the closing date for the receipt of applications.
(b) Write to every head of superior courts of record in Nigeria and every judicial officer of the court concerned asking for nominations of suitable candidates for the proposed judicial appointment. The notice shall specify the closing date for the receipt of nominations.
(c) Write to the President of the NBA or chairmen of branches of NBA in a state for appointment to the federal courts or state courts respectively, calling for nomination of suitable candidates for the proposed judicial appointment and requesting that they bring to the notice of suitable candidates the call for expression of interest by each of them. The notice shall specify the closing date for the receipt of applications and/or nominations.

128. Where the judicial officers to be appointed are for the Court of Appeal or SC, the heads of these courts (the President of the Court of Appeal or Chief Justice of Nigeria respectively) shall write to heads of courts, serving Justices of the Court of Appeal/SC, and President of the NBA asking for nomination of suitable judicial officers/legal practitioners for appointment as Justices of the Court of Appeal or SC.[114]

129. The nomination of a candidate is to be done in writing indicating clearly that the candidate is known to the person nominating in a personal and professional capacity for a reasonable period of time as to be in a position to nominate the candidate as a person possessing the requisite attributes needed of a judicial officer. The person nominating must expressly certify that from personal knowledge of the candidate, the candidate possesses the qualities set out in the guidelines which are:

- good character and reputation;
- diligence and hard work;
- honesty;
- integrity;
- sound knowledge of the law;
- consistent adherence to professional ethics;

---

112. Rule 2(5) NJC Revised Guidelines and Procedural Rules 2014.
113. Rule 3(1)(a) *ibid.*
114. Rule 3(1)(b) *ibid.*

- active successful practice at the Bar, including satisfactory presentation of cases in court either as a legal practitioner in private practice or as a legal officer in any public service or satisfactory and consistent display of sound and mature judgment in the office as a Chief Registrar or Chief Magistrate or credible record of teaching in a reputable University and publication of legal works; and
- where the appointment is to the office of Kadi of a Sharia Court of Appeal, knowledge of Arabic language and grammar.

130. After the closing date of receipts of applications and/or nominations, the chairman of the Judicial Service Commission/Committee or the head of court as the case may be shall make a provisional shortlist on the merit. This list shall contain not less than twice the number of judicial officers to be appointed at a particular time. In carrying out this exercise, the chairman of the Judicial Service Commission/Committee is expected to take into consideration as much as it is possible issues such as professional expertise and competence, sound knowledge of the law, seniority at the Bar and/or Bench and federal character or geographical spread where necessary and possible without compromising the independence of the judiciary or allowing politics to influence the appointment process.

131. In the case of appointment of judges from the HCs to the Court of Appeal or Justices of the Court of Appeal, Chief Judges/legal practitioners/academics to the SC, in addition to the above consideration, the issue of the quality of judgments and performance and demonstration of the judicial skill of the judge and in the case of appointment from the Bar, evidence of six contested cases in the last five years should be taken into consideration. Although no mention of the qualification for academics to be appointed to the SC, it is safe to say that such academics must possess a credible record of teaching in a reputable University and publication of legal works.

132. Moreover, the chairman of the Judicial Service Commission/Committee is enjoined not to shortlist any candidate whose reputation in the locality is low or has been tarnished and in the case of a candidate who is a serving judicial officer, where the performance of such had been consistently rated low or not satisfactory in judicial performance reports.[115] Where a candidate was excluded from the provisional shortlist on the basis of reputation or poor performance as a judicial officer, this fact must be stated in the provisional shortlist that is placed before the members of the Judicial Service Commission/Committee concerned.[116]

133. The list of the provisional shortlisted candidates shall be circulated to the following persons calling for comments from them on the suitability or otherwise of any of the shortlisted candidates:

(a) serving and retired judicial officers of the court to which the appointment of a judicial officer (other than the head of a court) is to be made;

115. Rule 3(7) *ibid.*
116. Rule 3(8) *ibid.*

(b) serving and retired heads of the relevant state or federal court including retired Chief Justices of Nigeria and President of the Court of Appeal in the case of appointment of a head of court;
(c) the NBA branches in the State concerned where the appointment is to a state court or the President of the NBA in the case of appointment to a federal court; and
(d) members of the State Judicial Service Commission/Committee concerned.

134. The Chairman of the Judicial Service Commission/Committee concerned shall forward or direct the Secretary to the State Judicial Service Commission/ Committee to forward to the shortlisted candidates the NJC Form A that is to be completed by them and returned to the chairman of the Judicial Service Commission/Committee together with all necessary attachments as specified in the Form. Following this, the chairman of the Judicial Service Commission/Committee shall table before the Judicial Service Commission/Committee for consideration a memorandum on each of the shortlisted candidates. Also attached to the memorandum are the following:[117]

- The duly completed NJC Form A and the necessary attachments to it.
- The comments of eligible persons who nominated the candidates.
- Any petition or protest against any of the shortlisted candidates, together with the response of the candidate, if the candidate has responded to them.
- Detailed medical certificate of fitness issued by a government hospital or medical institution.
- Report by the Department of State Security on the suitability of the candidate for appointment to a judicial office supported with verifiable facts on which the report is based. The report should also state clearly whether the Department of State Services kept a file on the candidate and if so, whether the file contains a report adverse to the candidate being appointed a judicial officer.

135. The Judicial Service Commission/Committee is at liberty to make further enquiries on any of the shortlisted candidates as to their suitability for judicial office from reputable sources.[118] In its consideration of the shortlisted candidates, the Judicial Service Commission/Committee shall take into consideration the qualities for selection of suitable candidates for judicial office in any superior court of record mentioned in paragraph 129 above.

136. The presence of any of the following facts will disqualify a candidate for recommendation for appointment as a judicial officer in any superior court of record:[119]

(1) involvement in canvassing or lobbying for the appointment directly or indirectly in any form and/or through any person or persons;

117. Rule 4(2) *ibid.*
118. Rule 4(3) *ibid.*
119. Rule 4(4)(ii) *ibid.*

(2) bad behaviour whether in or out of court;
(3) activity suggesting impecuniosity and/or display of lifestyle that indicates that the candidate is living above his means;
(4) influence peddling;
(5) acts of dishonesty or corruption or corrupt practices either on behalf of the candidate or any other judicial officer or professional colleague;
(6) rendering dishonest or questionable legal opinion or advice or suppression of truth and suggestion of falsehood in any legal matter regarding colleagues, clients, or the court of law;
(7) deliberate improper or wrong completion of the NJC Form A with the intention to deceive or mislead;
(8) submission of false credentials and or deceitful or fraudulent curriculum vitae; or
(9) the candidate is shown to have no or very limited exposure to practise at the Bar and conduct of cases in the superior court of record.

137. A candidate once rejected on these grounds shall not be presented again to the NJC for at least another two years or such time as the NJC may direct.[120]

138. The decision of the Judicial Service Commission/Committee after considering the shortlisted candidates in respect of nomination and advice for appointment as a judicial officer shall be authenticated by the minutes of the Judicial Service Commission/Committee meeting duly adopted and signed by the Chairman and Secretary.[121]

139. The next stage will be the Chairman of the Judicial Service Commission/Committee advising or recommending as the case may be to the NJC the shortlisted candidates. The advice/recommendation shall be in form of a memorandum. The memorandum must state the fact of whether a shortlisted candidate had on any previous occasion been presented to the NJC on recommendation for appointment as a judicial officer. Where a candidate had been previously recommended, the memorandum must contain particulars of such earlier presentation including the date of the earlier submission of the candidate's name to the NJC and the date of the NJC's decision on such earlier submission. The memorandum shall contain justification for the number of judicial officers to be appointed. It shall conclude with an explicit declaration that the 2014 NJC Guidelines and Procedural Rules have been strictly and fully complied with. The memorandum shall be accompanied by the following:[122]

(1) minutes of the meeting of the State Judicial Service Commission/Committee where the nomination of candidates was considered and a decision taken;
(2) all materials and documents placed before the State Judicial Service Commission/Committee as outlined above;

120. Rule 6(5) *ibid.*
121. Rule 4(5) *ibid.*
122. Rule 5(4) *ibid.*

(3) proof of the establishment prescribed by legislation for the particular court concerned;
(4) proof of adequate capital vote provision in the relevant approved budget for the superior court of record concerned;
(5) real and verifiable proof of availability of suitable court hall, judge's residence, car and library, etc.;
(6) a chart showing in a clear format, the essential particulars of the candidates shortlisted.

140. It is must be pointed out that the NJC has power in considering the number of judicial officers to be recommended for appointment, in addition to the conditions in (3)–(6) paragraph 139 above, consider factors such as the workload of the court in question and the performance of the current serving judicial officers of the court. The NJC may consequent upon such consideration, in its discretion, reduce the number of judicial officers to be recommended for appointment or consider that the proposed appointment is not at all justified by need or it may direct that no such advice to the NJC be made in future until such time as the NJC may decide having regard to factors such as absence of need, very low performance of judicial officers of the court concerned and low level of average judicial workload.[123]

141. The next stage is for the NJC to conduct interview for the shortlisted candidates to determine their suitability for the judicial office they are seeking. The mode of conducting the interview is determined by the NJC. In the last exercise for the appointment of judges to the Federal HC, the mode used was oral interview while the one to the National Industrial Court written and oral interviews were adopted. The result of the interview forms a major part of the decision on candidates' suitability for the judicial office for which they have been interviewed. As a result, a candidate who fails the interview shall not be recommended for appointment by the NJC.

142. The names of candidates recommended by the NJC for appointment are sent to the President of the Federal Republic of Nigeria in the case of appointment of judges of the superior courts of record in the federal courts including that of the Federal Capital Territory, Abuja or the Governor of the concerned state in the case of appointment to a superior court of record of a state. Upon the appointment, the names of the newly appointed judges are then made public, and they are subsequently sworn in as judges at the SC by the Chief Justice of Nigeria for the federal judges and at the HC of the relevant state by the Chief Judge of the state for the state judges.

---

123. Rule 5(5) *ibid.*

C. Appointment of Magistrates

143. The appointment of Magistrates in Nigeria like other judges of the inferior courts of record has no uniform procedure and is done in some cases informally. In Lagos State of Nigeria, the Lagos State Judicial Service Commission is responsible for the appointment of Magistrates. Legal practitioners of not less than five years post-call to the Nigerian Bar with relevant experience are eligible for appointment as Magistrates. The Magistrates appointed serves as judicial officers to the exclusion of any other function except as provided for in any other law.[124]

D. Appointment of Registrars, Legal Assistants, Court Clerks and Other Members of the Court Registry

144. There are other members of the judiciary who work in the various courts that ensure smooth administration of justice. They include the Chief Registrars of the various courts, registrars, legal assistants to judges, court clerks and bailiffs. The judges are the ones who preside and adjudicate over matters brought to court by aggrieved members of society. To aid the work of the judges, the support staff provides administrative services. The Chief Registrar is the Chief accounting officer of each court. The Chief Registrar is also referred to as the Sheriff of the court. The position of Chief Registrar is only available in the superior court of record. The office of the Chief Registrar of a superior court of record coordinates the duties of the administrative staff of the judiciary. These duties include the filing process of the court, service of court processes, enforcement of judgments of the courts, training of staff and other incidental matters. The Chief Registrar of superior courts of records through the various Deputy Chief Registrars also coordinates the activities of the inferior courts of records. The legal assistants to judges help the judges in conducting research, which goes a long way in helping the judges write erudite judgments. The Registrars handle the filing of court processes, enrolment of court orders, compiling of records of proceedings, interfacing with the police and prisons for the executions of bail bonds, committal warrants and production warrants. The court clerks are responsible for handling cases files, sitting in the open court during court proceedings, endorsing on the case files what transpired in a case on any given date, etc. the bailiffs are responsible for service of court processes.

145. The appointment of these officers is made by the Judicial Service Commission with regard to the states, the Judicial Service Committee of the Federal Capital Territory, Abuja or the Federal Judicial Service Commission for the federal courts.[125] The process of appointment into these offices is similar to the appointment of civil servants in the general civil service recruitments in Nigeria.

---

124. Section 4 Magistrates' Courts Law 2009 of Lagos State.
125. *See, e.g.*, the Judicial Service Committee of the Federal Capital Territory Regulations (Revised Edition 2018).

§2. MEMBERS OF THE JUDICIARY

I. Incompatibilities

A. *Judges of Superior and Inferior Courts of Record*

146. In this segment, the discussion will be on conducts and inactions that are not expected of judicial officers and members of the judiciary. These conducts or omissions are considered incompatible with the office of a judicial officer as it has the tendency to bring the office into public odium and impede the confidence of members of the public in the judicial system. In Nigeria, the Code of Conduct for Judicial Officers regulates the conduct of Judicial Officers. The current operative Code of Conduct for Judicial Officers in Nigeria is the Code of Conduct for Judicial Officers of the Federal Republic of Nigeria 2016. This Code makes provisions for acts incompatible with the office of a judicial office holder. The Code defines a judicial officer to include both judges of the superior and inferior courts of record.[126] The prescription of the Code shall now be discussed.

147. A judicial officer shall not hold membership in any organization that discriminates on the basis of race, sex, religion, ethnicity, national origin or other relevant cause contrary to the fundamental rights and the fundamental objectives and directive principles of state policy under the 1999 Nigerian Constn.[127] The reason for this is not far-fetched. A judicial officer is meant to dispense justice without fear or favour and devoid of any prejudices. Similarly, where for any reason, a judge will be seen not to dispense justice impartially, the judge must disqualify himself from such proceedings. In that light, a judge should disqualify himself from proceedings in the following circumstances:

(1) where any member of the judicial officer's family is a litigant in the case;
(2) where the judicial officer is socially involved in a dating relationship with a lawyer, cases involving such lawyer and members of the lawyer's family;
(3) cases handled by the law firm where the judicial officers had worked before the officer's appointment as a judicial officer;

126. The definition of a judicial officer in Item 1 of the Explanatory Notes in the Code means a holder of the office of Chief Justice of Nigeria, a Justice of the SC, the President or Justice of the Court of Appeal, the Chief Judge or Judge of the Federal HC, the President or Judge of the National Industrial Court of Nigeria, the Chief Judge or Judge of the HC of a state and the Federal Capital Territory, Abuja, the Grand Kadi or Kadi of a Sharia Court of Appeal of a state and the Federal Capital Territory, Abuja, the President or Judge of the Customary Court of Appeal of a state and the Federal Capital Territory, Abuja, and every holder of a similar office in any office and tribunal where the duties involves adjudication of any dispute or disagreement between person and person (natural or legal) or person and government at federal, state and local government levels, including the agents and privies of any such person.

127. Rule 1.6 Code of Code for Judicial Officers of the Federal Republic of Nigeria 2016.

(4) cases before a judge where it appears that the judge or members of the judge's family or other persons with whom the judge is in a fiduciary relationship[128] is likely to benefit financially.[129]

148. It is not permitted for a judicial officer to allow his residence to be used by a member of the legal profession to receive clients or other members of the profession. It is equally incompatible with a judicial office for a lawyer to be allowed to use the residence of a judicial officer to meet clients or use the telephone line of the judicial officer in connection with the lawyer's legal practice.[130]

149. A judicial officer shall not in or outside Nigeria accept accommodation provided by a lawyer either in the lawyer's house or in a hotel paid for by the lawyer nor should a lawyer who is likely to appear before a judicial officer host the officer.[131] A judicial officer must not associate with lawyers and litigants who come to the judicial officer's court in a manner that will affect the judicial officer's impartiality. In addition, the Code frowns at excessive close relationships with frequent litigants such as government ministers or their officials, municipal officials, police prosecutors in any court where the judge sits, if such relationship could reasonably create an appearance of partiality.[132]

150. A judicial officer shall not accept gifts from a lawyer who might appear in his court except gifts given generally to all judges at festive seasons such as Christmas or Salah as long as such gifts are not more than that ordinarily given or are not of a pecuniary nature.[133]

151. Gambling as leisure is an act that is incompatible with the office of a judicial officer.[134]

152. Involvement in public controversies is an act incompatible with a judicial office. As a result, a judge is not permitted to allow himself to be involved or entangled in public controversies by expressing opinions on controversial subjects, involving in disputes with public figures in the community or openly criticizing the government. This includes a judicial officer expressing an opinion on social media on government policies and controversial public discussions.

---

128. The Code of Code for Judicial Officers of the Federal Republic of Nigeria 2016 defines fiduciary to include such relationships as executor, administrator, trustee and guardian. *See* Rule 7.3 of the Code.
129. The Code of Code for Judicial Officers of the Federal Republic of Nigeria 2016 defines financial interest as ownership in a substantial manner of a legal or equitable interest, or a relationship as director, adviser or other active participation in the affairs of a party.
130. Rule 2.3 Code of Code for Judicial Officers of the Federal Republic of Nigeria 2016.
131. Rule 2.6 *ibid.*
132. Rule 2.8 *ibid.*
133. Rule 2.5 *ibid.*
134. Rule 1.7 *ibid.*

153. Taking or accepting of chieftaincy titles while in office is incompatible with a judicial office.[135] The customs and traditions of Nigerians recognize the conferment of chieftaincy titles on illustrious sons or daughters of different communities. The acceptance of such titles may put judicial officers in a position where their impartiality may be called to question where the conferring authorities have matters before such judicial officers or there are disputes between such communities and others. The impartiality of a judicial arbiter is one of the bedrock in the administration of justice. It must not be tampered with directly or indirectly.

154. A judicial officer is not allowed to publish a book (this include biographies, essays, collection of Judgments, textbooks, journals, articles and any publication which may attract financial benefit or otherwise to the judicial officer or author if such author is different from the judicial officer) nor can he permit persons acting on his behalf to publish such until he ceases to hold office where such publication may infringe in any manner the Code of Conduct for Judicial Officer. From the provision of the Code, it appears that there is no absolute bar on a judicial officer publishing a book while in office. Where a judicial officer publishes a book while in service such officer shall ensure that such publication is not used as a means of raising funds beyond the normal cover or market price or as a donation or gift to the judicial officer. It is an abuse of office for a judicial officer to take advantage of the judicial office for personal gain or for gain by the judge's relatives or relations.[136]

155. Besides the above-discussed areas, it is incompatible with the judicial office for a judicial officer to participate in an organization be it a charitable organization, university/school council, religious body, or sporting organization, where the object of such organization is political or can expose the judicial officer to public controversy, the organization's activities will make excessive demand of the judicial officer's time, where the judicial officer is required to serve as a legal adviser to the organization, where the judicial officer will be required to lend his name to any fundraising by the organization, or where the organization requires its members to solicit if the solicitation might reasonably be perceived as coercive or is essentially a fundraising mechanism. The judicial officer should not belong to a social union or group where lawyers who appear before such officers are also members.[137]

156. A judicial officer though can own properties and investments, provided that in the management of the investment the judicial officer cannot be an officer, director, manager, adviser or employee of any investment entity.

157. In addition a judicial officer shall not practice law while in office, as it is incompatible with the office. The practice of law by a judicial officer includes work performed outside of a court and which has no immediate bearing with court proceedings, conveyance, giving of legal advice on a wide range of subjects, preparing and executing legal instruments covering an extensive field of business and trust

135. Rule 13.2 *ibid.*
136. Rule 8.3 *ibid.*
137. Rule 2.9 *ibid.*

relations, and other affairs. Acting as an arbitrator, mediator or in other judicial functions in a private capacity is also incompatible with a judicial office. Moreover, a judicial officer shall not be a member of a Tenders Board nor engage in the award of contract. Acts of engaging in sexual harassment, nepotism and favouritism are also incompatible with a judicial office.

B. Other Members of the Judiciary

158. For other members of the judiciary such as registrars, legal assistants, clerks and secretaries, the general code of conduct for civil servants regulates their conduct which is the Code of Conduct for Public Officers enshrined in the Fifth Schedule, Part 1 of the 1999 Constitution of the Federal Republic of Nigeria (as amended) and the Public Service Rules.

II. End of Functions

A. Judges of Superior Courts of Records

159. A judge of superior courts of record in Nigeria is generally expected to function as one until the stipulated retirement age. For Justices of the SC and Court of Appeal, the retirement age is 70 years while for the other judges of superior courts of records it is 65 years. However, a judicial officer may also cease to function as a result of incapacity or by disciplinary action. This will be discussed shortly. With regard to a judicial officer of a superior court of record, irrespective of the mode that brings to an end the functions of such judicial officer, such officer cannot appear before any court of law in Nigeria again. For further discussion on the restriction of judicial officers in the superior court of records to practise law, *see* paragraphs 204–205 below.

B. Judges of Inferior Courts of Records

160. For judges of the inferior courts of record, the general civil service rules apply to them. They cease functioning in their judicial capacity upon the compulsory retirement age of 60 years[138] or after having put in a total of thirty-five years of service. A Magistrate shall also cease to act as a Magistrate if in the opinion of the relevant Judicial Service Commission the Magistrate is mentally impaired or otherwise unable or unfit to discharge the functions of a Magistrate.[139] In addition, a Magistrate shall cease to hold office if the relevant Judicial Service Commission determines that the Magistrate be removed due to indiscipline or misconduct or incapacity to continue to hold the office.[140]

138. Section 10(a) Magistrates' Court Law 2009 of Lagos State.
139. Section 10(b) Magistrates' Court Law 2009 of Lagos State.
140. Section 10(c) Magistrates' Court Law 2009 of Lagos State.

C. *Other Members of the Judiciary*

161. Registrars, legal assistants and secretaries act as such until their retirement age, which is 60 years of age or thirty-five years of service whichever comes first according to the general civil service rules. They can also cease functioning where the Judicial Service Commission dismisses them from the service on grounds of indiscipline, misconduct or incapacity to continue to hold the office.

III. Discipline

162. Every profession or organization has rules and regulations guiding its members. In the same vein, such organizations also have in place mechanisms for disciplining their members. The 1999 Nigerian Constn provides for the grounds under which judicial officers of superior courts of record can be removed from office before the age of retirement.[141]

A. *Grounds for Removal of Judicial Officers*

163. The grounds for removing a judicial officer are contained in the 1999 Nigerian Constn.[142] They are as follows.

1. Inability to Discharge the Functions of the Office of a Judicial Officer

164. Where a judicial officer is unable to discharge the duties of the office either by infirmity of the mind or body, such officer can be removed from office. Infirmity of the mind includes insanity, medical control that makes the judicial officer not to be in control of his mental faculty such as epileptic seizures, etc. Infirmity of the body includes situations where the officer becomes permanently bedridden or conditions that deny the judicial officer the ability to carry out the functions of the judicial office.

2. Misconduct

165. A judicial officer may be removed from office where such an officer commits acts of misconduct. Misconduct has been defined as a dereliction of duty, unlawful or improper conduct.[143] The misconduct that will necessitate the removal of a judge from office includes acceptance of bribe, abuse of office, improper private conduct such as habitual drunkenness, dependency on drugs such as cocaine, heroin and Indian hemp, etc. The court has held that there is no rule of law defining

141. Section 292 of the 1999 Nigerian Constn.
142. *Ibid.*
143. B.A. Garner (ed.), *Black's Law Dictionary* 1019 (8th ed., West 2004).

the degree of misconduct that will justify the removal of a judge rather each case is determined on merit.[144] Examples of misconduct for which the NJC has recommended dismissal of judicial officers include being a director/chief executive officer of a company for which the judicial officer is also the sole signatory of the company's account,[145] having ex parte communications with a lawyer who has a matter before the judicial officer,[146] and collecting money from lawyers/litigants who have cases before the judicial officer.[147] Also, the NJC has issued advice to a judge for unwarranted utterances in a case before the judge.[148]

3. Contravention of the Code of Conduct for Public Officers

166. The code of conduct for public officers in Nigeria also binds judicial officers, as they are also public officers as defined under the 1999 Nigerian Constn.[149] The code of conduct for public officers prohibits certain actions.[150] A breach of the Code makes a public officer upon a finding of guilty by the Code of Conduct Tribunal liable to imposition of punishment. The punishment includes vacation from office, disqualification from holding any public office for a period not exceeding ten years, and seizure and forfeiture to the state of properties acquired in abuse of office or corruption of office.[151] It is to be noted that many of the actions proscribed by the Code of Conduct are similar in character to the ones proscribed under the Code of Conduct for Judicial Officer 2016. However, there is a particularly significant provision under the Code of Conduct for a public officer that is worthy of mention. It is the requirement of the declaration of assets by prescribed public officers. It is the most known provision of the Code, the breach of which has received publicity compared to others. A public officer is required to immediately after taking office to make a written declaration of his assets. Thereafter at the end of every four years and at the end of the public officer's tenure, he must also declare his assets and submit the written declaration to the Code of Conduct Bureau. The declaration includes the declaration of his properties, assets, liabilities and those of the public officer's spouse if such spouse is not a public officer and the officer's unmarried children below 18 years of age. The following is a breach of the code of conduct requirement of declaration of assets:[152]

---

144. *A.G Cross River State of Nigeria v. Esin* (1991) 6 NWLR (Pt 197) 365.
145. A Judge of the Federal HC of Nigeria was recommended for dismissal on this ground in 2018. This information is available on https://njc.gov.ng/11/news-details, accessed on 26 Jul. 2019.
146. *Ibid.*
147. A Judge of the National Industrial Court was dismissed on this ground in 2018. This information is available on https://njc.gov.ng/11/news-details, accessed on 26 Jul. 2019.
148. An HC Judge in one of the states of the Federation of Nigeria was reprimanded on this ground. This information is available on https://njc.gov.ng/11/news-details, accessed on 26 Jul. 2019.
149. Item 5 of Part 11 of the Fifth Schedule to the 1999 Constn.
150. These are contained in paras 1–13 of Part 1 of the Fifth Schedule to the 1999 Nigerian Constn.
151. Paragraph 18(2) *ibid.*
152. Paragraphs 11(2)(3) and 13 *ibid.*

(1) Any statement in such declaration that is found to be false by any authority or person authorized on that behalf to verify it shall be deemed to be a breach of the code.
(2) Any property or assets acquired by a public officer after any declaration required under the 1999 Nigerian Constn and which is not fairly attributable to income, gift or loan approved by the Code of Conduct for public officers shall be deemed to have been acquired in breach of this code unless the contrary is proved.
(3) A public officer who does any act prohibited by the Code of Conduct for public officers through a nominee, trustee or other agent shall be deemed ipso facto to have committed a breach of the Code.

167. A judicial officer who breaches any provision of the Code of Conduct for judicial officers can also be removed from office. For discussions on the Code of Conduct for Judicial Officers, *see* paragraphs 146–157 above.

168. It must be noted that it is not every breach of the code of conduct that will make a judicial officer liable for removal. Other forms of sanctions such as compulsory retirement, suspension and reprimand may be imposed rather than removal from office.

B. Procedure for Discipline of Judicial Officers of the Superior Courts of Record

169. The process of disciplining a judicial officer is set in motion where a complaint is written against the officer and sent to the NJC. In addition to the 1999 Nigerian Constn, the Judicial Discipline Regulation 2017 made by the NJC on 9 March 2017 and which came into force on 29 June 2017 regulates the procedure for the discipline of judges of superior courts of record. By the Regulation, complaints must be made within six months of the event or matter complained of. However, where the state of affairs complained is of a continuing nature, the complaint can be brought at any time while the state of affairs continues or within six months after it ceases to continue. Any complaint brought outside the time limit shall be dismissed.[153] It must be pointed out that the chairman of the NJC has the discretion to extend the time for making the complaint whether the time limit has expired or not if there is a good reason to do so.[154] The complaint is required to be in writing unless the Chairman of the NJC or a Head of Court or the NJC considers that in the circumstances it is reasonable to accept a complaint in another form. A complaint must contain a concise statement of the specific facts on which the claim of misconduct or disability is based. The statement of facts should include a description of:

(a) what happened;
(b) when and where the relevant event happened;

---

153. Regulation 11 of the Judicial Discipline Regulation 2017.
154. Regulation 12 *ibid.*

(c) any information that would help the investigator to check the facts;
(d) nature of the misconduct alleged, itemized where several types of misconduct are alleged; and
(e) for an allegation of disability, any additional facts that form the basis of the allegation.

170. The complaint may be typewritten or otherwise presented in a legible form. The Secretary may not accept an illegible complaint about filing and may return it to the complainant with a request to resubmit it in a legible form.[155] The complaint must be signed by the complainant and accompanied by a verifying affidavit deposed by the complainant before a Court of Record (any complaint not so verified shall be rejected for filing by the Secretary or by the Preliminary Complaint Assessment Committee also known as the 'Sifting Committee'). In addition, the complaint must contain a contact address provided by the complainant. Such contact address must not be solely a postal box address, but must include an address where the complainant can be located. Failure to comply with this may make the Secretary reject the complaint. Where in addition to a contact address a telephone number is given, such telephone number must have been registered in the name of the complainant or an identifiable person whose name is stated.

171. A complaint against a Judicial Officer must be addressed to the Chairman of the NJC and filed at the Office of the Secretary to the NJC. It can also be submitted to the Office of the Chief Justice of Nigeria or to the Head of Court of the Judicial Officer to whom the complaint relates. The recipient of a complaint is required to make and retain a copy of the complaint and forward the original to the Secretary of the NJC within seven days of the receipt of a Complaint. The Secretary shall cause the complaint to be registered in a Register in a Complaint Registry established by the Secretary indicating the date of the complaint, the date of filing or receipt of the complaint, the serial number assigned to the complaint, the name of the complainant, the name of the Judicial Officer subject of the complaint, a remarks column recording action taken and such other information as the Secretary may prescribe. In addition, the Secretary shall open a file for the complaint and assign a serial number to it. The Secretary shall then promptly seek further directives from the chairman of the NJC with regard to the complaint in circumstances as the Chairman may from time to time prescribe. Unless the complaint is withdrawn, the next stage will be for the Chairman of the NJC to assess a complaint or, he may at his discretion, refer it to a Preliminary Complaint Assessment Committee where such has been established. Upon this assessment, the Chairman of the NJC or the Preliminary Complaint Assessment Committee will advise the NJC as to whether the complaints should be dismissed, terminated or whether they should be referred to an Investigative Committee to investigate it. The advice can also include the complaint be referred to the Subject judicial officer for the officer's response (the subject Judicial Officer is required to file a reply to the complaint within fourteen

155. Regulation 14 *ibid.*

days of the receipt of the complaint, and the reply shall be accompanied by an affidavit deposed to by subject judicial officer before a Court of Record). The reply of the subject Judicial Officer shall be served on the complainant.

172. Where the NJC decides that a complaint be referred to an Investigation Committee, it shall immediately appoint an Investigation Committee directing it to investigate the complaint or a particular part of it and report back to and make recommendations to the NJC regarding it. The Investigation Committee shall be made up of not less than three and not more than five members of the NJC. The Chairman of the Investigating Committee must be a member of the NJC, appointed by the NJC from among the members of the Committee. It should be noted that:

> the Chairman of the Investigating Committee must be of a higher Judicial rank than the subject of the disciplinary proceedings while the members of the Committee whether serving or retired Judicial Officers may be of a higher Judicial rank or of the same Judicial rank as the subject of the disciplinary proceedings. In relation to a retired Judicial Officer, his judicial rank will be the rank he held immediately before he ceased to hold Judicial Office. With regards to the Investigative Committee's hearings, the Committee has the power to notify a subject Judge and the complainant of its proposals for the conduct of the investigation.

173. The Committee can invite a subject judge and the complainant to make representations on its proposals and shall make a recording of any representations on the proposals, which they may make. The subject judge and the complainant have a right to counsel. It is at the discretion of the Committee to decide whether or not other witnesses may have counsel present when they testify. All testimonies taken at the hearing shall be given under oath or affirmation and recorded, however, the rules of evidence do not apply to the Investigating Committee's hearings. At the hearings, the complainant shall be given an opportunity to produce evidence and call witnesses. Also, the subject judge has the right to present evidence, to compel the attendance of witnesses, to compel the production of witnesses and to cross-examine, in person or by counsel, the Investigative Committee's witnesses. At the close of the hearings, the subject judge and the complainant may submit written arguments to the Investigating Committee and shall be given a reasonable opportunity to present oral arguments at an appropriate stage of the hearing.

174. The Investigating Committee may, if it deems fit, forward a copy of its draft report or a part of the report excluding its recommendations, to the subject judge and the complainant and invite each of them to make a representation about it within fourteen days of delivery of the draft report. After considering any representations made by them, the Investigating Committee shall within thirty days of the representations complete its report and shall immediately submit to the NJC through the NJC Chairman a comprehensive report of its investigation, including its findings and recommendation for the NJC's action. A statement of the vote by which it was adopted signed by the Chairman and all members of the Committee with any dissenting or separate statements of Committee members shall accompany the report. The Investigating Committee report to the NJC must contain:

(1) its findings of facts on each of the allegations in the complaint;
(2) whether the case is substantiated or not;
(3) if the case is substantiated the nature of misconduct or misconducts or disability found;
(4) whether disciplinary action should be taken, and if so what disciplinary action should be taken; and
(5) findings with regard to any other matters in its terms of reference.

175. The next stage is for the NJC to consider the report of the Investigating Committee. Consequently, upon this, it may do any of the following:

(a) decide that the case is unsubstantiated and dismiss it;
(b) decide that the case is substantiated wholly or in part, but does not require further action and dismiss it;
(c) decide that the case is substantiated wholly or in part, but should be dealt with informally by the Chief Justice/Chairman of the NJC or any person nominated by him where the misconduct is not grave;
(d) decide that the case is substantiated wholly or in part and the NJC will, depending on the nature of the infraction committed by the subject judge, exercise one or more of its disciplinary powers to:
   - censure or reprimand the subject judge; or
   - suspend the subject judge; or
   - direct that the subject judge be put on a ‘watch list’ for the purpose of monitoring and reporting his conduct or ability to perform the functions of his office for a period specified by the NJC; or
   - prohibit the nomination of the subject judge for appointment to a higher Judicial Office for a specified period or permanently; or
   - recommend to the President or Governor, as the case may be, that the subject judge be removed from judicial office.

176. The President or Governor upon the recommendation for dismissal of a judicial officer will dismiss such an officer. However, where the judicial officer recommended for dismissal is the head of a court, in the case of a federal court including the superior courts of record of the Federal Capital Territory, Abuja, the President will have to act on an address supported by a two-thirds majority of the Senate of the Federal Republic of Nigeria to remove such head of court.[156] With respect to the states in Nigeria, where the judicial officer recommended by the NJC for dismissal by the Governor is the head of court in a state, the Governor of the state will only do so upon an address supported by a two-thirds majority of the House of Assembly of the state.[157]

156. Section 292(1)(a)(i) of the 1999 Nigerian Constn.
157. Section 292(1)(a)(ii) *ibid.*

177. The decision taken by the NJC shall be communicated to the subject judge, the complainant and the relevant head of court. Also, where a request is made to the NJC, the decision may be notified to any other person. The grant or refusal of such a request is at the absolute discretion of the NJC. The Secretary of the NJC usually communicates disciplinary decisions of the NJC to members of the public in a press conference.[158]

158. Regulation 27 of the Judicial Discipline Regulation 2017.

Chapter 2. The Bar

178. The bar in Nigeria refers to the legal profession. This profession is important in the governance structure of the country, as members of the profession constitute the third arm of government. A look at the conditions for admission into the profession, the rights and duties of a member of the profession, how members of the profession are disciplined and the bar in public institutions and private organizations shall be undertaken in this chapter.

§1. Exercise of the Legal Profession

I. Conditions for Admission

179. The Legal Practitioners Act (LPA) defines a Legal Practitioners as a 'person entitled in accordance with the LPA to practise as a barrister and solicitor either generally or for the purpose of any particular office or proceedings'.[159] By this definition, there are three categories of persons who can practice law in Nigeria namely: those entitled to practise generally, those entitled to practise for the purpose of any particular office and those entitled to practise for the purpose of any particular proceedings.

A. *Persons Entitled to Practise as Legal Practitioners Generally*

180. There are two sects of persons entitled to practise law generally in Nigeria. The first sect are those whose names have been enrolled in the roll of Legal Practitioners kept by the Chief Registrar of the SC by reason of their having been called to the Bar upon presentation of a qualifying certificate.[160] A person shall be entitled to be called to the Bar if such a person produces to the Body of Benchers a qualifying certificate stating that such person is qualified to be called to the Bar. The Council of Legal Education is the body responsible for issuing qualifying certificates to persons seeking to be called to the Nigerian Bar. In addition, the Body of Benchers must be satisfied that the person seeking to be called to the Nigerian Bar is of good character. For the Council of Legal Education to issue a qualifying certificate to a person, such must have successfully completed a practical training course for one academic year at the Nigerian Law School. The one-academic year training programme is made up of compulsory practical lectures on procedural laws in Nigeria, mock trials, attachment as law externs to court and in law offices for about four weeks and eight weeks respectively and a mandatory keeping of three dinning terms. In addition, such a person must be of good conduct and must have been sponsored by two members of the Body of Benchers. However, the Council of

159. Section 24 Legal Practitioners Act (LPA) as amended Cap L11 LFN 2004.
160. Section 2(1) *ibid.*

Legal Education may in certain cases waive the mandatory one academic year attendance at the Nigerian Law School under certain conditions.[161]

181. The conditions are:

(1) The person must be a Nigerian citizen.
(2) Such a person must be qualified for admission into the Nigerian Law School and fulfil the requirement of the qualifying subjects for admission into the Nigerian Law School including the core subjects prescribed by the Council of Legal Education.
(3) At the time of the application for exemption, the Council of Legal Education is satisfied that the applicant has acquired knowledge and experience over a period of at least five years fitting such a person for enrolment and that it will be unreasonable, having regard to all circumstances, to require such person to go through the Nigerian Law School.
(4) At the time the person was qualified to attend the Nigerian Law School or so soon thereafter, such person lost the opportunity of doing so by reasons beyond the person's control.[162]

A person who has been granted this exemption will not be required to fulfil the condition of presenting a qualifying certificate for a call to the Nigerian Bar. What the person will be required to produce will be the exemption certificate that the Council of Legal Education will issue to such a person.

It is pertinent to state here that partial exemption is granted to law teachers teaching in Nigerian universities who had obtained their Bachelor of Law degree outside Nigeria where they meet certain conditions. The exemption is only from attendance of the Bar Part 1 programme of the Nigerian Law School which ordinarily persons in a similar situation have to go through before they are qualified to be admitted into the Bar Part 11 programme. The conditions to be met for this partial exemption are:

(1) For law teachers who had their law degrees from a Common Law jurisdiction, they must have taught in a Nigerian University for at least five years.
(2) For law teachers who had their law degrees from a Civil Law jurisdiction, they must have taught law in a Nigerian university for at least ten years.

182. The law teacher, who gets the exemption, will then be required to only attend the Bar Part 11 programme. The rationale for requiring persons who obtained their law degrees in universities outside Nigeria to compulsorily attend the Bar Part 1 programme is to acquaint them with core Nigerian Law subjects which their training abroad may not necessarily have exposed them to. A law teacher's exemption from going through it is in my opinion on the basis that such a teacher would have by reason of exposure to these subjects while teaching in a Nigerian university garner sufficient knowledge of these subjects to warrant exemption from taking them.

---

161. The Council of Legal Education exercises this powers under ss 2(5) and 5(b) of the Legal Education (Consolidation) Act Cap L10 LFN 2004.
162. Legal Notice 439 of 5 Jul. 1989.

183. The second category of persons who can practice law generally are persons whose names are enrolled in the roll of lawyers by reason of a regulation made by the AG which provides for the enrolment of their names.[163] The persons under this category are non-Nigerians practising law in countries with which Nigeria has such reciprocal arrangements. The said Regulation is made at the discretion of the AG after consultation with the Bar Council and the Body of Benchers. The regulation may require such persons to pass such examinations and pay such fees as may be prescribed by or under the regulations and also provide for the cancellations of enrolments made pursuant to the regulation where in the opinion of the AG the facilities are altered or withdrawn.

B. Persons Entitled to Practise by Virtue of Office

184. It is appropriate to give a brief background on those entitled to practise by reason of their office. In 1962, when the law providing for this provision was made, there was a dearth of legal practitioners in Nigeria to cover the various government offices at the federal and state levels. To fill the obvious gap, the provision was made to allow certain persons to practise as barristers and solicitors by reason of the office they occupy. There are two categories of person who may be allowed to practise law by reason of their office. They are legal practitioners employed by the government as legal officers and second, persons who exercise the functions of an AG, Solicitor-General and Director of Public Prosecution whether at the federal or state level. They are entitled to practise as a barrister and solicitor for the purpose of their offices.[164] The importance of this provision is that a person occupying this position though not a legal practitioner is allowed to practise as one. Following this provision, the AGF has by an order designated some offices in the public service as ones for which the occupants can practice as barristers and solicitors for the purposes of their offices. This includes law officers in the Federal Ministry of Justice, legal practitioners employed in the Legal Services Department of the National Assembly,[165] Road Safety Commission,[166] Federal Housing Authority,[167] etc. With the Nigerian Law School having trained over 100,000 lawyers since its establishment this provision seems to have lost its least relevance and should be deleted.

C. Persons Entitled to Practise in Particular Proceedings

185. By section 2(2) LPA 2004, the Chief Justice of Nigeria may upon application by or on behalf of a person appearing to the Chief Justice of Nigeria to be

163. Section 7(2) LPA 2004.
164. Section 2(3)(a) of the LPA 2004.
165. Entitlement to Practice as Barristers and Solicitors (National Assembly Office) (Legal Practitioners) Order 1995.
166. Entitlement to Practice as Barristers and Solicitors (Federal Road Safety Commission) (Legal Officers) Order 1997.
167. Entitlement to Practice as Barristers and Solicitors (Federal Housing Authority) (Legal Practitioners) Order 1995.

entitled to practise as an advocate in any country where the legal system is similar to that of Nigeria. Where the Chief Justice of Nigeria is of the opinion that it is expedient to permit that person to practise as a barrister in Nigeria for the purposes of particular proceedings as indicated in the person's application, the Chief Justice of Nigeria can issue a warrant under his hand authorizing that person to practise as a barrister in Nigeria for the purposes of those specific proceedings and any appeal arising therefrom provided the person pays to the Registrar such fee not exceeding Naira (NGN) 50. This provision is in consonance with section 36(6)(c) of the 1999 Nigerian Constn that guarantees a choice of legal representation to a person charged with an offence. Where a person charged with an offence chooses a lawyer in a foreign country, such can come to Nigeria to practise in such proceedings. However, the court has held that the issuance of a warrant for a legal practitioner in a foreign jurisdiction to come into Nigeria and practise in a particular proceeding does not obviate the obligation on such legal practitioner to meet Nigerian immigration conditions and be allowed lawful entry into the country.[168]

II. Rights and Duties of a Legal Practitioner in Nigeria

186. A legal practitioner practising in Nigeria is conferred with certain rights as provided for by the LPA 2004 and other relevant laws. Consequently, the legal practitioner is under certain obligations towards the legal practitioner clients, the legal profession, the Nigerian State and fellow colleagues.

A. Rights of a Legal Practitioner in Nigeria

187. By reason of being admitted into the noble profession of law in Nigeria certain rights and privileges are accorded to members of the profession that other persons do not enjoy. These rights and privileges are as follows

1. Rights of Audience in Any Court in Nigeria

188. A legal practitioner is entitled to appear in any court of law to represent his client and be accorded a right of audience. Section 8(1) LPA 2004 provides that a legal practitioner shall have the right of audience in all courts of law sitting in Nigeria. This right has its roots in the 1999 Constn. As such any law that makes any provision to the contrary is void to the extent of the inconsistency. This situation played out in *Uzodinma v. C.O.P.*[169] where section 28 of the Area Court Edict 1967 and section 390 of the Criminal Procedure Code Act were subject to the court's interpretation. Both sections prohibit the appearance of a legal practitioner before a native court, which in this case was the Area Court. The court held that both sections were unconstitutional and void to the extent of their inconsistency with the

168. *Awolowo v. Minister of Internal Affairs* (1966) NSCC 209.
169. (1982) 1 NCR 27 (HC Benue State).

constitutional practitioner entitling a person to legal representation of choice. Closely related to this right, is the right of a legal practitioner who appears in court on behalf of a client to charge professional fees if the legal practitioner so desires.

189. The right to audience before any court in Nigeria enjoyed by a legal practitioner has some limitations. A legal practitioner is required to pay yearly practising fees.[170] Lawyers in Nigeria are required to pay their annual practising fees not later than 31 March of every year.[171] For new wigs that get enrolled during the year, they are required to pay their practising fees within a month of enrolment. This provision for payment of practising fees not later than 31 March of every year and within one month for new wigs has recently been affected by the deletion of Rule 9(2) from the RPC 2007 by the Rules of Professional Conduct for Legal Practitioners (Amendment) Rules 2020.[172] Section 12 (4) of the LPA 2004 empowers the Bar Council to make rules regulating professional conduct in the legal profession in Nigeria from time to time. The General Bar Council is made up of the Attorney General of the Federation who is the president of the Bar Council, the Attorney General of the thirty-six states in Nigeria and twenty members of the NBA.[173] The twenty members of the NBA are elected to serve on the Bar Council at elections in which members of the NBA are entitled to vote in the manner prescribed in the NBA's constitution.[174] The twenty members of the NBA holds office in the Bar Council for such a period as determined under the NBA constitution. The LPA requires that not less than seven of these twenty NBA members shall be legal practitioners of not less than ten years standing at the Nigerian Bar.[175] The quorum of the Bar Council shall be eight members.[176]

Rule 9(2) prohibits a lawyer who has not paid his practising fees from signing documents, pleadings, affidavits, letters, or similar documents and such a lawyer shall not file processes or documents as a legal practitioner, legal officer or legal adviser of any government department. The deletion of this rule appears to take away the obligation in Rule 9 (1) RPC that requires legal practitioners to pay their practising fees not later than 31 March of each year. This is because if a legal practitioner can draft documents, court processes and file them without having paid his practising fees, then the need to pay the fees is taken away. Perhaps, it is only legal practitioners who would be appearing in court that may see the need to pay their practising fees as section 8(2) of the LPA makes payment of practising fees a condition precedent to a right of audience before any court. It should be noted that the

170. Section 8(2) LPA 2004.
171. Rule 9(1) RPC 2007.
172. The gazette which amended the RPC 2007 is marked S.I No. 15 of 2020 dated 3 Sep. 2020.
173. Section 1 (2) LPA 2004.
174. Section 1(3)(a) LPA 2004.
175. Section 1(3)(b) LPA 2004.
176. When the amendment was gazetted, issues about the legality of the process that birthed it were raised by many members of the legal profession. However, there is yet no decision of any court in Nigeria declaring the amendment illegal and void. As such it stands as the extant position of the law.

payment of practising fees by legal practitioners in Nigeria being a statutory provision cannot be amended by the Bar Council as it is an Act of Parliament. The purport of deleting Rule 9(2) from the RPC 2007 was not stated in the amending instrument.

2. Right to Prepare Court Processes on Behalf of Their Client

190. Legal practitioners in Nigeria have the right to prepare court processes for their client and file them in court for a fee if the legal practitioner so desires. These court processes range from writ of summons, originating summons, pleadings, election petitions, divorce petitions motions, etc. Some of these court processes require the name and signature of the legal practitioner who prepared it. Formerly, the law required that court processes should bear the stamp and seal of the lawyer who prepared them.[177] This provision has been deleted from the RPC 2007 by the Rules of Professional Conduct for Legal Practitioners (Amendment) Rules 2020. The processes were also required to carry the National Identification Number (NIN) of the lawyer.[178] The SC has held that the Regulation of the National Identity Management Commission requiring court processes to carry NIN of counsel, who filed the action or that of the claimant where such sues in person, are not part of the Rules of court and can therefore not apply to the processes filed in court.[179] Section 22(1)(d) LPA 2004 provides that:

> Any person other than a legal practitioner who prepares for or in expectation of reward any instrument relating to immovable property, or relating to or with a view to the grant of probate or letters of administration, or relating to or with a view to proceedings in any court of record commits an offence and liable on a second or subsequent offence to a fine of an amount not exceeding N200 or term of imprisonment not exceeding two years or both.

As such it is only legal practitioners that can render these services. In doing this the legal practitioner can act pro bono or for a fee.

3. Right to Prepare Documents on Behalf of Their Client

191. A legal practitioner has the right to prepare legal documents such as instruments relating to grant of probate or letters of administration, instruments relating to immovable properties such as deed of assignment, Power of Attorney, etc. for a fee. Section 22(1)(d) LPA 2004 confers this right. The fees to be charged with regard to some legal documents are regulated by the Legal Practitioners (Remuneration for Legal Documentation and Other Land Matters) Order 1991. The

---

177. Rule 10 RPC 2007.
178. Regulation 1(u) of Part 1 of the Mandatory Use of the National Identification Number Regulation 2017.
179. *APC & Anor v. Marafa* (2020) 6 NWLR (Pt 1721) 383 SC.

requirement in Rule 10 RPC 2007 for a lawyer to affix his stamp and seal on legal documents prepared by him has been deleted from the RPC 2007 by the Rules of Professional Conduct for Legal Practitioners (Amendment) Rules 2020.

4. A Legal Practitioner Is Entitled to Sign the Statutory Declaration of Compliance with the Companies and Allied Matters Act in Registration of Companies Form

192. The incorporation of companies in Nigeria requires among other steps, the filling and filing of incorporation Form CAC 1.1, which is the form for registration of companies. Though an applicant or his agent for incorporation of a company are the persons required to make a declaration as to compliance with the requirement for incorporation, a legal practitioner is accepted as one who could make a statutory declaration of compliance with the requirement of the Companies and Allied Matters Act 2020[180] for registration of a company before a Commissioner for Oath or Notary Public.[181]

5. Right to Be Appointed a Member of Some Statutory Bodies

193. There are some statutory bodies in Nigeria that the law establishing them provides as part of its membership, members of the legal profession. Examples include the Council of Legal Education, the Body of Benchers, etc.

6. Right to Be Appointed an AG

194. The 1999 Nigerian Constn of Nigeria creates the office of the AG either of the Federation[182] or of a state.[183] For a person to be qualified to hold or perform the functions of an AG whether at the federal or state level, such must have been qualified to practise as a legal practitioner in Nigeria and have been so qualified for not less than ten years.[184] From these provisions, it is clear that only a legal practitioner can be appointed as an AG in Nigeria.

7. Appointment as a Judge of a Superior Court of Record

195. The 1999 Nigerian Constn provides for the appointment of and qualification for appointment of persons as judges of the superior courts of record such as

---

180. The Companies and Allied Matters Act 2020 repealed the Companies and Allied Matters Act 1990 Cap C20 LFN 2004.
181. Section 40(3) *Companies and Allied Matters Act 2020.*
182. Section 150(1) of the 1999 Nigerian Constn.
183. Section 195(1) of the 1999 Nigerian Constn.
184. Sections 150(2) and 195(2) of the 1999 Nigerian Constn respectively.

the SC,[185] Court of Appeal,[186] Federal HC,[187] National Industrial Court,[188] HC of the Federal Capital Territory,[189] HC of a state,[190] Sharia Court of Appeal[191] and Customary Court of Appeal.[192] It is obvious that only legal practitioners can be appointed to these courts. It must be noted also that qualification as a legal practitioner is required for appointment as judges of some inferior courts. For example, by section 4(2) of the Magistrates' Court Law of Lagos State 2009, only legal practitioner of not less than five years post call to the Bar experience is eligible for appointment as a Magistrate by the Lagos State Judicial Service Commission.

8. Appointment as a Notary Public

196. Legal practitioners who have consistently paid practising fees for seven years within the period stated by law (which is on or before 31 March of each year) and are adjudged fit and proper are eligible to be appointed as Notary Publics. As a Notary Public a legal practitioner is entitled to notarize affidavits and documents requiring notarization for a fee.

9. Conferment with the Rank of Senior Advocate of Nigeria

197. The distinguished rank of senior advocate of Nigeria can only be conferred on a legal practitioner.[193] The rank is conferred on legal practitioners who have distinguished themselves in the practice of law or in academics. The selection of legal

185. Such person must be qualified to practice as a legal practitioner in Nigeria and has been so qualified for a period of not less than fifteen years. *See* s. 231(3) of the 1999 Nigerian Constn.
186. Such person must be qualified to practice as a legal practitioner in Nigeria and has been so qualified for a period of not less than twelve years. *See* s. 238(3) of the 1999 Nigerian Constn.
187. Such person must be qualified to practice as a legal practitioner in Nigeria and has been so qualified for a period of not less than ten years. *See* s. 250(3) of the 1999 Nigerian Constn.
188. One of the qualifications is that such person must be qualified to practice as a legal practitioner in Nigeria and has been so qualified for a period of not less than ten years. *See* s. 254B(4) of the 1999 Nigerian Constn as amended by Section 6 of the Constitution of the Federal Republic of Nigeria (Third Alteration) Act 2010.
189. Such person must be qualified to practice as a legal practitioner in Nigeria and has been so qualified for a period of not less than ten years. *See* s. 256(3) of the 1999 Nigerian Constn.
190. Such person must be qualified to practice as a legal practitioner in Nigeria and has been so qualified for a period of not less than ten years. *See* s. 271(3) of the 1999 Nigerian Constn.
191. One of the qualifications is that such person must be qualified to practice as a legal practitioner in Nigeria and has been so qualified for a period of not less than ten years. *See* s. 261(3) of the 1999 Nigerian Constn for Sharia Court of Appeal of the Federal Capital Territory and s. 276(3) of the 1999 Nigerian Constn for that of the State.
192. One of the qualifications is that such person must be qualified to practice as a legal practitioner in Nigeria and has been so qualified for a period of not less than ten years. *See* s. 266(3) of the 1999 Nigerian Constn for Customary Court of Appeal of the Federal Capital Territory and s. 281(3) of the 1999 Nigerian Constn for that of the State.
193. Section 5(2) LPA 2004.

practitioners to be accorded this privilege and the conferment of the rank on them is the responsibility of the Legal Practitioners Privileges Committee.[194] The process is usually conducted yearly.

B. Restrictions on the Rights of Legal Practitioners in Nigeria

198. The rights that a legal practitioner enjoys as discussed above are not without restriction. It is trite that there are no absolute rights. The limitations are as follows.

1. Payment of Practising Fees

199. A legal practitioner is required to pay a yearly practising fee, and this is to be done no later than 31 March of each year except newly enrolled legal practitioners who are required to pay their practising fees within one month from the date of enrolment.[195] A legal practitioner who had not paid his practising fees would be denied right of audience before the court. Before the amendment to the RPC 2007, such a legal practitioner cannot sign court processes, documents, deeds, reports, legal opinions, etc.[196] The practising fees are paid to the Registrar of the SC who issues a receipt to the legal practitioner. To make this process simpler and in line with best practices, legal practitioners obtain SC customized tellers from designated banks and use them to pay their practising fees. The retained copy of the teller serves as the receipt for the payment of practising fees. However, the requirement that payment of annual practising fees is to be done not later than 31 March of every year has been greatly affected by the deletion of Rule 9(2) from the RPC 2007. *See* paragraph 189 above. By section 8(3) LPA 2004, the Registrar of the SC shall as soon as reasonably practicable after the end of January in each year and thereafter from time to time during the year publish the list of legal practitioners who have paid their practising fees. This provision appears not to have been effectively implemented, as the fact of payment of practising fees by a legal practitioner is not readily in the public domain. In the past, some judges resorted to requesting that lawyers produced the receipts of payment of practising fees before they grant them audience in court. The NBA by Rule 12 RPC 2007 also had the responsibility of compiling a list of lawyers who had paid their practising fees for the year not later than a date in every year specified by the NBA. However, this provision has been deleted from the rules by the Rules of Professional Conduct for Legal Practitioners (Amendment) Rules 2020.

200. The NBA has in a bid to ensure compliance and also rid the profession of non-lawyers posing as one, introduced in 2016, the legal practitioner's stamp and seal. However, as stated in paragraph 190 above, this requirement has been deleted

194. Section 5(1) *ibid.*
195. Rule 9(1) RPC 2007.
196. Section 8(2) LPA and Rule 9 RPC 2007.

from the rules. A pre-condition to obtaining this stamp and seal apart from paying for it is evidence of payment of practising fees. No reasons were given for deletion of this requirement from the RPC in the amending instrument.

2. Restrictions on Involvement in Business

201. A legal practitioner is prohibited from engaging in business and at the same practise the legal profession. A legal practitioner cannot be practising law and at the same time be personally engaged in buying and selling commodities, acting as a commission agent or involved in such other trade or business as the General Council of the Bar may from time to time declare as incompatible with the legal profession.[197] There are exceptions to this position. First, the restriction does not however extend to when a legal practitioner is a member of the board of directors of a company that does not require the legal practitioner to undertake executive, administrative or clerical functions.[198] Second, it does not affect a legal practitioner who is a secretary to a company. In addition, a legal practitioner can be a shareholder in a company without being in breach of this position.

3. A Legal Practitioner Cannot Practise Law Together with Another Profession

202. The RPC guiding the conduct of legal practitioners in Nigeria prohibits a lawyer from practising law at the same time as practise any other profession except the legal practitioner concerned gets the approval of the General Council of the Bar to so do.[199] Situations are rife where a person already trained and involved in the practise of another profession decides to get a law degree and subsequently gets called to the Nigerian Bar. Such may want to practise both professions simultaneously. This is not allowed except as already mentioned.

4. Restrictions on Lawyers in Full-Time Salaried Employment

203. A legal practitioner while in salaried employment cannot appear as counsel in a court or judicial tribunal on behalf of his employer.[200] This includes a director of a registered company.[201] The exception to this rule is legal practitioners employed as legal officers in Government Departments. However, a legal practitioner in salaried employment but not in the public service can appear in court, frank processes or documents on behalf of persons who are not such a legal practitioner's employer. Lawyers in salaried employment may represent their employer as an officer or agent where the law allows such employer to appear by its officers. But in

197. Rule 7(2) RPC 2007.
198. Rule 7(3) *ibid.*
199. Rule 7(1) *ibid.*
200. Rule 8(1) *ibid.*
201. Rule 8(3) *ibid.*

such cases the lawyer will not appear robed in court.[202] A legal practitioner who is an officer in the Armed Forces can discharge any duty imposed on such legal practitioner by reason of his position and can appear in a court martial but as an officer and not as a lawyer.[203] Also, a legal practitioner in salaried employment cannot while in the employment prepare, sign or frank pleadings, applications, instruments, agreements, contracts, deeds, letters, legal opinion, etc. or file them on behalf of his employer.[204]

204. A legal practitioner who is employed in the public service is prohibited from engaging in private legal practice. Paragraph 2(b) of Part 1 of the Fifth Schedule to the 1999 Nigerian Constn prohibits any public officer employed on a full-time basis from engaging in the management or running of any private business, profession or trade. The public officer can however engage in farming.

5. Restriction on Legal Practitioners Appointed to the Bench as Judges of Superior Courts

205. A legal practitioner who is appointed to the higher bench is upon leaving the bench for whatever reason barred from appearing before and/or frank any processes for filing in any court of law in Nigeria. Section 292(2) of the 1999 Nigerian Constn provides:

> Any person who has held office as a judicial officer shall not on ceasing to be a judicial officer for any reason whatsoever thereafter appear or act as a legal practitioner before any court of law or tribunal in Nigeria.

Judicial officers for the purpose of this section refer to judges of the superior courts of record in Nigeria. It is pertinent to point out that this restriction does not extend to situations where such judicial officers represent themselves in actions where they are a party. Former judicial officers can represent themselves in court as in such situations they will not be representing a client. Supporting this position, in *Justice F.O.M. Atake v. Chief N.A. Afejuku*,[205] the SC considering section 296(2) of the 1979 Nigerian Constn (which provision is in *pari materia* with section 294(2) of the 1999 Nigerian Constn) stated that:

> To appear or act as a legal practitioner within the purview of the Section, the legal practitioner must appear or act for and on behalf of a client. The Section does not deprive the complainant of his right of audience to conduct and prosecute his case in person … and that though the appellant as a retired judicial

202. Rule 8(4) *ibid.*
203. Rule 8(5) RPC.
204. Rule 8(2) RPC 2007.
205. (1994) 12 SCNJ 1 at 11.

officer had no right of audience in any court in Nigeria, he was entitled to represent himself in court. The court held further that the 'proposition that a barrister litigant who conducts his case in person is acting as a legal practitioner is misconceived'.

206. There is no prohibition however on such judicial officers engaging in solicitors' work or consultancy services as long as they do not pertain to any matter they may have presided over as a judicial officer. The restriction of not taking up matters that they have handled as judicial officers also affects Magistrates and Law Officers. Though they can engage in the practice of law after leaving their positions as Magistrates and law officers, they are not allowed to handle cases connected to matters they had handled when they were Magistrates and Law officers.

6. Restrictions on Lawyers Conferred with the Rank of Senior Advocate of Nigeria

207. A lawyer conferred with the rank of Senior Advocate of Nigeria enjoys certain privileges as well as is subject to certain restrictions. First, such legal practitioners do not have the right of audience nor can settle documents before inferior courts of records in civil matters. The application of this rule was tested in the case of *Registered Trustee of ECWA v. Ijesha*,[206] where objections were raised against the appearance of a learned silk before an Area Customary Court (an inferior court of record). The Court of Appeal of Nigeria held that a Senior Advocate of Nigeria is not entitled to appear on behalf of his client before an inferior court of record. However, this restriction no longer apply to the Magistrates' Court in Lagos State as section 9 of the Magistrates' Court Law of Lagos State 2009 expressly allows a Senior Advocate of Nigeria to appear before the Magistrate Court though it is an inferior court of records and the court have pronounced on this provision holding that a Senior Advocate of Nigeria can appear before the Magistrate Court in Lagos State.[207] Second, a Senior Advocate shall not appear as counsel in any civil matter before any superior court of record alone but must appear either with a junior legal practitioner or with another silk.[208]

208. But a learned silk can appear alone in any motion or other civil cause or matter in a judge's chambers or elsewhere that is not an open courtroom.[209] In addition, a Senior Advocate of Nigeria is barred from accepting a brief to draft any instrument (such as any agreement, will, lease, mortgage, charge, power of attorney, settlement or any other document having or intended to have legal implications) where the appropriate or prescribed fees are less than NGN 400. The exceptions to this restriction are that the learned Senior Advocate can draft such

206. (1999) 13 NWLR (Pt 653) 368 (CA).
207. *A.G. Lagos State v. Persons Unknown & Okwudiri Uzodike* (2016) AFWLR (Pt 815) 245 (MC Lagos State).
208. Rule 2(1) of the Senior Advocate of Nigeria (Privileges and Functions) Rules 2004.
209. Rule 2(2) *ibid.*

instrument if it is done for free or where such document is connected with parliamentary processes and it is drafted for a fee lesser than the prescribed charges.[210] This provision is long overdue for revision of the amount upward as it is not possible to have any legal document drafted as at the time of writing this work for a fee of NGN 400.

7. Restriction Imposed by the Use of Stamp and Seal

209. One of the rights of a legal practitioner already discussed above is the right to draft certain documents. Formerly, for any of such document to be deemed to be properly signed or filed by a legal practitioner, such document or process must have affixed on them the stamp and seal of that legal practitioner as approved by the NBA.[211] A process filed or document signed without the stamp and seal of the legal practitioner that filed or signed it was deemed not properly filed or signed.[212] However, this requirement has been deleted from the RPC 2007 by the Rules of Professional Conduct for Legal Practitioners (Amendment) Rules 2020. *See* paragraph 190 above. A legal practitioner obtains the stamp and seal by applying to the NBA for it. The application shall have annexed to it evidence of payment of practising fees for the year and receipt of payment for the stamps and seals. There are situations where a lawyer who needs to sign and file processes has applied for and paid for the stamp and seal but has not been issued with one. In the case of *RE: Alhaja Safurat Olufunke Yakubu & Anor*,[213] court has held that where counsel attaches evidence of payment for the stamp to the court processes filed, the process is not incompetent as a party cannot be punished for the tardiness of the NBA in issuing the stamps.

8. Restriction Imposed by the Use of NIN

210. Under the Mandatory Use of the National Identification Number Regulation 2017, a legal practitioner requires a NIN to be able to file or register criminal and civil actions in courts or other arbitration processes.[214] However, the SC has held that this Regulation cannot apply to court processes. This has been earlier discussed in paragraph 190 above.

210. Rule 5 *ibid.*
211. Rule 10 of the RPC 2007.
212. Rule 10(3) *ibid.*
213. (2018) LPELR-43678 (CA). *See also Yaki v. Bagudu* (2015) LPELR-25721 (SC), *Todays Cars Ltd v. LASACO Assurance PLC* (2016) LPELR-41260 (CA).
214. *See* Regulation 1(u) of Part 1 of the Mandatory Use of the National Identification Number Regulation 2017.

9. Mandatory Continuing Professional Development Programme

211. The need to ensure that there is continuous capacity building for lawyers in Nigeria to align them with best practices globally, there is a mandatory prescription for lawyers who wish to carry on practice as a legal practitioner to participate in and satisfy the requirement of the mandatory Continuing Professional Development (CPD) Programme operated by the NBA.[215] Rule 11 RPC 2007 which provides for mandatory continuing legal education for lawyers in Nigeria has been deleted from the RPC by the Rules of Professional Conduct for Legal Practitioners (Amendment) Rules 2020. No reasons were given for the deletion of this provision from the RPC 2007. Under the deleted rule, the activities which a lawyer was expected to participate in with regard to the CPD are: attendance and participation in accredited courses; lectures, seminars, workshops and conferences on law approved by the NBA; writing on the law and its practice in books or journals and newspapers approved by the NBA; study towards professional qualifications approved by the NBA; and other approved means of acquiring legal professional knowledge and experience.[216]

212. For a lawyer to qualify for certification as having satisfied the requirement of the CPD programme, such a lawyer must during the relevant year, earn such number of credit hours of participation in the programme as required by any rules made by the NBA in furtherance of the CPD programme.[217] The NBA is expected to issue an annual practising certificate to a legal practitioner whose name is on the Annual Practising List. For a legal practitioner's name to be on this list, such must have paid the practising fee for the year and complied with the requirements of the CPD Programme. A lawyer who does not hold an annual practising certificate shall not conduct or take part in any proceedings in court, judicial tribunal or panel of enquiry. Such a lawyer cannot also sign any documents, pleadings, affidavit, depositions, applications, instruments, agreement, letters, memorandum, legal opinion or similar documents and processes nor file such documents as a legal practitioner, legal adviser or adviser of any government Department or Ministry or any company or corporation.[218]

213. The NBA is empowered to set up a CPD Department in its office for the operation of the programme.[219] This power however does seem to conflict with the

215. Rule 11(1) of the RPC 2007. This Rule has been deleted from the RPC 2007 by the Rules of Professional Conduct for Legal Practitioners (Amendment) Rules 2020.
216. Rule 11(2) *ibid.* This Rule has been deleted from the RPC 2007 by the Rules of Professional Conduct for Legal Practitioners (Amendment) Rules 2020.
217. Rule 11(3) *ibid.* This Rule has been deleted from the RPC 2007 by the Rules of Professional Conduct for Legal Practitioners (Amendment) Rules 2020.
218. Rule 12(3) *ibid.* This Rule has been deleted from the RPC 2007 by the Rules of Professional Conduct for Legal Practitioners (Amendment) Rules 2020.
219. Rule 11(5) *ibid.* This Rule has been deleted from the RPC 2007 by the Rules of Professional Conduct for Legal Practitioners (Amendment) Rules 2020.

powers conferred on the Council of Legal Education to undertake continuing legal education for members of the legal profession.[220]

10. Restriction on Legal Practitioner from Handling a Case Where He Is Likely to Be Called as a Witness

214. The RPC in Nigeria prohibits a lawyer from taking a brief where there is a likelihood of such legal practitioner or a lawyer from their firm appearing as a witness in the case.[221] However, there are situations where a lawyer is allowed to take a brief despite the possibility of being called as a witness. This is the case where the testimony of the lawyer will relate solely to an uncounted matter; or a matter of formality and there is no reason to believe that substantial evidence will be offered in opposition to the testimony; or where the testimony will relate solely to the nature and value of legal services rendered in the case by the lawyer or his firm to the client; or as to any matter if refusal would work a substantial hardship on the client because of the distinctive value of the lawyer or his firm as a lawyer in the particular case.[222]

215. Where the fact of the possibility of becoming a witness came to the knowledge of the lawyer after taking the brief, the lawyer and his firm shall withdraw from representing the client but a lawyer is allowed to testify with regard to the exceptions discussed above. There will be no need to withdraw if the testimony the lawyer is to give in the case is not on behalf of his client except it is apparent that the testimony will be prejudicial to his client.[223] Where during the trial, the ends of justice requires that a lawyer testifies in his client's case, he should from that point on leave further conduct of the case to another counsel. Where this is not practicable and the lawyer continues to represent the client, he shall not argue the credibility of his own testimony.[224]

11. Restriction on Mode of Carrying Out Legal Practice

216. In Nigeria, it is unlawful to carry out the practice of law as a corporation.[225] This means a law firm cannot be incorporated as a legal personality. Lawyers are however allowed to form partnerships that can be registered as a business name. The partnership can only be one made up of lawyers. This is because a lawyer is not allowed to form a partnership with a non-lawyer or a lawyer who has not

220. *See* s. 3 of the Legal Education (Consolidation etc.) Act 2004.
221. Rule 20(1) RPC 2007.
222. Rule 20(2) *ibid.*
223. Rule 20(4) and (5) *Ibid.*
224. Rule 20(6) *ibid.*
225. Rule 5(5) *ibid.*

been admitted to practise law in Nigeria.[226] Where a lawyer in a partnership has been appointed as a judge who is not allowed to practise, his name must be taken off the name of the partnership.[227]

12. Rule Requiring Appearance in Lawyers Robes Before Superior Courts of Records

217. A lawyer is required to appear robed in his wig and gown with the accessories accompanying them before a superior court of record. The court will not grant audience to a lawyer who is not properly robed. For the inferior court of records, though lawyers are not required to appear robed, they must however be attired in dark suits.

C. Duties of a Lawyer

218. In this segment, the duties of a lawyer as obtainable in Nigeria under the relevant laws shall be discussed under five headings namely; duty to the Nigerian state, duty to the Legal profession, duty to the court, duty to fellow colleagues, and duty to client.

1. A Lawyers' Duty to the Nigerian State

219. Legal practitioner owes a duty to the state where they practise to see to it that in the conduct of their legal practice, the laws of the state are upheld. In his representation of his client, the lawyer must not counsel, aid or participate in unlawful conduct. The lawyer must in the conduct of the client's case keep strictly within the bounds of the law even in the face of contrary instructions from his client. Though the general position is that a lawyer must carry out his clients' instructions, this is only to the extent that such instructions are within the bounds of the law. Where a client insists on a line of action that is in breach of the law, the lawyer must withdraw representation. A lawyer is also under an obligation to do all within his powers to prevent and restrain his client from breaching the law. Particular emphasis is placed on the conduct of a lawyer's client towards judicial officers, witnesses and litigants. A lawyer must neither give advice nor assist his client to do anything that is capable of bringing disrespect to the holder of a judicial office or involving corruption of a public officer. Where a lawyer assist or advice his client to participate in conduct that tends to amount to impinging on the impartiality of a judicial officer, such a legal practitioner can be sanctioned by the Legal Practitioners' Disciplinary Committee. Counsel must not assist his client in conduct that is illegal or fraudulent. Counsel is also under obligation where in the representation of a client,

226. Rule 5(1) *ibid.*
227. Rule 5(3) *ibid.*

he receives clearly established information that the client has perpetrated a fraud on a person or tribunal to reveal it to the affected entity except where such information is a privileged one.

2. A Lawyer's Duty to the Legal Profession

220. Lawyers have a duty to maintain a high standard of professional conduct and must not engage in conducts unbecoming of a member of the legal profession. They owe a duty to guide jealously the traditions of the profession. A lawyer's duties in this regard include the following.

(i) Duty not to allow their conduct or omission to lead to the admission of unsuitable persons to the Nigerian Bar

221. Every lawyer is under obligation to do all that is within their power to ensure that no unscrupulous individual finds their way into the profession. In this sense, they are to act as watchdogs for the profession. The noble profession of law admits only persons of integrity and high moral standing. It is the duty of any legal practitioner therefore to notify entities like the Nigerian Law School and the Body of Benchers when a person who does not meet that standard is trying to gain entrance into the profession. As such a lawyer shall not knowingly do any act or make any omission or engage in any conduct that leads to the admission into the legal profession unsuitable persons. Unsuitability can be by reason of their moral character, insufficient qualification, or for any other reason.[228]

(ii) Duty not to aid unauthorized practice of law

222. A lawyer should not assist persons who are not qualified to practise law in the practice of law. A lawyer must not send interns into their law offices that are yet to be called to the Nigerian Bar to court to handle cases, as it would amount to aiding an unauthorized practice of law.

(iii) Duty not to take brief at client's home or office

223. In order to uphold the dignity of the profession, a lawyer is under a duty not to take the brief or give advice to a client in the client's house or office. It is unethical for a lawyer to call at a client's house or place of business for the purpose of giving advice to or taking instructions from the client except in special circumstances or for some other urgent reason preventing the client from coming to the lawyer's office.[229] Special circumstances in this regard will include extreme old age, sickness or incapacity of the client, and such like issues.

228. Rule 2 *ibid.*
229. Rule 22 RPC 2007.

(iv) Duty not to instigate litigation or controversy

224. A legal practitioner shall not foment strife or instigate litigation and except in the case of close relations or where he is in a position of trust, the legal practitioner should not proffer advice or file a law suit for a person without being consulted.[230] The bar against a legal practitioner giving unsolicited legal services extends to the following:[231]

(a) Searching Land Registries or other registries for defects in titles with a view to employment or litigation.
(b) Seeking out claimants in respect of personal injuries or any other cause of action with a view to being employed by the prospective client.
(c) Engaging in, aiding or encouraging an agent or any other person to follow up accidents with a view to employment.
(d) Offering or agreeing to offer rewards to a person in a position to influence legal work in favour of a lawyer.

Any of the above acts amounts to professional misconduct and such conducts are to be reported for appropriate disciplinary action.

(v) Duty not to solicit for briefs

225. Lawyers are under obligation not to solicit for briefs either directly or indirectly. A legal practitioner is not allowed to solicit for professional employment through circulars, handbills, advertisements, services of touts or by personal communication or interview. Lawyers are not permitted to furnish, permit or inspire newspaper, radio or television comments in relation to their practice of the law. The prohibition also extends to acts of procuring photographs to be published in connection with matters in which they have been or are engaged, or concerning the manner of their conduct, the magnitude of the interest involved or the importance of the lawyer's position. Besides, a lawyer must not permit or inspire sound recordings in relation to their practice of law or such similar self-aggrandisement.[232]

(vi) Duty to advertise within the confines of acceptable standards in the profession

226. A lawyer is allowed to engage in advertising or promotion with regard to his practice as long as such is fair and proper in all circumstances and it is done in accordance with the rules.

227. Lawyers in Nigeria are allowed to publish in a reputable law list or law dictionary a brief biographical or informative data of themselves, including all or any of the following; their names or names of their professional association, their

230. Rule 47(1) *ibid.*
231. Rule 47(2) *ibid.*
232. Rule 39(3) *ibid.*

addresses, telephone number, telex number, email addresses, the schools, colleges or other institutions attended with dates of graduation, degrees or other educational or academic distinctions obtained, date and place of births, date of admission to practise law, any public or quasi-public or post of honour held, any legal teaching position held, any National Honours held, any membership and office in the Bar Association held and duties thereon, and any position held in scientific societies.

228. It is permitted for lawyers to print on their note-papers, envelopes, visiting cards, complimentary cards their names, addresses, academic and professional qualifications and titles including the words 'Barrister and Solicitor', 'Barrister-at-law', 'Solicitor and Advocate', 'Legal Practitioner', and any National Honours held.[233]

229. Lawyers or law firms are permitted to display a sign or notice of reasonable size and sober design containing their names and professional qualifications at the entrance of, or outside any building or offices where they carry on business.[234] Lawyers who have written books or articles on law are allowed to add their professional qualifications after their names.[235] Where a lawyer changes address, phone number or any other thing connected with the lawyers' practice, a notice of this change can be sent to clients and an advertisement of such change in a newspaper or journal is allowed.[236] Lawyers who are available to act as associates of other lawyers whether generally or in a particular branch of the law are allowed to send a brief and dignified announcement of their availability to lawyers in their locality and publish this fact in their local journals as long as such announcements are not calculated to attract business improperly.[237]

230. By Rule 46(1) RPC 2007, a legal practitioner is permitted to write articles, publications or participate in radio or television programmes in which he gives information on the law, but he shall not accept employment from any such publication or programme to advice on inquiries in respect of their individual rights. In addition, a lawyer cannot place an advert in any newspaper, periodical or any other publication offering as a lawyer to undertake confidential enquiries. He cannot also write for publication or caused to be published except in a legal periodical any information about his practice or earnings in the courts or in a case where he is engaged as a lawyer where the time for appeal in such cases has not expired. Moreover, a lawyer must not procure the publication of his photograph as a lawyer to the press or any periodical.[238] However, a lawyer can include his name, address, academic and professional qualification in an advertisement or notice that his client has instructed him to publish.[239]

233. Rule 40 *ibid.*
234. Rule 41 *ibid.*
235. Rule 42 *ibid.*
236. Rule 43 *ibid.*
237. Rule 44 *ibid.*
238. Rule 46(2) *ibid.*
239. Rule 46(3) *ibid.*

231. By Rule 45(2) RPC 2007 a lawyer can only wear the Barrister or Senior Advocates' robe in court or as may be directed or permitted by the Bar Council. A legal practitioner is not allowed to wear his robes when conducting his own case as a party in action nor where he is testifying as a witness in a proceeding in court.

By Rule 39(2) RPC 2007 whatever advertisement or promotion of a lawyer's legal practice that is allowed by the rules, a lawyer has a duty to ensure that:

(a) such is not inaccurate or likely to mislead;
(b) such is not likely to diminish public confidence in the legal profession, or the administration of justice, or otherwise bring the legal profession into disrepute;
(c) such advertisement or promotion does not make comparison with or criticizes other lawyers or other professions and professionals;
(d) such advertisement does not contain statements about the quality of the lawyer's work, the success of his practice or his success rate in handling of cases;
(e) such advertisement is not so frequent as to constitute annoyance to the target audience.

3. Duty to Court

232. A lawyer is a minister in the temple of justice and must do all it takes to uphold the dignity of the court. Rules 29–36 of the RPC 2007 generally provide for the duties of lawyers to the court. Lawyers should not do any act or conduct themselves in any manner that may obstruct, delay or adversely affect the administration of justice. A lawyer should treat the court with respect, courtesy, dignity and honour at all times. A lawyer must not discuss a pending case with a judge trying the case unless the opposing lawyer is present. This may however be dispensed with where the opposing lawyer is aware but fails or refuses to turn up and the judge is advised of the circumstances. Lawyers should not do anything or conduct themselves in such a manner as to give the impression that such action or conduct is calculated to gain or have the appearance of gaining special personal consideration of favour from a judge. This rule springs from the maxim that 'justice must not only be done it must also be seen to be done'. A neutral person following a proceeding must at all times have the impression that justice was done in each case, and there should be nothing to suggest that the judge had favoured one party against the other.[240] A lawyer shall not deliver to the judge any letter, memorandum, brief or other written communication without also delivering a copy to the opposing lawyer except as provided by a rule or order of court.

233. Lawyers are also required to deal candidly and fairly with a court or tribunal where they are appearing in their professional capacity. Lawyers must comply with any undertaking given by them either personally or on behalf of their client

240. Rule 34 *ibid.*

to a court. Failure to do this makes a lawyer prima facie guilty of professional misconduct. Moreover, in representing a matter to the court, lawyers are required to disclose any legal authority in the jurisdiction known to them though such authority is adverse to their client and has not been disclosed by the opposing counsel. Counsel shall also disclose the identities of the client they represent and of the persons who employed them unless such disclosure is privileged or irrelevant. When handling a matter before a court or tribunal, counsel shall not allude to any matter that they have no reasonable ground to believe is relevant to the case or would not be supported by admissible evidence. Counsel shall not ask any question that they have no reasonable ground to believe is relevant to the case and is intended to degrade a witness or other person. It is unethical for a counsel to assert his personal knowledge of the facts in issue except when testifying as a witness and they are allowed to assert their personal opinion as to the justness of a case, or as to the credibility of a witness, or as to the culpability of a party in a civil suit or the guilt, or innocence of an accused person. But counsel can rightly argue on their analysis of the evidence for any position or conclusion with respect to the matters stated therein.

234. A counsel must comply with known customs and traditions of the Bar or of particular courts. Where counsel is unable/unwilling to do this, they must give adequate notice of such to the opposing lawyer. A lawyer must not intentionally or habitually violate any established rule of procedure or evidence nor should a lawyer knowingly misquote the content of a paper, testimony of a witness, language of an opposing counsel or language of a court's decision or textbook. Counsel must not cite authorities that they know to be invalid, has been overruled or repealed with the intention to mislead the court. When making submissions to court in a matter, a counsel must not assert as a fact that which has not been proved, conceal or withhold positions they intend to rely on during their opening statements. This particular provision of the rules has little relevance in Nigeria given that counsel most often than not does not make opening statements as this is better suited to trial before a jury which is not practised in Nigeria.

235. A counsel must not produce evidence which they know the court should reject nor should they promote a case that they know to be false or in any other way do any act which may obviously amount to an abuse of the process of the court or is dishonourable and unworthy of an officer in the temple of justice with a duty to aid the administration of justice.[241]

236. While in a courtroom, counsel must be properly attired and not wear any apparel calculated to draw attention to them. In this respect, male lawyers in Nigeria are expected to be attired in their black or dark-blue suit or a black jacket/ sleeved vest over a black and grey striped trousers, a white collarless shirt or white shirt with wing collar white wing collar, white band, two studs (for affixing the winged collar to the shirt), black shoes with black socks. Female lawyers are to be attired in black or dark blue suit/black dress/black jacket over a black skirt with a white camisole if jacket has an opening in front, a white collaret/ladies white band

241. Rule 32 *ibid.*

and black shoes. When appearing in the superior courts of record, in addition to the outlined attire, counsel must wear the lawyers' wig and gown. When appearing before an inferior court of record, a male lawyer is not required to wear the collarless shirt, wing collar and studs. A white shirt with a dark tie will suffice. A female lawyer does not need to wear the collaret when appearing before an inferior court of record. The lawyers' wig and gowns are not worn before inferior courts of record.

237. Very importantly, while in a courtroom, lawyers must conduct themselves with decency and decorum observing the customs, code and conduct of behaviour of the court and custom of practice at the bar regarding appearance, dress, manners and courtesy. A lawyer should be properly robed before a court resumes session for the day as it is discourteous to the court to be seen going through the rudiments of wearing the wig and gown right in court when the court is already in session. A lawyer must address the court with the proper appellation as dictated by law or rules of practice. The following are the appropriate modes of addressing the judges of the different courts with civil jurisdiction in Nigeria:

- Justices of the SC: My Lords or Your Lordships.
- Justices of the Court of Appeal: My Lords or Your Lordships.
- Judges of the Federal HC / National Industrial Court / HC of the Federal Capital Territory / HC of states: My Lord / Your Lordship.
- Magistrates as well as District Court Judges: Your Worship. In Lagos State, Magistrates are addressed as 'Your Honour' (This is provided for in section 8(1) of the Magistrates' Court Law of Lagos State 2009 and section 349 of the Administration of Criminal Justice Law of Lagos State 2011).
- Area Court / Customary Court Judges: Your Honour.

238. Counsel is expected to show respect to the court even where the ruling/judgment of the court does not favour their client's case by thanking the judge for the ruling. A lawyer must rise when addressing the judge or being addressed by the judge. Counsel must address their objections, requests, arguments and observations to the judge and should not engage in an exchange of banter, personality display, arguments or controversy with the opposition lawyer and must not engage in conduct that is degrading to a court or tribunal.

239. When a lawyer is a party in an action, he must not remain in the bar (sit at position for lawyers in the courtroom) or wear the lawyer's robes when conducting a case in which he is a party. The same applies to where counsel is giving evidence in a case.[242]

240. A lawyer engaged or associated with a civil action in court must not while litigation is anticipated or pending make or participate in making any extra-judicial statement that is calculated to prejudice or interfere with, or is reasonably capable

242. Rule 36(f) *ibid.*

of prejudicing or interfering with the fair trial of the case. Where in the course of a litigation, there is a change of counsel; both the new and old lawyers have a duty to inform the court of this fact.[243]

4. Duty to Fellow Lawyers

241. Lawyers being ministers in the temple of justice are expected to exhibit the spirit of comradeship among themselves irrespective of their duties to their client. This is because litigants come and go but counsel remain in the temple of justice. As such lawyers must at all times not allow themselves to descend into the arena of conflict. The RPC requires lawyers to treat one another with respect, fairness, consideration and dignity and should not allow any ill feelings between their clients to influence their conduct, demeanour towards one another or towards the opposing client.[244] Lawyers are expected to treat themselves equally subject to the rules of precedence in the order of seating and handling of cases in court. The order of precedence with regard to the order in which lawyers may call their cases (motions or matters for mention that are not otherwise listed for hearing) in court out of turn is as follows:

(a) The AGF.
(b) The AG of a state in the HC of a state or any court established by that state law.
(c) Senior Advocate of Nigeria in order of seniority. Note that where a Life Bencher is in court, he will take precedence over a Senior Advocate of Nigeria. This is because section 6(3) of the LPA 2004 confers the same right and privileges conferred on law officers on them. This takes precedence over regulations conferring same privilege.
(d) Persons authorized to practise by reason of their office.
(e) Persons enrolled as barrister and solicitors of the SC in the roll of lawyers in the order of seniority of enrolment.
(f) Persons authorized to practise by warrant.

242. A lawyer shall deal with his fellow lawyer in all good faith and fairness. As such, a lawyer shall strictly observe all promises and agreements made to opposing counsel whether oral or in writing and whether made in court or outside court. This also includes agreement implied by the circumstances of the case. Where a lawyer gives personal undertaking and has not expressly and clearly disclaimed personal liability, such a lawyer shall promptly honour such undertaking. In addition, a lawyer must not take undue advantage of the predicament or misfortune of the opposing party or client.[245]

243. Rule 27(3) RPC 2007 provides that lawyers who intend that another lawyer hold their brief in a case because they are unable to personally attend court on

243. Rule 29(2) *ibid.*
244. Rule 26(1) *ibid.*
245. Rule 27(2)(a)–(c) *ibid.*

the given date should hand over the brief in reasonable time to enable the receiving lawyers enough time to acquaint themselves with the matter. Where a counsel is or ought reasonably to be aware that a person is already represented by another lawyer in a case, such counsel shall not have any dealings with such a person with regard to the same matter without first notifying the other lawyer. Where the litigant decides to change counsel, the new lawyer shall promptly give notice of it to the former lawyer and use his best endeavour to ensure that the former lawyer is paid his earned fees. A client has the right to engage an additional lawyer in a matter whether at the client's instance or on advice of the client's lawyer. However, the new lawyer shall decline the employment if the original lawyer finds it objectionable. The original lawyer may withdraw either on self-volition or upon being debriefed by the client. In such an instance, the new lawyer may come into the matter and shall use his best endeavour to ensure that outstanding fees due to the original lawyer are paid. Where lawyers jointly handling a matter disagree on a matter vital to the interest of the client, the conflict of opinion shall be frankly communicated to the client and the decision of the client shall be final. Where, however, the nature of differences between the lawyers makes it impracticable for the lawyer whose opinion has been overruled to work together with the other lawyer, such a lawyer shall withdraw from the employment.[246]

244. A lawyer during the course of his representation of a client shall not communicate or cause another to communicate on the subject of the representation with the other party that the lawyer knows is represented by a counsel in that matter unless with the prior consent of the lawyer representing such party or such communication is authorized by law. Also, a lawyer is not allowed to give advice to a person who is not represented by a lawyer in the matter or cause where he is representing one of the parties.[247]

5. Duty to Clients

245. A legal practitioner has a duty to efficiently represent the overall interest of his client. Rule 14 RPC 2007 provides that:

> It is the duty of a lawyer to devote his attention, energy and expertise to the service of his client and, subject to any rule of law, to act in a manner consistent with the best interest of the client.

To achieve the above provision, lawyers must consult with their clients in all questions of doubts that are not within their discretion. Counsel must keep the client informed of the progress of the case and important development as it may be reasonably necessary and must respond promptly as reasonably possible to any request for information by the client. Counsel is under obligation to warn the client of any particular risk that is likely to occur in the course of the matter and must not

246. Rules 27(4), 28 and 29(1) RPC 2007.
247. Rule 27(5) *ibid.*

fail to inform the client of their opinion as to the hopelessness of the claim or defence. In fact, the HCCPR Abuja makes it mandatory to file a pre-action counselling certificate alongside the originating process for the process to be acceptable for filing. The import of the certificate is to the effect that counsel shall be personally liable if the case turns out to be frivolous.[248]

246. Counsel has a duty to ensure that the client is properly represented throughout the case by being personally present in court or ensuring proper representation of the client. A lawyer is not permitted to abandon or withdraw from employment by his client once he has accepted the brief except for good cause. The RPC 2007 lists what amounts to a good cause to be a conflict of interest between the lawyer and the client; where the client insists on an unjust or immoral course in the conduct of his case; where the client persists against the lawyer's advice in pressing frivolous defences; or where the client deliberately disregards an agreement or obligation as to payment of fees or expenses. Where a legal practitioner is justified in withdrawing from an employments, such legal practitioner is under obligation to give the client reasonable notice of this fact to allow the client to employ another lawyer.[249] The HCCPR provides that an application for a change of counsel or withdrawal by any party in an action or an application by a legal practitioner to withdraw his services may be made not less than three clear days before the date fixed for hearing.[250] Where counsel makes such application it shall be served on all the parties in the action and on the outgoing legal practitioner if he is not the applicant. A legal practitioner who withdraws his appearance for a party in an action may reappear for the same party with the leave of court.[251]

247. Counsel is under obligation to inform his client of all available options in resolving the disputes. Where ADR is the best option to resolve a client's dispute, a lawyer must advise the client appropriately. Counsel must advise his clients not to breach the law and where in the course of their representation of a client, counsel receives established information that a client has perpetrated fraud upon a person or tribunal, counsel should promptly call on the client to rectify the fraud and if the client insists on that line of action or is unable to rectify it, the lawyer should reveal the fraud to the affected person or tribunal. But such information must not fall under the class of privilege information for which counsel is not permitted to disclose.[252]

248. A lawyer owes a client a duty to handle the client's matter with competence and must seek the assistance of another lawyer if the lawyer lacks the requisite competence to handle the matter. Counsel must be adequately prepared at all times to handle the client's case and must never go to court unprepared.

---

248. Order 2 Rule 8 HCCPR Abuja.
249. Rule 21(3) RPC 2007.
250. Order 55 Rule 2 HCCPR Abuja; Order 52 Rule 2 HCCPR Lagos.
251. Order 55 Rule 4 HCCPR Abuja.
252. Rule 15(4) RPC 2007.

249. A legal practitioner must disclose any conflict of interest that may exist with regard to a client brief, which may influence the client in the choice of the lawyer to handle the case. A lawyer shall not accept a retainer if the exercise of the lawyer's professional judgment on behalf of the client will or may be reasonably affected by the lawyer's own financial, business, property or personal interest. In this light, a lawyer shall not acquire a proprietary interest in the cause of action or subject matter of litigation that he is conducting for a client.[253] The exception to this rule is that a lawyer is allowed to acquire a lien granted by law to secure the lawyer's fees and expenses or the lawyer can enter into an agreement with the client for a reasonable contingency fee in a civil matter. To eliminate possibilities of conflict of interest, a lawyer shall not accept a proffered employment if the exercise of an independent professional judgment on behalf of the client will be or is likely to be affected negatively by the lawyer's acceptance of the proffered employment or if it will lead to representation of differing interest. The exception to this provision is where it is obvious that such a lawyer can effectively represent the interest of each of the clients and they consent after full disclosure of this possible conflict. In addition, a lawyer shall not appear as counsel for a client in a matter in which the lawyer is himself a party. Where based on a situation of possible conflict of interest a lawyer is required to decline employment of a client, his associate, partners and any lawyer affiliated with him are also expected to decline employment with regard to the same.

250. A lawyer is expected to honour a contract between him and his client whether it is reduced into writing or not.

251. A lawyer shall not knowingly reveal a confidence or secret of his client, use such confidence or secret to the disadvantage of the client or use such confidence or secret to the advantage of the lawyer himself or a third person except with the consent of the client after full disclosure.[254] Section 192(1) of the Evidence Act 2011 provides that:

> No legal practitioner shall at any time be permitted unless with his client's express consent, to disclose any communication made to him in the course and for the purpose of his employment as such legal practitioner by or on behalf of his client, or to state the contents or condition of any document with which he has become acquainted in the course and for the purpose of his professional employment or to disclose any advice given by him to his client in the course and for purpose of such employment … .

This duty on a lawyer not to disclose confidences of his client continues even after termination of the lawyer's employment and it applies to the interpreters and clerks of the lawyer.[255]

---

253. Rule 17(1)(2) *ibid.*
254. Rule 19(1)(2) *ibid.*
255. Sections 192(3) and 193 of the Evidence Act 2011.

The law however provides for exceptions to the rule of a lawyer not revealing confidences or secrets of his client. They are:

(1) A lawyer can reveal confidences or secrets either by himself or through his employees when permitted under the RPC or a law or a court order. By the proviso to section 192 of the Evidence Act 2011, a lawyer can reveal confidence of his client in the form of communications made to him in the course of his employment where any of such communications was made in furtherance of any illegal purpose or they show that any crime or fraud has been committed since the commencement of the lawyer's employment.
(2) A lawyer may reveal either by himself or through his employees the intention of the client to commit a crime and the information necessary to prevent the crime.
(3) A lawyer can reveal either by himself or through his employees confidences or secrets necessary to establish or collect his fee or to defend himself or his employees or associates against an accusation of wrongful conduct.

252. Lawyers owe a duty to their clients not to communicate with the other party on the subject of controversy and should not negotiate or compromise their client's case with the other party. A lawyer should only deal with the lawyer of the other party with regard to the matter.[256]

III. Discipline of Lawyers

253. Like every other profession, actions and inactions of members of the legal profession are regulated. It has been said: 'For a profession that has far-reaching effect on the fate of consumers of legal services and the society in general, the need for regulation is obvious.'[257] Statutes regulate discipline in the legal profession in Nigeria. The LPA 2004 provides for acts that amount to misconduct on the part of a lawyer and the procedure for disciplining an erring legal practitioner. There are four offences under the LPA for which a lawyer can face disciplinary actions before the appropriate disciplinary body.[258] These offences are described below.

(1) Infamous Conduct in a Professional Respect

254. Infamous conduct in a professional respect refers to an act or omission that in the opinion of the disciplinary body is such that will bring the legal profession into disrepute.[259] Acts, which have been held by the disciplinary body to amount to infamous conduct in a professional respect, include misappropriation of client's money, breach of the RPC, etc.

---

256. Rule 19(5) RPC 2007.
257. C. Oba & O. Ikwuanusi, *Expanding the Frontiers of Discipline of Lawyers in Nigeria: An Overview*, 2(3) Miyetti Q. L. Rev. 49 et seq. at 50 (2017).
258. Section 12 LPA 2004.
259. *NBA v. Alabi* (2006) 14 NWLR (Pt 1000) 841.

(2) Conviction by Any Court in Nigeria for an Offence Incompatible with the Status of a Legal Practitioner

255. Where a lawyer has been convicted by a court in Nigeria having the power to impose term of imprisonment for any offence that is considered incompatible with the status of a lawyer, such a lawyer is liable to be disciplined professionally. The offences that will come under this category include financial dishonesty, dealing in hard drugs, maintaining a brothel, etc. It is pertinent to state that for a lawyer to be liable to discipline under this head there must be no pending appeal against the conviction and the time of appeal must have passed. Also, the offence for which the lawyer is convicted need not be one that attracts a term of imprisonment. Even where the penalty for the offence is a fine, the legal practitioner can still be disciplined.

(3) Fraudulent Enrolment as a Barrister and Solicitor of the SC

256. Where a lawyer fraudulently got his name on the roll of lawyers in Nigeria by either misrepresenting material facts or presenting forged certificates to get enrolled or admitted into a university or the Nigerian Law School, such a lawyer will have committed an offence for which the lawyer can be disciplined.

(4) Misconduct incompatible with the status of a legal practitioner

257. Under this category, the misconduct committed by a lawyer is not one committed in the cause of the practice of the legal profession or connected with it, but the act is considered by the disciplinary body as incompatible with the status of a legal practitioner. Acts that have been held by the disciplinary body to amount to misconduct incompatible with the status of a lawyer include street fighting, seduction of a client's wife, habitual drunkenness, etc.

A. Bodies Responsible for Discipline in the Legal Profession in Nigeria

1. The NBA

258. This is the body of lawyers in Nigeria. Though not a creation of statutes, but is recognized by the Legal Practitioner Act 2004 and the Legal Education (Consolidation) Act 2004. The NBA receives complaints against legal practitioners from members of the public. This is sent to its disciplinary panel. There are currently, nine disciplinary panels of the NBA located in different zones in Nigeria. The role of the NBA disciplinary panel is to find out whether a prima facie case is made out against a legal practitioner with respect to the petition received against the lawyer.

Where the panel finds in the affirmative, the petition against the legal practitioner is forwarded to the Legal Practitioner Disciplinary Committee of the Body of Benchers.[260]

2. The Body of Benchers

259. This is the body of the highest distinction in the legal profession in Nigeria. It is made up of distinguished legal practitioners either on the Bench or the Bar in Nigeria. By section 3(1) of the LPA 2004, it comprises of the following members: the Chief Justice of Nigeria, all Justices of the SC, President of the Court of Appeal, the AGF, the presiding Justices of Court of Appeal Divisions, the Chief Judge of the Federal HC, the Chief Judge of the National Industrial Court, the Chief Judge of the Federal Capital Territory, Abuja, the Chief Judges of the states of the Federation, the Attorneys General of the states of the Federation, the President of the NBA, the Chairman of the Council of Legal Education, thirty Legal Practitioners nominated by the NBA, and such number of persons not exceeding ten who appear to the Body of Benchers to be eminent members of the Legal profession in Nigeria of not less than fifteen years' post-call standing.

260. The Body of Benchers is responsible for the formal call to the Bar of an aspirant to the Bar and for the discipline of members of the profession. With respect to its role of seeing to the discipline of members of the legal profession, the body performs this role through the LPDC, which is a Committee of the Body of Benchers. The Committee is made up of a Chairman who shall neither be the Chief Justice of Nigeria nor any Justice of the SC (the reason for this been that appeal from the Committee ultimately gets to the SC and it is in the interest of justice that they do not sit over the trial and also over an appeal based on the trial), two Justices of the Court of Appeal (one of whom shall be the President of the Court of Appeal), two Chief Judges, the AGF and an AG of the state or two AGs of states and four members of the NBA who are not connected with either the investigation of a complaint or the decision of the NBA to present the complaint to the LPDC.[261] The Committee hears petitions forwarded to it by the Disciplinary Panel of the NBA. The NBA is the official prosecutor in the proceedings before the LPDC. The legal practitioner facing the LPDC referred to as the respondent is entitled to defend himself in person or by a legal practitioner of his choice. Where the LPDC finds that a complaint against a lawyer before it has been proved, the LPDC has the power to reprimand the lawyer, suspend the lawyer from practice for a given period of time or strike out the name of the lawyer from the roll of lawyers in Nigeria. Any of these

260. Rules 3–4 of the Legal Practitioners Disciplinary Committee Rules 2006.
261. Section 11(2) LPA 2004.

sanctions may also include an order of refund of money or handing over of documents or any other thing as dictated by the circumstance.[262] Appeals from the LPDC go to the SC.[263]

3. The SC

261. By section 12 of LPA 2004, where it appears to the SC that a lawyer is guilty of infamous conduct in any professional respect with regard to matters before any court of record in Nigeria, the SC may if it thinks fit, after hearing any representations made and evidence adduced by or on behalf of that person and such other persons as the court considers appropriate, give such direction as it deems fit (these are same as any of the directions that the LPDC is empowered to make which have already been discussed in paragraph 259 above). The direction shall take effect immediately and the SC shall cause the direction to be published in the Federal Gazette except where the direction is an admonition.

§2. Public Institutions and Organization

262. Every person called to the Nigerian Bar is a member of the NBA. The association, though not a creation of statutes, is recognized by the LPA 2004. The association has a national body headed by a President and has branches in major cities and towns throughout the federation, which are headed by chairmen. Every legal practitioner is expected to belong to a local Bar. The RPC 2007 mandates a person who establishes a private legal practice either alone or in association or partnership with others to not later than thirty days after commencement of such legal practice and if such a person continues to carry on the practice, send a notice in the prescribed form to the local Bar in the jurisdiction where the law office is situated.[264] The notice should contain the following:

(1) the name of the legal practitioner;
(2) the address where the legal practice is carried on;
(3) the date when the legal practitioner was called to Bar in Nigeria; and
(4) the date when his name was entered in the Roll of legal practitioners in Nigeria.

262. Section 11 LPA 2004.
263. Section 12(7) LPA as amended by the Legal practitioners (Amendment) Decree No. 21 of 1994, Cap L11 LFN 2004, Revised Edition (Incorporating the provisions of the Legal practitioners (Amendment) Decree No. 21 of 1994) published as supplementary to the LFN 2004 by the Federal Ministry of Justice, Abuja.
264. Rule 13 RPC 2007.

The local Bar that receives such notice shall enter the particulars in the notice in a Register or Database kept for that purpose. Rule 13 of the RPC 2007 which prescribes the requirement outlined in this paragraph has been deleted from the RPC 2007 by the Rules of Professional Conduct for Legal Practitioners (Amendment) Rules 2020.

263. The association is entitled to over 70% of the practising fees paid by lawyers in Nigeria. The local Bars organizes yearly law week, while at the national level, the Annual National Convention of the association is held usually on the last week of August. The Law Week and National Convention are forums for continuing legal education for lawyers. The President of the NBA and other members of the national executives are elected for a term of two years. The position is the same for the tenure of officers at the local Bar. The NBA being the umbrella body for all lawyers in Nigeria is the voice for lawyers in Nigeria and promotes the collective interest of lawyers. It also issues communiqués and press statement on the position of lawyers regarding government policies and programme. The association also plays a crucial role in the training of aspirants to the Bar as students at the Nigerian Law School are sent to law firms as part of their practical training programme. In addition, the association is involved in the discipline of lawyers in Nigeria as already discussed in paragraph 257 above.

Chapter 3. Bailiffs

264. Bailiffs are officers of the Sheriff department of an HC responsible for the service of court processes and execution of court judgments. The SCPA empowers the Sheriff to appoint such number of persons as bailiffs as may be necessary.[265] The Sheriff can perform any of the functions of his office through officers of his department including the bailiffs.

§1. Exercise of the Profession

265. The exercise of the bailiff's profession discussed here is with regard to the functions of the office of the Sheriff as delegated to the bailiff. Every bailiff authorized to intermeddle with the execution of writs issued by any court of record shall before he does so make a declaration, which shall be exempt from stamp duty. The declaration shall be in Form 2 of the First Schedule to the SCPA or to the like effect, and it is made before a judge or Magistrate for the division or district in which the bailiff exercises such authority.[266] In the exercise of his duty, a bailiff acting on the instruction of the Sheriff may command any person to arrest a person who has committed or is suspected of having committed a felony and any person failing to obey such command shall on conviction be liable to a fine of NGN 200 or to imprisonment for one year or both.[267] He can also receive writs and process of a court issued in accordance with the SCPA, and in such instance, the bailiff shall be charged with making returns with respect to such writs or court process. Acting on behalf of the Sheriff, he can direct sufficient number of police constables to be posted to the court premises when the court is in session. The bailiff at the request of a person delivering a writ to him for execution shall give a receipt for that writ stating the hour and the day of its delivery.

266. The law protects a bailiff in the exercise of his duties. Where any goods in the possession of a judgment debtor at the time of seizure by the bailiff who is charged with the enforcement of a writ, warrant or other processes of execution are sold by the bailiff without any claim having been made to such goods, good title shall pass to the purchaser of the goods. The bailiff cannot be sued for the sale of such goods or for paying over the proceeds thereof.[268] All fees received by the bailiff in respect of any duty performed by him in the discharge of his official duties shall be paid into and form part of the Consolidated Revenue Fund of the state or part of the Federation in respect of which the fees is prescribed.[269]

265. Section 5 SCPA Cap S6 LFN 2004.
266. Section 6 *ibid.*
267. Section 7 *ibid.*
268. Section 16 *ibid.*
269. Section 18 *ibid.*

§2. PUBLIC INSTITUTIONS AND ORGANIZATION

267. There is no known organization of bailiffs in Nigeria. In courts in each district within a jurisdiction, there are bailiffs appointed as court staff. They like other support staff in the judiciary come under the umbrella body of the Judicial Staff Union of Nigeria (JUSUN).

Part II. Jurisdiction

Chapter 1. Domestic Jurisdiction

268. When a lawyer handling a matter decides that the appropriate way to resolve his client's case is through litigation, the issues of which court in Nigeria the lawyer will approach and what will influence that choice comes into play. A step in the wrong direction will lead to a waste of time, energy and resources.

269. Jurisdiction is the power or competence of a court to adjudicate over a cause or matter. It is the live wire of any case and is a threshold issue. It is so fundamental that where a court gives a decision in a case without the court having the jurisdiction to try that case, it is a nullity.[270] There can be no exercise of justice delivery within the framework of jurisdiction that does not exist. The SC has stated that:

> The jurisdiction of a court or tribunal is not inferred or imagined but statutory. Courts are set up under the Constitution, Decrees, Acts, Laws and Edicts and these are the instruments that cloak the courts with the powers and jurisdiction of adjudication. Therefore, where statutes have not donated jurisdiction to a court or tribunal, the court cannot operate. This is because jurisdiction is not endowed by the consent of parties but confined, limited and circumscribed by the statute creating it.[271]

270. The issue of jurisdiction is so fundamental to a case that it can be raised at any stage of a proceeding even for the first time on appeal. Generally, no issue can be raised for the first time on appeal without the leave of the court. The issue of jurisdiction is an exception to this position. The SC has said that due to the fundamental nature of jurisdiction, leave is not required before it can be raised for the first time on appeal.[272] When an objection is raised to the jurisdiction of a court in a case, the court is under obligation to hear it before going on with the case. A court is said to have jurisdiction to hear a matter when:

- the court is properly constituted with respect to the number and qualification of its members; and

---

270. *Okorocha v. U.B.A. Plc* (2018) 17 NWLR (Pt 1649) 441 (SC).
271. *Oloruntoba-Oju v. Abdul-Raheem* (2009) 13 NWLR (Pt 1157) 83 (SC).
272. *A.G. Kwara v. Adeyemo* (2017) 1 NWLR (Pt 1546) 210 at 240 (SC).

- the subject matter of the case is within the court's jurisdiction and there is no feature in the case which robs the court of jurisdiction; and
- the action is initiated by due process of law and every condition precedent for the court to exercise jurisdiction has been fulfilled.

The SC in *Madukolu v. Nkemdilim* enunciated the above position on jurisdiction.[273] Subsequent cases like *Nyesom v. Peterside*[274] and *Durbar Hotel Plc v. Ityough*[275] have adopted this position. Where a court lacks jurisdiction over the principal issue in a dispute, the court cannot assume jurisdiction over an ancillary matter in the same case. The court has held that the incompetence of the court to entertain and determine the principal question is enough to nullify the whole proceedings and the judgment given as there is no room for half judgment in any matter.[276] The issue of jurisdiction can be raised at any time even before an appellate court irrespective of the fact that it was not raised at the trial court and the lower appellate court provided the procedure of raising it was properly followed by the party choosing to raise it. A party raises the issue of lack of jurisdiction of a court by filing a preliminary objection stating the grounds of the objection and accompanying it with a written address. Where the party raising the objection will be relying on facts, then the party has to attach an affidavit stating facts the applicant seeks to rely on in asking the court to decline jurisdiction.

§1. Subject-Matter Jurisdiction

271. This is also known as substantive jurisdiction. It is jurisdiction conferred on a court by the Constitution or statute setting up the court. The statute setting up a court cloaks the court with the powers and jurisdiction for adjudication with regard to the matters it can handle and the power of the court is circumscribed by the same statute. For example section 251(1) of the 1999 Nigerian Const. vests the Federal HC of Nigeria with exclusive civil jurisdiction with regard to the subject matters contained therein namely:

(a) Matters relating to the revenue of the Government of the Federation in which the said Government or any organ thereof or a person suing or being sued on behalf of the said Government is a party.
(b) Matters connected with or pertaining to the taxation of companies and other bodies established or carrying on business in Nigeria and other persons subject to federal taxation.
(c) Matters connected with or pertaining to customs and excise duties and export duties, including any claim by or against the Nigerian Customs Service or any member or officer thereof, arising from the performance of any duty imposed under any regulation relating to customs and excise duties and export duties.

---

273. (1962) 2 SCNLR 341.
274. (2016) 7 NWLR (Pt 1512) 452 (SC).
275. (2017) 7 NWLR (Pt 1564) 256 (SC).
276. *Mailantarki v. Tongo* (2018) 6 NWLR (Pt 1614) 69 (SC).

(d) Connected with or pertaining to banking, banks, other financial institutions, including any action between one bank and another, any action by or against the Central Bank of Nigeria (CBN) arising from banking, foreign exchange coinage, legal tender, bills of exchange, letters of credit, promissory notes and other fiscal measures: Provided, however, that this paragraph shall not apply to any dispute between an individual customer and the bank. Following this provision, the SC has held in *NDIC v. Okem Enterprise Ltd*[277] that in dispute bordering on banker customer relationship both the Federal HC and the HC of states including that of the Federal Capital Territory, Abuja, have concurrent jurisdiction.
(e) Matters arising from the operation of the Companies and Allied Matters Act or any other enactments replacing the Act or regulating the operation of companies incorporated under the Companies and Allied Matters Act.
(f) Matters on any federal enactment relating to copyright, patent, designs, trademarks, and passing-off, industrial designs and merchandise marks, business names, commercial and industrial monopolies, combines and trusts, standards of goods and commodities and industrial standards.
(g) Matters arising from any admiralty jurisdiction, including shipping and navigation on the River Niger or River Benue and their effluents and on such other inland waterway as may be designated by any enactment to be an international waterway, all federal ports(including the constitution and powers of the port authorities for federal ports) and carriage by sea.
(h) Matters relating to diplomatic, consular and trade representation.
(i) Matters on citizenship, naturalization and aliens, deportation of persons of persons who are not citizens of Nigeria, extradition, immigration into and emigration from Nigeria, passport and visa.
(j) Bankruptcy and insolvency matters.
(k) Aviation and safety aircraft matters.
(l) Matters relating to arms, ammunitions and explosives.
(m) Matters relating to drugs and poisons.
(n) Matters relating to mines and minerals (including oil fields, oil mining, geological surveys and natural gas).
(o) Matters relating to weights and measures.
(p) Matters relating to the administration or the management and control of the Federal Government or any of its agencies.
(q) Matters relating to the operation and interpretation of the 1999 Nigerian Constn in so far as it affects the Federal Government of Nigeria or any of its agencies.
(r) Any action or proceeding for a declaration or injunction affecting the validity of any executive or administrative action or decision by the Federal Government or any of its agencies.
(s) Such other civil jurisdictions that may be conferred by an Act of the National Assembly.

277. (2004) 10 NWLR (Pt 880) 107 (SC).

I. Factors to Be Taken into Account in Determining Subject-Matter Jurisdiction

A. *Statutes Creating the Court*

272. The statute creating a court expressly confers it with the power to adjudicate certain matters. In Nigeria, the superior courts of records are established under the 1999 Constn, which also expressly confers them with jurisdiction. For the inferior courts of record, there are laws at the state level establishing them, which also confers them with jurisdiction. For example, the Magistrates' Court Law of Lagos State 2009 establishes the Magistrates' Courts in Lagos State. Section 28 of the law expressly confers the court with jurisdiction. By this section, the Magistrates' Court in Lagos has jurisdiction to adjudicate upon the following matters:

(1) All personal actions arising from contract, tort or both where the debt or damages claimed do not exceed NGN 10 million at the time of filling the action.
(2) All actions between landlord and tenant for the possession of any land, agricultural, residential or business premises or house claimed under an agreement where the annual rental value does not exceed NGN 10 million at the time of filling the action. With regard to this category of actions, what confers the court with jurisdiction is the annual rental value of the property. This is because the proviso to section 28(1)(b) that confers this power on the court says, that the landlord is allowed to claim in addition to recovery of the premises, arrears of rent and *mesne* profit notwithstanding the fact that the total amount claimed exceeds NGN 10 million. This statutory provision is a codification of a decision in *Joyland Ltd v. Wemabod Estates Ltd*[278] to the effect that what confers jurisdiction on the court in this situation is the annual rental value of the property and not the amount claimed. Once the annual rental value is NGN 10 million and below then the court has jurisdiction to entertain the matter.
(3) Proceeding to appoint guardian ad litem (for persons under legal disability) and orders, issues and directions relating to their appointment.
(4) With regard to matters before the court, the court has the powers to make orders of injunction, orders to stay, waste or alienate or for the detention and preservation of any property, orders to restrain breaches of contract and tort.
(5) To hear appeals from Customary Courts.
(6) Recovering of penalties, charges, rates, taxes, expenses, cost of enforcement of statutory provisions that may be recoverable by virtue of any existing law provided that the jurisdiction to hear them is not expressly conferred on another court and the amount to be recovered does not exceed NGN 10 million.
(7) To issue, process and make any order or give such directions for the due enforcement of the regulatory provisions and any other legislation and subsidiary legislation contained in any of the following legislation:

---

278. (2001) 18 NWLR (Pt 744) 22 (SC).

(a) Urban and Regional Planning Development Law No. 9 of 2005 and subsidiary legislations;
(b) Lagos State Lotteries Law 2004 Cap L89, Laws of Lagos State of Nigeria;
(c) Land Use Charge Law Cap L61, Laws of Lagos State of Nigeria 2003; and
(d) any other regulatory legislation as may be prescribed from time to time.

For the jurisdiction of the various courts with civil jurisdiction in Nigeria has conferred on them by statutes *see* paragraphs 280–305 below.

B. Value of the Claim

273. The value of the claim is an important consideration with regards to the jurisdiction of the inferior courts of records to handle a matter. This is because the superior courts of records are unlimited in the jurisdiction with respect to financial limits. The two Magistrates' Courts used as a reference for the Magistrate Courts in Nigeria namely the Magistrate Court in Lagos and the District Court (where a Magistrates' Court in Abuja sits in its civil jurisdiction it is referred to as the District Court) in Abuja have financial jurisdiction. For the Magistrates' Court in Lagos State, the limit of its financial jurisdiction is NGN 10 million.[279] The Magistrate Court in Lagos State is not graded as such all Magistrates in the state have the jurisdiction to entertain any claim the amount of which is not more than NGN 10 million. It was earlier pointed out in paragraph 271 above that there is an exception to this position with regard to claims for recovery of premises by a landlord. In such cases, what confers jurisdiction on the court is the rental value of the property to be recovered and not the amount claimed. With regard to the District Court in Abuja, its financial limit is NGN 5 million.[280] The different grades of District Judges have financial limits of their jurisdiction in the following order as shown in the below table:

Chief District Judge Grade 1	5 million
Chief District Judge Grade 11	4 million
Senior District Judge Grade 1	3 million
Senior District Judge Grade 11	2 million
District Judge Grade 1	1 million

C. Limitation of Actions

274. The issue of limitation of action is one that affects the jurisdiction of a court. Different actions have different limitation periods. The various states of the

279. Section 28 of the Magistrate Court Law of Lagos State 2009.
280. By the District Courts (Increase of Jurisdiction of District Judges) Order 2014.

Federation of Nigeria have their limitation laws, and there is also the limitation Act that applies to the Federal Capital Territory, Abuja.[281] These laws are essentially the same in content with minor variations. The Limitation Law of Lagos State and the Limitation Act with regard to some actions are as stated in the below table:

Action	*Limitation Period*
Simple contract	Six years
Damages for negligence	Three years
Damages for Nuisance	Three years
Action by state authority to recover land in Abuja	Twelve years
Action upon an instrument under seal	Twelve years

275. The court has held that where an action is filed outside the limitation period, a court will lack jurisdiction to entertain it.[282] The claimant's right to pursue his claim becomes 'dead' when the time to bring the action as dictated by the limitation law lapses. Time begins to run for the purpose of limitation law when the cause of action arose. It has been held by the court that where an employee was first suspended before the employee's employment was eventually terminated, time for the purpose of the limitation law will start running from the notice of termination of the employment.[283] Time ceases to run upon the filing of an action by a claimant in respect of a cause of action for the purpose of limitation laws. As such where a claimant's action is struck out when the matter has not been heard on the merit, for any reason such as for want of jurisdiction, the claimant can file the action in the appropriate court irrespective of the fact that at the time of filing the action the second time, time to file the action would have lapsed having regard to the statute of limitation. The rationale behind this position is that time stopped running at the time the action was first filed as long as the action was filed within time, the first time it was filed. This position has been given judicial credence in *Sifax Nig Ltd v. Migfo Nig Ltd*[284] where the SC held that:

> Where an aggrieved person commences an action within the period prescribed by the statute and such action is subsequently struck out for one reason or the other without being heard on the merit or subjected to an outright dismissal, such action is still open to be recommenced at the instance of the claimant and the limitation period shall not count during the pendency of the earlier suit.

276. There is a limitation period to bring actions against public officers.[285] Section 2(a) of the Public Officers Protection Act provides that:

281. Limitation Act Abuja Cap 542 Laws of the Federal Capital Territory Abuja.
282. *Adetula v. Akinyosoye* (2017) 16 NWLR (Pt 1592) 492 (CA).
283. *Nweke v. Unizik, Akwa* (2017) 18 NWLR (Pt 1598) 454 (SC).
284. (2018) 9 NWLR (Pt 1623) 138 (SC). *See also CBN v. Harris* (2017) 11 NWLR (Pt 1575) 54 (CA).
285. The Public Officers Protection Act Cap P41 LFN 2004.

> Where any action, prosecution, or other proceeding is commenced against any person for any act done in pursuance or execution or intended execution of any Act or Law or of any public duty or authority, or in respect of any alleged neglect or default in the execution of any such Act, Law, duty or authority –
>
> (a) The action, prosecution, or proceeding shall not lie or be instituted unless it is commenced within three months next after the act, neglect or default complained of, or in case of a continuance of damage or injury within three months next after the ceasing thereof …

However, this limitation period does not apply where an action is brought against a public officer for an act done outside the public officer's statutory or constitutional duty. It will also not apply when the wrong act of the public officer on which the action is based is continuing as time will only begin to count when the wrong ceases. Moreover, actions based on contract or recovery of land against a public officer is not affected by the limitation period prescribed under the Public Officers Protection Act. The Public Officers Protection Act applies to both human beings and institutions. This was the position of the court in *A.G Rivers State v. A.G Bayelsa State*.[286]

D. Condition Precedent

277. Payment of filing fees is a condition precedent to a court assuming jurisdiction in a case. Where filing fees are not paid, a court of law has no jurisdiction to entertain the matter before it and would be entitled to discountenance the process filed. This is because the Rules of court make payment of filing fees mandatory. However, where it is a case of not paying in full the prescribed filing fees it is a mere irregularity that does not vitiate the court's proceedings.[287] Similarly, the affixing of the stamp and seal of the lawyer who prepared a court process on the process is a condition precedent for a court to have jurisdiction to adjudicate on the matter. However, this provision has been deleted from the RPC 2007. *See* paragraph 190 above for information on this. There is also the regulation requiring the NIN of the lawyer who is filing a process on the court process. These have earlier been discussed in paragraphs 190 and 209 above.

278. Where parties had by agreement stated that in the event of a dispute arising from their contractual or other relationship, the parties must first resort to a particular means of resolving the dispute before considering litigation, then a court will lack jurisdiction unless and until the parties had explored the particular means stated. In practice, a claimant in a situation like this may file an action in court without first exploring the option of resolving the dispute stated in the contractual agreement. This is to avoid a situation where the limitation period may lapse while the parties are exploring the means of resolving the dispute stated in the agreement.

286. (2014) AFWLR (Pt 699) 1087 (SC).
287. *Green Fingers Ltd v. Musawa* (2017) 5 NWLR (Pt 1558) 308 (CA).

When an objection to the jurisdiction of the court is raised, the court will adjourn *sine die* to give the parties enough time to comply with the agreed means of resolving their dispute. The court does not strike out the action because it has jurisdiction to hear the matter. The issue is that the time to invoke the jurisdiction of the court was not ripe, as a condition precedent had not done.

II. Main Claims and Ancillary Claims

279. A court must have jurisdiction over the main claim of a claimant in court before it can entertain the matter. A court cannot adjudicate on ancillary reliefs where it has no jurisdiction to entertain the main claim, especially where the determination of the ancillary claim must necessarily involve the consideration of the main claim.[288] The SC has held that it is a well-settled law that, where a court does not have jurisdiction over the principal claims, it cannot adjudicate over the suit.[289] The main claim of a party must be within the purview of a court's jurisdiction for the court to exercise its authority to hear the suit.

III. Overview of the Jurisdiction of the Different Courts in Nigeria with Civil Jurisdiction

280. In this segment, the discussions will be on the various courts in Nigeria having civil jurisdiction and the jurisdiction conferred on them by the 1999 Nigerian Constn or by statutes. It must be noted that in Nigeria, courts generally exercise both civil and criminal jurisdiction. Only a few courts/tribunals exercise only criminal[290] or civil jurisdiction.[291] The courts with civil jurisdiction in Nigeria are described as follows.

A. *Superior Courts of Records*

1. The SC

281. Section 230 of the 1999 Nigerian Constn of the Federal Republic of Nigeria established the SC. The Court has both original and appellate civil jurisdiction. Section 232(1) of the 1999 Nigerian Constn confers the court with original civil Jurisdiction. Under this provision, the SC to the exclusion of any other court has two original jurisdictions namely: where there is a dispute between the federation and a state or between states if and in so far as that dispute involves any question (whether of law or fact) on which the existence or extent of a legal right depends.

288. *Adu v. L.S.T.F.E.* (2017) 11 NWLR (Pt 1575) 32 (CA).
289. *Ufomba v. I.N.E.C.* (2017) 13 NWLR (Pt 1582) 175 (SC).
290. Court Martials, Code of Conduct Tribunal and Juvenile Courts.
291. Election Petition Tribunals, Customary Court of Appeal, Sharia Court of Appeal, Districts Courts in the Northern part of Nigeria including the Federal Capital Territory, Abuja.

By section 232(2) of the 1999 Nigerian Constn, the National Assembly of Nigeria is empowered to confer additional original jurisdiction on the court. In exercise of this power, the National Assembly enacted the SC (Additional Original Jurisdiction) Act No. 3 of 2002 conferred the court with three more additional jurisdictions. As such the SC now has five original jurisdictions namely:

(1) where there is a dispute between the Federation and a state;
(2) where there is a dispute between two states;
(3) in dispute between the National Assembly and the President;
(4) in dispute between the National Assembly and a state; and
(5) in dispute between the National Assembly and a State House of Assembly.

The areas of original jurisdiction of the SC seem very clear except for the first one. The issue of when it can be said that there is a dispute between the Federation and a state has been a subject of interpretation before the SC in a couple of cases. The SC in *A.G Lagos State v. A.G.F*[292] distinguished Federation used in section 232(1) for the purpose of invoking its original jurisdiction from the Federal Government of Nigeria and held that 'it must be a dispute between the Federation and/ or more States as component parts of the federation or between, states inter se'. More recently, the SC pronouncing on this issue has held that:

> For a dispute to come under the original jurisdiction of the Supreme Court under this head, the subject matter of the dispute must be a matter in which the interest of the Federation as a unit consisting of the interest of the thirty-six States of the Federation and the Federal Capital Territory, Abuja is in issue as opposed to Federal Government of Nigeria or Government of the Federation where ministries and departments of the three arms of government are agencies of government.[293]

282. In invoking the original jurisdiction of the SC, the Federation sues or is sued through the AGF and a state sues or is sued through the AG of the state.[294] In *Plateau State v. AG (Fed)*,[295] the SC held that it was wrong that the action was commenced in the name of the principal rather than the nominal party. In the case of the National Assembly, it sues or is sued as the National Assembly, and a State House of Assembly sues or is sued through the Speaker of the State House of Assembly.[296] Before the National Assembly can invoke the original jurisdiction of the SC, there must be a resolution to that effect passed by a simple majority of members of each Chamber of the National Assembly present and voting at the sitting where the resolution is put to vote. For a State House of Assembly to bring an action under the original jurisdiction of the SC, there must be a resolution in that regard passed by

292. (2014) FWLR (Pt 740) 1296 (SC). *AG Kano v. AGF* (2007) 3 SC 59.
293. *A.G Federation v. A.G Anambra State* (2018) 6 NWLR (Pt 1615) 304 (SC).
294. S.20 Supreme Court Act Cap S16 LFN 2004.
295. (2006) 3 NWLR (Pt 967) 346 (SC).
296. Section 3 Supreme Court (Additional Original Jurisdiction) Act No. 2, 2002.

a simple majority of members of that State's House of Assembly present and voting at the sitting where the issue is put to vote.

283. In its appellate jurisdiction, the SC is constitutionally empowered to hear all appeals arising from the decision of the Court of Appeal that is appealable to the SC. The SC is properly constituted when it consists of not less than five justices of the court. However, when it is sitting in its original jurisdiction or it is sitting over matters bordering on interpretation or application of the 1999 Nigerian Constn, or matters on whether any of the rights in Chapter IV of the 1999 Nigerian Constn has been, is being or likely to be breached the SC shall be properly constituted by seven justices of the court.[297] This is usually referred to as the full court.

2. Court of Appeal

284. Section 237 of the 1999 Nigerian Constn establishes the Court of Appeal of Nigeria. The Court has both original and appellate jurisdiction. Section 239(1) of the 1999 Nigerian Constn confers the court with original jurisdiction. Under this provision, the Court of Appeal has jurisdiction to the exclusion of any other court of law in Nigeria, to hear and determine any question as to whether any person has been validly elected to the office of President or Vice President, or whether the term of office of the President or Vice President has ceased, or whether the office of the President or Vice President has become vacant.

285. In its appellate jurisdiction, the Court of Appeal to the exclusion of any other court hears civil appeals from the Federal HC, the HC of the Federal Capital Territory, the National Industrial Court, HCs of states, Sharia Court of Appeal of the Federal Capital Territory, Abuja, Sharia Court of Appeal of states, Customary Court of Appeal of the Federal Capital Territory, Customary Court of Appeal of states, the Governorship Election Tribunals, the National Assembly and State Houses of Assembly Election Tribunals and other tribunals as may be prescribed by an Act of the National Assembly.[298] With regard to the National Assembly and State Houses of Assembly Election Tribunal, the Court of Appeal's decision is final.[299] The SC in *PDP v. Umeh*[300] held that the interpretation of section 246(3) with regard to the jurisdiction of the SC is that an appeal in respect of a decision of the National Assembly and State Houses of Assembly Election Tribunal ends at the Court of Appeal of Nigeria for all purpose in line with section 246(3) of the 1999 Nigerian Const. The court has held that this applies to both final and interlocutory appeals

297. Section 234 of the 1999 Nigerian Constn.
298. Sections 240 and 246(1) of the 1999 Nigerian Constn as amended by s. 8 of the Constitution of the Federal Republic of Nigeria (Second Alteration) Act.
299. Section 246(3) of the 1999 Nigerian Constn as amended by s. 8 of the Constitution of the Federal Republic of Nigeria (Second Alteration) Act.
300. (2017) 12 NWLR (Pt 1579) 272 (SC).

from decisions of the National Assembly and State Houses of Assembly Election Tribunal.[301] However, with regard to the appeals from the Governorship Election Tribunal, it goes further to the SC.[302]

286. For the purpose of exercising any of the jurisdictions conferred upon it by the 1999 Nigerian Constn or any other law, the Court of Appeal of Nigeria is properly constituted if it consists of not less than three justices of the court. In the case of appeals from a Sharia Court of Appeal, the Court of Appeal of Nigeria shall be properly constituted if it consists of not less than three justices of the court learned in Islamic personal law. Also in the case of appeals from a Customary Court of Appeal, the Court of Appeal of Nigeria shall be properly constituted if it consists of not less than three justices of the court learned in customary law.[303]

3. Federal HC

287. Section 249 of the 1999 Nigerian Constn establishes the Federal HC of Nigeria. Section 251(1) of the 1999 Nigerian Constn confers exclusive civil jurisdiction on the court with respect to matters listed in section 251(1)(a)–(s). These matters have earlier been mentioned in paragraph 270 above. In addition by section 251(4),[304] the Federal HC exercises jurisdiction to determine any question as to whether the term of office or a seat of a member of the Senate or the House of Representatives has ceased or the seat has become vacant. Also, section 272(3)[305] confers the Federal HC of Nigeria with jurisdiction to determine questions of whether the term of office of a member of a State House of Assembly, Governor or Deputy Governor has ceased or become vacant. This particular provision is somewhat confusing. This is because section 272 of the 1999 Nigerian Constn relates to the HC of states. As such conferring jurisdiction on the Federal HC under the section looks untidy. It is hoped that future amendments to the 1999 Nigerian Constn will address the issue.

288. The Federal HC of Nigeria is duly constituted if it consists of at least one judge of the court sitting.[306] By section 22(3) of the Federal High Court Act, where the Federal HC finds that it lacks jurisdiction to entertain a matter but the proper court to hear and determine it is the HC of a state, the proper order it should make is one transferring the matter to the appropriate HC. The SC has held in *Fasakin Foods (Nig) Ltd v. Martins Babatunde Shosanya*[307] that this provision is a saving

301. *See APC v. Kerfi* (2017) 16 NWLR (Pt 1592) 457 (SC).
302. Section 233 of the 1999 Nigerian Constn as amended by s. 6 of the Constitution of the Federal Republic of Nigeria (Second Alteration) Act.
303. Section 247 of the 1999 Nigerian Constn.
304. As amended by s. 27 of the Constitution of the Federal Republic of Nigeria (Second Alteration) Act.
305. As amended by s. 28 of the Constitution of the Federal Republic of Nigeria (Second Alteration) Act.
306. Section 253 of the 1999 Nigerian Constn.
307. (2006) 10 NWLR (Pt 987) 126 at 161 (SC).

provision as it saves a matter duly and properly filed in a court of law from being struck out. The court however noted that this provision is only valid with regard to the Federal HC transferring matters to the State HC. For the provision to empower a State HC to transfer matters to the Federal HC in this circumstance the House of Assembly of the state must have adopted that provision or something similar to it. This is because the provisions of section 22(3) of the Federal High Court Act empowering a State HC to transfer matters to the Federal HC is inconsistent with the 1999 Nigerian Constn as it is the State House of Assembly that can legislate on such. The issue of transfer of cases is usually regulated by rules of procedure of the State HCs. In this light, the HC of the Federal Capital Territory, Abuja, by Order 41 Rule 6 empowers a judge when it has no jurisdiction to hear a matter by an order transfer the matter to a court with competent jurisdiction.

4. HC

289. The discussion on the HC here is in reference to the HC of the Federal Capital Territory and HC of the thirty-six states of the Federation. Section 255 of the 1999 Nigerian Constn establishes the HC of the Federal Capital Territory while section 270 of the 1999 Constn establishes the HC of a state. The HC has jurisdiction to hear and determine any civil matter in which the existence or extent of a legal right, power, duty, liability, privilege, interest, obligation or claim is in issue subject to sections 251(which confers exclusive jurisdiction on the Federal HC in some civil matters), 254C (which confers exclusive jurisdiction on the National Industrial Court in some civil matters) and such other provisions of the 1999 Nigerian Const. The HC has appellate jurisdiction to hear appeals from the courts under it such as the Magistrate Courts, District Courts and Area Courts. The court is duly constituted when it consists of at least one judge of the court sitting.[308]

290. As noted earlier, the jurisdiction of the HC is subject to the exclusive jurisdiction of the Federal HC. Expectedly, this has generated some sort of controversy in some of these areas necessitating the pronouncements of the courts. The areas where the two courts have concurrent jurisdiction or areas where their jurisdictions have been the subject of frequent controversies before the court will now be discussed.

Banker/Customer Related Disputes

291. An exclusive jurisdiction of the Federal HC are matters connected with or pertaining to banking, banks, other financial institutions including any action between one bank and another, any action by or against the CBN arising from banking, foreign exchange, coinage, legal tender, bills of exchange, letters of credit promissory notes and other fiscal measures.[309] However, this area of the exclusive jurisdiction of the Federal HC comes with a proviso. The 1999 Nigerian Constn

308. Section 273 of the 1999 Nigerian Constn.
309. Section 251(1)(d) *ibid.*

exempts disputes between an individual customer and his bank with respect to transactions between the individual customer and the bank from the exclusive jurisdiction of the Federal HC. The controversy then was what is the implication of the proviso. Does it take away the jurisdiction of the Federal HC to hear such matters and confer it on the HC or does is that both courts have concurrent jurisdiction to hear such matters? The SC in *NDIC v. Okem Enterprises Ltd*[310] held that what the proviso to section 251(1)(d) did was to take away the exclusive jurisdiction of the Federal HC from such cases such that both the Federal HC and the HC of states (including HC of the Federal Capital Territory, Abuja) can handle such matters. In effect, both courts have concurrent jurisdiction to hear and determine such matters.

Reference of Questions of Law as to Interpretation and Application of the 1999 Nigerian Constn in a Dispute Before an Inferior Court of Record

292. Where any question as to the interpretation or application of the 1999 Nigerian Constn arises in any proceedings in any court of law in any part of Nigeria (other than in the SC, Court of Appeal, Federal HC or an HC) and the court is of the opinion that the question involves a substantial question of law, the court may *suo motu* refer the question to the Federal HC or HC having jurisdictions in that part of Nigeria. Where the parties or any of the party in the proceedings is the one who requests the reference to be made, the court shall refer the matter to the Federal HC or HC. The implication of this is that in matters of reference to a higher court both the Federal HC and the State HC (including the HC of the Federal Capital Territory, Abuja) have concurrent jurisdiction. This is provided for in section 295(1) of the 1999 Nigerian Constn. On receipt of the questions referred, the Federal HC or the State HC shall do either of two things namely:

(1) if it is of the opinion that the question involves a substantial question of law, refer the question to the Court of Appeal; or
(2) if it is of the opinion that the question does not involve a substantial question of law, remit the question to the court that made the reference to be disposed of in accordance with such direction as the Federal HC or the State HC may deem fit to give.

Fundamental Rights Cases

293. Chapter IV of the 1999 Nigerian Constn provides for the fundamental rights of every person in Nigeria. Section 46 thereof confers jurisdiction on the HC to hear and determine any application made to it in pursuance of the provisions of Chapter IV. The 1999 Nigerian Constn does not define what it meant by HC. By section 46(3) of the 1999 Nigerian Constn the Chief Justice of Nigeria is empowered to make rules with respect to the practice and procedure of an HC for the purposes of enforcement of any of the rights as enshrined in Chapter IV. Based on this

310. (2004) 10 NWLR (Pt 880) 107 (SC).

empowerment, the Fundamental Rights (Enforcement Procedure) Rules 2009 were made. The Rules clearly define the HC to mean the Federal HC or the HC of a state or the HC of the Federal Capital Territory.[311] The question then will be when can the Federal HC exercise jurisdiction over a matter for enforcement of fundamental rights and when will the State HCs / HC of the Federal Capital Territory exercise jurisdiction? In *Tukur v. Government of Gongola State*,[312] the SC held that though both the Federal HC and the State HCs have jurisdiction to hear matters of enforcement of fundamental rights, the jurisdiction of the Federal HC is restricted to fundamental right issues arising from those areas where it has been conferred with exclusive civil jurisdiction. For example, if a fundamental right issue is arising from narcotics (such as a person arrested and detained at the Airport on allegation of being in possession and transporting cocaine), it is the Federal HC that should have jurisdiction as issues of drugs and poisons are under the exclusive jurisdiction of the Federal HC.

294. But in *Grace Jack v. University of Agriculture Makurdi*,[313] the same SC held that in matters of enforcement of fundamental rights both the Federal HC and the State HCs have concurrent jurisdiction irrespective of the subject matter. In *Adetona v. Igele General Enterprises Ltd.*,[314] the SC appears to have gone back to its position in *Tukur v. Government of Gongola State's* case by holding that the Federal HC's jurisdiction in the enforcement of fundamental rights issues is restricted to the areas covered by section 251 of the 1999 Nigerian Constn. It is pertinent to point out that the decision in *Adetona v. Igele General Enterprises Ltd* was an obiter dictum of the SC. However, in *FUT Minna v. Olutayo*[315] the SC did a U-turn and appeared to have gone back to its position in *Grace Jack v. University of Agriculture Makurdi* when it held that in fundamental rights issues, both the Federal HC and the HC have concurrent jurisdiction. When later decisions of the SC are at variance with its previous decisions, it means that the previous decisions have been overruled to the extent of the variation.[316] As it stands, the position of the law is that with respect to fundamental rights matters both the Federal HC and the State HC / HC of the Federal Capital Territory have concurrent jurisdiction to hear and determine such matters. An applicant seeking to enforce his fundamental right is at liberty to choose either of the courts to approach.

295. It is observed that the SC did not consider section 46(2) of the 1999 Nigerian Constn which makes the exercise of the HC jurisdiction to entertain fundamental right enforcement matters subject to the provisions of the 1999 Nigerian Constn and Order 1 Rule 2 of the Fundamental Right Enforcement Procedure Rules 2009, that define HC to mean the Federal HC, the HC of the Federal Capital Territory, Abuja, and the HC of a state. However, to the extent that the SC did not consider

311. Order 1 Rule 2 Fundamental Rights (Enforcement Procedure) Rules 2009.
312. (1989) 4 NWLR (Pt 117) 517 (SC).
313. (2004) 5 NWLR (Pt 865) 208 (SC).
314. (2011) 7 NWLR (Pt 1247) 535 (SC).
315. (2018) 7 NWLR (Pt 1617) 176 (SC).
316. *Osude v. Azodo* (2017) 15 NWLR (Pt 1588) 293 (SC).

the said provisions, it can be argued that the decision of the court in *FUT Minna v. Olutayo* cannot be said to have overruled the decision in *Tukur v. Govt of Gongola State.*

296. Attention is also drawn to the fact that given the amendment to the 1999 Nigerian Constn and the consequent conferring of the National Industrial Court with jurisdiction to entertain matters related to or connected with any dispute bordering on the interpretation and application of the provisions of the 1999 Constn on fundamental rights as it relates to any employment, labour, industrial relations, trade unionism, employer's association or any other matter, which the court has jurisdiction to hear and determine,[317] the courts that have jurisdiction to entertain actions for enforcement of fundamental rights now includes the National Industrial Court.

Matters Where the Federal Government of Nigeria or Any of Its Agencies Is a Party

297. Section 251(1)(p)–(r) of the 1999 Nigerian Constn confers exclusive jurisdiction on the Federal HC on issues relating to the administration and control of the Federal Government or any of its agencies, the operation and interpretation of the said Constn as it affects the Federal Government or any of its agencies, and any action for a declaration or injunction affecting the validity of any executive or administrative action or decision of the Federal Government or any of its agencies. The underlying contention is whether, for every action where the Federation Government or any of its agencies is a party, it is the Federal HC that has jurisdiction to entertain it? In *NEPA v. Edengbenro*,[318] the SC held that once one of the parties in a dispute is the Federal Government or any of its agencies, it is the Federal HC that should have jurisdiction to hear the case. But in *Onuorah v. KRPC*,[319] the same SC held that what should be considered in determining which court has jurisdiction are both the parties in the action and the subject matter of the dispute. The court went further to state that, though KRPC is a Federal Government agency, the subject matter of the dispute is a simple contract and as such it is the HC that has jurisdiction. Some subsequent SC decisions on the issue followed *NEPA v. Edengbenro's* case (e.g., the case of *Osakwe v. FCE Asaba*[320]) while others followed *Onuorah's case* (e.g., the case of *NUEE v. BPE*).[321] The position of the SC that both the parties and the subject matter be considered to determine which court has jurisdiction is the current position.

317. Section 254C(1)(D) of the 1999 Nigerian Constn as amended by *See* s. 6 of the Constitution of the Federal Republic of Nigeria (Third Alteration) Act 2010, Act No. 3.
318. (2002) 18 NWLR (Pt 798) 79 (SC).
319. (2005) 6 NWLR (Pt 921) 393 (SC).
320. (2010) 10 NWLR (Pt 1201) 1 (SC).
321. (2010) 7 NWLR (Pt 1194) 538 (SC).

5. National Industrial Court

298. The National Industrial Court is established as a superior court of record by section 254A of the 1999 Nigerian Constn.[322] Section 254C of the 1999 Nigerian Constn provides for the jurisdiction of the court. Like the Federal HC, the National Industrial Court is a court of special civil jurisdiction in the sense that its jurisdiction is specified in the 1999 Nigerian Constn or other statutes. This is as distinct from the HC whose jurisdiction is only limited by the express jurisdiction conferred on the Federal HC and the National Industrial Court. The National Industrial Court by section 24(3) of the National Industrial Court Act is empowered to when it finds that it lacks jurisdiction, transfer a matter before it to the appropriate court.[323] This section also empowers a State HC to do the same if there is a corresponding provision in the State HC laws or rules of procedure. Where a State HC does not have provisions in the state laws or rules of procedure, a judge in a State HC transferring a matter to the National Industrial Court will be doing so without jurisdiction.[324] The National Industrial Court is duly constituted if it consists of a single judge or not more than three judges as the President of the National Industrial Court may direct.[325]

6. Sharia Court of Appeal

299. Another court with civil jurisdiction is the Sharia Court of Appeal. The Court is conferred with both appellate and supervisory jurisdictions in civil proceedings involving questions of Islamic personal law.

Specifically, the Sharia Court of Appeal whether of the Federal Capital Territory, Abuja,[326] or of the states[327] have jurisdiction with regard to the following:

(a) any question of Islamic personal law regarding a marriage concluded in accordance with that law, including a question relating to the validity or dissolution of such a marriage or a question that depends on such a marriage and relating to family relationship or the guardianship of an infant;
(b) where all the parties to the proceedings are Muslims, any question of Islamic personal law regarding a marriage, including the validity or dissolution of that marriage, or regarding family relationship, a foundling or the guardianship of an infant;
(c) any question of Islamic personal law regarding a wakf, gift, will or succession where the endower, donor, testator or deceased person is a Muslim;

---

322. Amended by *See* s. 6 of the Constitution of the Federal Republic of Nigeria (Third Alteration) Act 2010.
323. Section 24(3) National Industrial Court Act 2006.
324. University of *Ado-Ekiti v. Isijola* (2017) 15 NWLR (Pt 1588) 334 at 343–344.
325. Section 254E(1) of the 1999 Nigerian Constn.
326. Section 262(2) *ibid.*
327. Section 277(2) *ibid.*

(d) any question of Islamic personal law regarding an infant, prodigal or person of unsound mind who is a Muslim or the maintenance or the guardianship of a Muslim who is physically or mentally infirm; or

(e) where all parties to the proceedings, being Muslims, have requested the court that hears the case in the first instance to determine, that case is in accordance with Islamic personal law.

By sections 263 and 278 of the 1999 Nigerian Constn, the Sharia Court of Appeal of the Federal Capital Territory, Abuja, and the Sharia Court of Appeal of a state respectively shall be duly constituted, when it consists of at least three Kadis of the court.

7. Customary Court of Appeal

300. Sections 265 and 280 of the 1999 Nigerian Constn establish the Customary Court of Appeal of the Federal Capital Territory, Abuja, and Customary Court of Appeal of the states respectively. The Customary Court of Appeal shall in addition to such other jurisdiction conferred on it by an Act of the National Assembly or law of a State House of Assembly exercise appellate and supervisory jurisdiction in civil proceedings involving questions of customary law.[328] The Customary Court of Appeal is properly constituted when it consists of at least three judges of the court. *See* sections 268 and 283 of the 1999 Nigerian Const.

B. Inferior Courts of Record

1. Magistrates' Court / District Court

301. They are referred to as courts of summary jurisdiction because matters are dispensed with expeditiously for the procedure in the court is simple as there is no filing of pleadings. When Magistrates in the north preside over criminal matters they are referred to as Magistrate, but when they sit over civil matters they are regarded as District Judges. In the south, the Magistrate is regarded as a Magistrate when they preside over both criminal and civil cases. Section 28 Magistrate Court Law Lagos 2003 confers jurisdiction on the court with its financial limit being NGN 10 million for all Magistrates as there is no cadre of Magistrates in Lagos State.[329] By section 30 of the Magistrate Court Law of Lagos State, the AG of Lagos State on the recommendation of the Lagos State Judicial Service Commission is empowered by notice in the Gazette to increase the jurisdiction of the Magistrates' Court in Lagos.

328. Sections 267 and 282 of the 1999 Nigerian Constn respectively.
329. Section 93(1) Magistrate Court Law 2009 of Lagos State.

302. For the District Court in the Federal Capital Territory, the financial limit is NGN 5 million.[330] The financial limit of the various grades of District Courts has earlier been discussed in paragraph 272 above. The Minister of the Federal Capital Territory, Abuja, is by section 17 of the District Court Act[331] and section 18(b) of the Federal Capital Territory Act[332] conferred with powers to increase the jurisdiction of the Magistrates' Court in the Federal Capital Territory, Abuja.

303. It is to be noted that the Magistrates' Court/District Court does not have jurisdiction to entertain any matter bordering on the declaration of title to land, any interest in land or the validity of any devise, bequest or limitation under any will or settlement.[333]

2. Customary Courts

304. There is Customary Court Grade A or B. They are found in the southern states in Nigeria and the Federal Capital Territory, Abuja.[334] These exercise jurisdiction over matters bordering on native laws and customs and over persons subject to customary law. For example under the Customary Court Law of Lagos State 2003, the customary court in Lagos exercises unlimited jurisdiction in Matrimonial Causes and other related matters with respect to persons married under customary law, or arising from or connected with a union contracted under customary law. The court also has jurisdiction in suits relating to guardianship and custody of children under customary. Its jurisdiction also extends to causes and matters relating to inheritance upon intestacy and the administration of intestate estate under customary law where the amount does not exceed NGN 500. Its jurisdiction also covers debt demand or damages not exceeding NGN 500.[335] The Jurisdiction of the Customary Court in the Federal Capital Territory is similar save for the financial limits, which is unlimited for the Grade A Customary Courts and NGN 200,000 and NGN 100,000 for Grade B and Grade C Customary Courts respectively.[336]

3. Area Courts

305. In the Federal Capital Territory, Abuja, there are four Grades of Area Court namely Upper Area Court, Area Court Grade 1, Area Court Grade 11 and Area Court Grade 111. The Area Courts are found in the northern states in Nigeria and the Federal Capital Territory, Abuja. They exercise unlimited jurisdiction in matrimonial matters between persons married under customary law but not matters arising from

---

330. By the District Courts (Increase of Jurisdiction of District Judges) Order 2014.
331. Cap 495 LFN (Abuja) 1990.
332. Cap 503 LFN (Abuja) 2006.
333. Section 28(7) Magistrates' Court Law of Lagos State 2009.
334. The Federal Capital Territory Abuja has Customary Court Grade A, B and C.
335. *See* s. 16 and Part 1 of the Second Schedule to the Customary Court Laws of Lagos State 2003.
336. Sections 1 and 14 and Part 1 of the Schedule of the Customary Court Act of the Federal Capital Territory, Abuja.

Christian marriages, etc.[337] An Area Court consists of an Area Court Judge sitting alone or with one or two members but for the Area Courts in the Federal Capital Territory, Abuja the court consists of a single judge.[338]

4. Sharia Courts

306. These are established in some states in northern Nigeria. They exercise jurisdiction over persons who are Muslims or non-Muslims that voluntarily submit to the jurisdiction of the court. They exercise jurisdiction over matters of Islamic law.

§2. Venue/Territorial Jurisdiction

307. This refers to jurisdiction vested on courts within a particular geographic description. Courts are usually not seized of matters that occur outside their territory. For example, a cause of action arising in Edo State on the southern part of Nigeria is within the jurisdiction of the court in Edo State and cannot be adjudicated upon by the courts in Lagos State, which is another state in the southern part of Nigeria. In *Mailantarki v. Tongo & ORS*,[339] the SC held that the Federal Capital Territory, Abuja HC lacked jurisdiction to entertain a cause of action that arose in Gombe State and that it amounted to forum shopping to have filed the action in the Federal Capital Territory HC. In the words of the SC 'forum shopping denotes a rather reprehensible practice of choosing the most favourable territorial jurisdiction or court in which a matter or cause may be entertained and adjudicated upon'. It has been held that though the Federal HC is one and has jurisdiction throughout Nigeria, matters should be commenced in the judicial division where the cause of action arose, if not, it will amount to forum shopping.[340] The SC in *Tukur v. Government of Gongola State*,[341] brought out the essentials of jurisdictions to include:

(a) the legal capacity, the power and authority of a court to hear and determine a judicial proceeding; and
(b) the geographical area in which and over which the legal jurisdiction of the court can be exercised. This area of authority is called the area of geographical jurisdiction or venue.

337. *See* s. 18 and Part 2 of the First Schedule to the Area Court Act of the Federal Capital Territory, Abuja.
338. Section 2 Federal Capital Territory, Abuja Area Courts (Repeal and Enactment) Act 2010.
339. (2017) LPELR-42467 (SC).
340. *Ibori v. FRN* (2009) AFWLR (Pt 487) 159 (CA).
341. (1989) 4 NWLR (Pt 117) 517 at 560–561 (SC).

The issue of venue of commencing an action indicates that a court having jurisdiction to hear and determine matters over which it has been conferred with authority to adjudicate can only do so with respect to a given geographical area. This is determined by the Rules of Court. Certain factors determine the issue of venue. This shall now be considered.

I. Factors to Be Taken into Account

A. Where the Cause of Action Arose

308. Where a cause of action arose is a factor in determining where the action should be commenced as the court in such territory is the court with jurisdiction. The HCCPR of the Federal Capital Territory, Abuja and of Lagos State provides that with regard to actions for recovery of penalties, forfeitures and all actions against public officers, such may be commenced and tried in the judicial division in which the cause of action arose.[342] With respect to the Federal HC, the appropriate judicial division to commence an action is the one where the cause of action arose irrespective of the fact that there is only one Federal HC in Nigeria.

B. Where the Contract Ought to Have Been Performed

309. With regard to disputes arising from breach of contract, where the contract ought to have been performed as opposed to where the contract was entered into is a relevant consideration in determining the court that has jurisdiction to hear the matter. The HCCPR provides that 'all suits for the specific performance, or upon the breach of any contract, may be commenced and determined in the judicial division in which such contract ought to have been performed or in which the defendant resides or carries on business'.[343]

C. Where the Defendant Resides or Carries on Business

310. This is by far the most common consideration with respect to the issue of which venue to commence an action within the territory of a particular state. For example, in actions bordering on specific performance of a contract or breach of any contract apart from the consideration of where the contract ought to have performed, the other consideration is where the defendant residence or carries on business (for non-natural defendants). Also apart from actions regarding land or personal property distrained or seized, actions for recovery of penalties, forfeitures and against public officers, all other action may be commenced where the defendant resides or carries on business.[344] In the event that there are several defendants who

342. Order 3 Rule 2 HCCPR Abuja.
343. Order 3 Rule 3 HCCPR Abuja and Order 4 Rule 3 Lagos.
344. Order 3 Rule 4 HCCPR Abuja and Order 4 Rule 4 Lagos.

reside or carry on business in different judicial divisions, the action may be commenced in any one of those judicial divisions subject to any direction the court may make regarding the most convenient venue for the trial.

D. *Where the Land Is Situated*

311. Actions relating to land or any mortgage or charge on land, any interest in land, inquiry or damage to land, personal property distrained or seized for any cause may be commenced where the land is situated or where the distrained or seizure took place.

E. *Domicile of a Party*

312. In matrimonial matters, the domicile of the petitioner determines the jurisdiction of the court. Any HC in Nigeria has jurisdiction to entertain a divorce petition or any other relief under the Matrimonial Causes Act 2004[345] where the petitioner is domiciled in Nigeria.[346] For the purpose of the Matrimonial Causes Act, a person domiciled in any state of the federation of Nigeria is domiciled in Nigeria. The court has held that the whole of Nigeria is taken as one territory for the purpose of matrimonial proceedings.[347] However, an HC of a state for the purpose of convenience may transfer a matrimonial matter filed before it to another State HC.

II. Main Claims and Ancillary Claims

313. The rules set out in paragraph 278 above with regard to the court's subject-matter jurisdiction apply accordingly.

III. Overview of the Different Rules

314. The Rules of the various courts make provisions for the venue of commencing an action. This segment takes a look at these rules with regard to the issue of venue for commencement of action. Necessarily, the rules that will be discussed are rules of trial courts. As such only the HCCPR of Lagos and the Federal Capital Territory, Abuja will be reviewed. Suffice to say that in form and content the HCCPR of the various are essentially similar. The Civil Procedure Rules of the Federal HC and the National Industrial Court will also be looked at. In addition, the Civil Procedure Rules of the Magistrates' Courts in Lagos State in the southern part of Nigeria and the District Court Rules of the Federal Capital Territory, Abuja in the

345. Cap M7 LFN 2004.
346. Section 2(2) Matrimonial Causes Act *ibid.*
347. *Adegoroye v. Adegoroye* (1996) 4 NWLR (Pt 433) 712 (CA).

northern part of Nigeria will be discussed. The Customary Court Rules of Lagos State and the Federal Capital Territory, Abuja and Area Court Rules of the Federal Capital Territory, Abuja will also be mentioned.

A. *The Federal HCCPR 2019*

315. The Federal HC of Nigeria is one court and has the whole of Nigeria has its territory. However, for the purpose of administrative convenience, it sits in different judicial divisions across the states in Nigeria. The Federal HC of Nigeria Civil Procedure Rules 2019 provides for the appropriate judicial division to commence an action. Subject to the provisions of any law with respect to the transfer of suits or to specific subject matters, the place for the trial of any suit or matter shall be as follows:[348]

(a) all suits or actions relating to taxation of companies and of other bodies established or carrying on business in Nigeria and of all other persons subject to federal taxation shall be commenced and determined in the judicial division of the court in which the headquarters or the principal office of the company or body is situated and in the case of a person subject to federal taxation, where the person resides or carries on substantial part of the person's business;
(b) all actions for recovery of revenue, penalties and forfeitures, actions against public officers shall be commenced in the judicial division of the court where the cause of action arose;
(c) all suits for specific performance or upon the breach of any contract shall be commenced and determined in the judicial division of the court in which the contract is meant to be performed or in which the defendant resides or carries on substantial part of the person's business;
(d) all suits and actions relating to customs, excise, tariff, etc. shall be commenced and determined in the jurisdiction of the judicial division of the court in which the breach of the law, or contract took place or the port or border where the breach took place;
(e) all suits and actions in respect of diplomatic, consular or foreign trade representation shall be commenced and determined in the judicial division in which the diplomatic, consular or foreign trade is carried out;
(f) all suits and actions in respect of citizenship, naturalization and aliens, repatriation of persons who are not citizens of Nigeria, passport and visas shall be commenced and determined in the judicial division in which the person resides;
(g) all suits and actions relating to copyright, patents, designs, trademarks and merchandise marks shall be commenced and determined in the judicial division in which the defendant resides or where the alleged passing-off or infringement took place; and

---

348. Order 2 Rule 1 of the Federal High Court Civil Procedure Rules 2019.

(h) all other suits shall be commenced and determined in the judicial division in which the defendant resides or carries on substantial part of the defendant's business or in which the cause of action arose.

316. In situations where there are several defendants who reside in different judicial divisions, the suit or action may be commenced in any of the judicial divisions subject to any order the court may deem fit to make upon the application of any of the parties or by the court *suo motu* with a view to the most convenient place of trial of the action.[349] In the event that a suit is commenced in a judicial division other than the one that it ought to have been commenced, it may notwithstanding be tried in the judicial division in which it was commenced unless the court otherwise directs or the defendant pleads especially in objection to the jurisdiction before or at the time when the defendant is required to state his answer or to plead in the cause. However, no proceedings that have been taken before the plea in objection shall be in any way affected but the judge may order that the cause be transferred to the judicial division to which it is proved to the judge's satisfaction to belong. Where such proof is not made, the judge may order that the suit be retained and proceeded with in the court where it was commenced.

B. The National Industrial Court of Nigeria Civil Procedure Rules 2016

317. The National Industrial Court in Nigeria is one court and has the whole of Nigeria as its territory. However, for the purpose of administrative convenience, it sits in different judicial divisions across the states in Nigeria. The National Industrial Court of Nigeria Civil Procedure Rules 2016 provides for the appropriate judicial division to commence an action. Subject to provisions of the National Industrial Court Act on the transfer of suit, actions are instituted/filed in any Registry of the court nearest to where the defendant or respondent resides or has a presence or in which the defendant or respondent carries on business. There is, however, an exception to this provision. In cases where economic, security, environmental or other exigencies warrants actions may be filed in the Registry of the court in a judicial division other than the one closest to the place of residence or business of the defendant or respondent. Where there are several defendants or respondents who reside or carry on business in different judicial divisions, the suit may be commenced in any one of those judicial divisions subject to any order or direction of the court as to the most convenient arrangement for the trial of the suit. Where a suit is commenced in a wrong judicial division, it may be tried in that division unless the President of the court otherwise directs.[350] Where a party has justifiable grounds for a suit commenced in a particular judicial division to be tried in a different one, the party makes an application to the President personally or through the party's counsel for consideration and directions as to the appropriate judicial division in which the suit may be heard. The decision of the President of the court in this regard is

349. Order 2 Rule 2 of the Federal High Court Civil Procedure 2019.
350. Order 2 Rule 5 National Industrial Court of Nigeria Civil Procedure Rules 2016.

final.[351] Notwithstanding the provision that suits are to be filed in the judicial division closest to where the defendant/respondent resides or carries on business, the President of the National Industrial Court may in the interest of justice, fairness, balance of convenience, equity and security of parties and the court direct that a case be heard in a judicial division other than where the case was filed.[352]

C. The HCCPR of Lagos State 2019

318. The HC of Lagos State only has jurisdiction with regard to suits and action arising in Lagos. The whole of Lagos State is its jurisdiction. However, for administrative convenience, the HC of Lagos State is divided into judicial divisions. Order 4 of the HCCPR of Lagos State 2019 makes provision for which judicial division has jurisdiction to entertain a matter. By the rules, an action relating to land or any mortgage or charge or any interest in land or any inquiry or damage to land and actions relating to personal property distrained or seized for any cause shall be commenced in the judicial division in which the land is situated or where the distrain took place. Where the action is one for recovery of penalties, forfeitures and actions against public officers it shall be commenced and tried in the judicial division in which the cause of action arose. Actions for specific performance or breach of contract can be commenced and determined in the judicial division in which the contract ought to have been performed or in which the defendant resides or carries on business. Any action not falling under the ones that have been specifically mentioned may be commenced in the judicial division where the defendant resides or carries on business.

319. Where there are several defendants who reside or carry on business in different judicial divisions the action may be commenced in any of the judicial divisions but this is subject to any order or direction a judge may make with respect to the most convenient place for the trial of the action.[353] However, in the event that a claimant files an action in contravention of these provisions, that is, a claimant files an action in the wrong judicial division, the action is not defeated by this fact as the case may be held in that 'wrong judicial division' except the Chief Judge of Lagos State directs otherwise.[354]

D. The HCCPR of the Federal Capital Territory, Abuja 2018

320. The HC of the Federal Capital Territory, Abuja has jurisdiction over matters arising from the whole of the Federal Capital Territory, Abuja. That is to say, the whole of the Federal Capital Territory, Abuja is its jurisdiction. However, like in Lagos State, it is divided into judicial divisions for administrative convenience.

---

351. Order 2 Rule 6 National Industrial Court of Nigeria Civil Procedure Rules 2016.
352. Order 2 Rule 4(2) National Industrial Court of Nigeria Civil Procedure Rules 2016.
353. Order 4 Rule 2 HCCPR Lagos State 2019.
354. Order 4 Rule 3 *ibid.*

Order 3 of the HCCPR of the Federal Capital Territory, Abuja provides for the appropriate venue to commence an action. Where the suit is with regard to land or any mortgage or charge or any interest in land or any inquiry or damage to land and actions relating to personal property distrained or seized for any cause shall be commenced in the judicial division in which the land is situated or the distraint or seizure took place. Where the action is one for recovery of penalties, forfeitures and all actions against public officers it shall be commenced and tried in the judicial division in which the cause of action arose. Actions for specific performance or breach of contract may be commenced and determined in the judicial division in which such contract ought to have been performed or in which the defendant carries on business. Any action not falling under the ones that have been specifically mentioned may be commenced in the judicial division where the defendant resides or carries on business.

321. Where there are several defendants who reside or carry on business in different judicial divisions the action may be commenced in any of the judicial divisions but this is subject to any order or direction a judge may make with respect to the most convenient place for the trial of the action.[355] However, a suit filed in a wrong judicial division may be tried in that division except if the Chief Judge of the Federal Capital Territory, Abuja directs otherwise.[356]

E. Magistrates' Court Civil Procedure Rules of Lagos 2009

322. The Magistrates' Court in Lagos State is divided into ten Magisterial Districts namely: Lagos Magisterial District, Yaba Magisterial District, Surulere Magisterial District, Apapa Magisterial District, Mushin Magisterial District, Ikeja Magisterial District, Badagry Magisterial District, Ikorodu Magisterial District, Epe Magisterial District and Agege Magisterial District. However, the Magistrates' Court Law of Lagos State 2009 grants a Magistrate jurisdiction throughout Lagos State. In that light, once the Magistrates' Court in Lagos has jurisdiction to hear a matter, it can be filed in any Magisterial District. So the issue of venue in the Magistrates Court in Lagos State is discussed in the context that the whole of Lagos State is one venue. Order 1 of the Magistrate Court Civil Procedure Rules 2009 makes provision for when an action can be commenced in the Magistrates' Court in Lagos State. Except any law or rule provides otherwise, an action may be commenced by claim in a Magistrates' Court if the defendant or one of the defendants resides or carries on business in Lagos. A claim can also be commenced in the Magistrates' Court in Lagos where the cause of action arose wholly or in part in Lagos. Also, a claim can be brought before the Magistrates' Court in Lagos in a situation where the claimant sue as an assignee of a debt or other thing in action, if the action may have been commenced in Lagos by the assignor. Moreover, an action may be commenced by an originating application in the Magistrates' Court in Lagos, if the claimant or one of them resides in Lagos, or the subject matter of the application is

---

355. Order 3 Rule 4(2) HCCPR Abuja 2018.
356. Order 3 Rule 6 *ibid.*

situated in Lagos. Additionally, in the Small Claims Court in Lagos (Fast Tract division of the Magistrates' Court in Lagos State) an action may be commenced in the Small Claims Court where the claimant or one of the claimants resides or carries on business in Lagos State, the defendant or one of the defendant carries on business in Lagos State and the cause of action arose wholly or in part in Lagos State.

F. District Court Civil Procedure Rules of the Federal Capital Territory, Abuja 2021

323. The District Court Act of the Federal Capital Territory, Abuja grants a District Judge jurisdiction throughout the Federal Capital Territory, Abuja.[357] For purposes of venue, an action can be commenced in the District Court having jurisdiction in the District in which the defendant or any of the defendants resides or carries on his business at the time of commencing the action or the cause of action or claim arose wholly or in part or the subject matter of the action is located.[358] There is a central registry at every district where an intending litigant can file his action.[359]

G. Customary Court Rules of Lagos State

324. The Customary Court in Lagos has jurisdiction throughout the states. Its jurisdiction, therefore, is prescribed by law, which has been discussed in paragraph 303 above. However, the court still reserves the discretion to transfer a matter filed in one district to another on the basis of convenience.

H. Customary Court Rules of the Federal Capital Territory, Abuja

325. The position under the Customary Court in the Federal Capital Territory, Abuja is similar to that in Lagos as outlined in paragraph 323 above save for the monetary limits which were pointed out in paragraph 303 above.

326. From the overview of the different rules, there is one common denominator that runs through them all. That is the issue of where the defendant resides or carries on a business being a major determinant as to the venue to commence an action. Where it has to do with a contract, it is where the contract ought to have been performed. It is also noted that commencing an action in the wrong venue does not automatically lead to the action being struck out. The bottom line is that the action may still be heard in the wrong judicial division where it was filed. It is only under the Federal HC Rules that provision is made allowing the defendant to raise the issue of jurisdiction due to commencing the action in the wrong venue.

357. Section 8(1) District Court Act Cap 495 LFN (Abuja) 1990.
358. Section 40(1) District Court Act Cap 495 LFN (Abuja) 1990.
359. Order 2 Rule 1 District Court Civil Procedure Rules of the Federal Capital Territory, Abuja 2021.

Resolution of Jurisdictional Conflict

327. There are instances where more than one court has jurisdiction with regard to a particular subject matter. A good example is the enforcement of fundamental rights in Nigeria. By the provision of the law, both the HC (including the HC of the Federal Capital Territory, Abuja) and the Federal HC have jurisdiction to entertain the matter.[360] More recently, the National Industrial Court of Nigeria also has jurisdiction to entertain matters on enforcement of fundamental rights where the alleged breach of fundamental right rose from an employer and employee relationship. The SC has in some cases attempted to resolve the jurisdictional conflict arising from this by holding that in fundamental right cases, both the Federal HC and the HC have concurrent jurisdiction.[361] As such *forum conveniens is used in resolving the conflict.* By such decisions, claimants are at liberty to approach any of the two courts that they find more convenient. However, in some other line of cases, the SC has held that the Federal HC jurisdiction with respect to fundamental right cases is limited to the subject matter for which the Federal HC has been conferred with exclusive jurisdiction under the 1999 Nigerian Constn.[362] As such when the fundamental right issue did not arise from any of the subjects over which exclusive jurisdiction had been conferred on the Federal HC, the court would not have jurisdiction. In such a situation it is the HC that will have jurisdiction. The issue is not yet a settled area of law, but it can safely be said that the current position by a recent decision of the SC is that both the Federal HC and the HC have concurrent jurisdiction.[363]

328. Another area of jurisdictional conflict between the Federal HC and the State HC is in matters arising from banker/customer relationship. The SC in *NDIC v. Okem Enterprise*,[364] where the issue came up for its determination held that both courts have concurrent jurisdiction to hear such suit. Again the court has towed the line of allowing the principle of *forum conveniens* to resolve the conflict.

329. It has been mentioned earlier in paragraph 272 above that Magistrates' Court in Lagos State has a financial jurisdictional limit of NGN 10 million. This does not however mean that it has exclusive jurisdiction to entertain claims in Lagos that is less than NGN 10 million. In the same vein the jurisdictional limit of the District Court in the Federal Capital Territory, Abuja is NGN 5 million. The jurisdiction of the HC in Lagos State and HC of the Federal Capital Territory, Abuja is not affected by the financial jurisdiction of the Magistrates' Court. The HC has unlimited financial jurisdiction in monetary claims. The effect of this is that for matters

360. Order 1 Rule 2 Fundamental Rights Enforcement Procedure Rules 2009.
361. *Grace Jack v. University of Agriculture Makurdi* (2004) 5 NWLR (Pt 865) 208 SC; *FUT Minna v. Olutayo* (2018) 7 NWLR (Pt 1617) 176 (SC).
362. *Tukur v. Government of Gongola State* 1989) 4 NWLR (Pt 117) 517 (SC); *Adetona v. Igele General Enterprises Ltd* (2011) 7 NWLR (Pt 1247) 535 (SC).
363. *FUT Minna v. Olutayo* (2018) 7 NWLR (Pt 1617) 176 (SC).
364. (2004) 10 NWLR (Pt 880) 107 (SC).

such as contractual claims, recovery of debt and recovery of premises there is jurisdictional conflict between the HC and the Magistrates' Court in Lagos State and between the HC and District Courts in the Federal Capital Territory, Abuja. How is this jurisdictional conflict resolved? The answer is in the principle of *forum conveniens*. Claimants are free to choose the court that they find more convenient to them. Convenience here is not just a function of the proximity of court to the parties it includes the practice and procedure of the court that the claimant finds convenient.

330. Where a party intends to challenge the jurisdiction of a court to entertain a matter, such party brings an application to the court whose jurisdiction is being challenged by way of a notice of preliminary objection stating the grounds for objecting to the jurisdiction of the court and the notice is supported with a written address. This is deployed where the party attacking the jurisdiction of the court is not relying on facts for the objection but purely on points of law. Where a party will be relying on facts, the party should come by way of motion on notice supported by an affidavit containing the facts that the party seeks to rely on for the grant of the application and a written address.

331. The issue of jurisdictional conflict can be raised by any of the parties or by the court upon its own motion. In *Tony-Anthony Holding Limited v. C.B.A.* the Court of Appeal of Nigeria held that:

> When there are sufficient facts *ex facie* on the record establishing a want of competence or jurisdiction in a court, it is the duty of the Judge or Justices to raise the issue *suo motu* if the parties fail to draw the court's attention to it.[365]

The objection to the jurisdiction of a court should be raised at the earliest opportunity. However, issues of jurisdiction can be raised at any time even for the first time on appeal. The court whose jurisdiction is attacked hears the objection to its jurisdiction. There are no special courts to hear issues on jurisdictional conflict. It is the court before which the issue of jurisdiction is raised that hears the application and gives a ruling whether or not it has jurisdiction. A party not satisfied with the court's decision can appeal against it to the appellate court. Issues of jurisdiction when raised are given prime place as the court must hear and determine it before proceeding further with the case. Where any of the parties is not satisfied with the way the court resolved the issue, it can appeal against the decision.

332. When a court rules that it has jurisdiction to adjudicate over a matter, the ruling of the court is an interlocutory ruling that can be appealed against in the manner prescribed by law for appealing against interlocutory rulings. The court thereafter proceeds with the matter except there is an order of stay of proceedings. Where a court rules that it has no jurisdiction to entertain a matter, it is a final decision of the court and the court becomes *functus officio* with regard to the case.

365. (2013) AFWLR (Pt 698) 944 at 963 (CA).

Chapter 2. International Jurisdiction

§1. Rules Applicable in the Absence of a Treaty

333. Where there is an international conflict whether or not Nigeria has jurisdiction to adjudicate over it is largely a function of the intention of the parties has can be deciphered from their contractual agreement. Generally, the Nigerian Courts will give effect to party's choice of foreign law and court to determine any issue arising from a contract. Where parties had agreed in a written contract that in the event of a dispute that it is the court in the UK that should adjudicate over it, the Nigerian courts would generally decline to entertain such cases. However, in limited cases, the courts in Nigeria may despite party's agreement assume jurisdiction in an international conflict. In *Sonnar (Nig) Ltd v. Partnereedri M.S. Nordwind*,[366] the SC held *inter alia* that:

> Our courts should not be too eager to divest themselves of jurisdiction conferred on them by the Constitution and by other laws simply because parties in their private contract chose a foreign forum and a foreign law.

334. The rules that will determine whether a court in Nigeria will assume jurisdiction in an international conflict were stated in *Sonnar (Nig) Ltd v. Partnereedri M.S. Nordwind.*[367] They are:

(a) the countries with which the parties are connected;
(b) the location of the evidence needed in the case and the convenience in terms of accessibility and expenses between the domestic and foreign courts;
(c) whether the party seeking to stay the proceedings in Nigeria is only seeking procedural advantages;
(d) whether the claimant would be prejudiced having to sue in the foreign court because the claimant would:
   - be deprived of security for the claim;
   - be unable to enforce any judgment obtained;
   - be faced with a time-bar not applicable to the domestic court; or
   - for political, racial, religious or other reasons be unlikely to get a fair trial in the foreign court.

§2. International Treaties

335. Nigeria has ratified the Convention on the Recognition and Enforcement of Foreign Arbitral Award (the New York Convention 1958), which is incorporated

366. (1987) 9-11 SC 121.
367. *Supra.*

into the Arbitration and Conciliation Act 2004 (ACA). So where parties opt for arbitration in the resolution of cross-border disputes the provisions of this Convention will apply.

Part III. Actions and Claims

Chapter 1. Actions

§1. Definition

336. An action is a civil suit stating a legal cause of action and seeking only a legal remedy.[368] The court has said that an action is the medium through which a claimant litigates his bundle of facts (cause of action).[369] A party's right to take a legal action eventuates from when a cause of action has arisen. The cause of action is the aggregate of facts the existence of which when proved gives rise to a remedy in law. The person who commences an action is termed the claimant and the person against whom the action is brought is called the defendant. What determines who should be claimants in an action and who should be defendants are guided by the principles of parties to an action. Basically, there are four types of parties to an action. First, there are proper parties in an action. These are persons made parties in an action because of their direct involvement in the cause of action. This was the decision of the SC in *Mobil Producing (Nig) Unltd v. LASEPA*.[370] Second, there are also desirable parties. They are persons who will be affected by the outcome of a suit. They usually apply to be joined in an action on the ground that their interest is likely to be affected by the decision of the court. Third, there are necessary parties who are persons whose presence is necessary in an action. They will not only be affected by the result of the case, but also the court cannot effectively and completely determine the questions it is called upon to decide without them. Lastly, there are persons who are parties in an action by virtue of their office. They are termed nominal parties. For example in a suit by or against the Federal Government of Nigeria, the AGF is a party by reason of his office. The same goes for AG of a State in suits by or against a state government. The SC held in *Plateau State v. Attorney General of the Federation*[371] that it is irregular for the action to have been commenced by the principal rather than the AG of the State.

368. B.A. Garner (ed.), *Black's Law Dictionary* 31 (West 2004).
369. *Sifax (Nig) Ltd v. Migfo (Nig) Ltd* (2018) 9 NWLR (Pt 1623) 138 at 183 (SC).
370. (2002) 12 SCNJ 1.
371. (2006) 3 NWLR (Pt 967) 346 at 394 (SC).

§2. ADMISSIBILITY

337. The law does not allow for meddlesome interlopers infiltrating the administration of justice system. For a person to approach the courts of law, the action the party brings should be one that affects the party initiating the action directly and personally. A party must have *locus standi* to bring an action. *Locus standi* means the legal right to bring an action. The SC in *Wushishi v. Imam*[372] reiterated its earlier position when it stated:

> To have a locus standi to sue, the plaintiff must show sufficient interest in the suit. One criterion of sufficient interest is whether the party could have been joined as a party to the suit. Another criterion is whether the party seeking redress or remedy will suffer some injury or hardship from the litigation. If the court is satisfied that he will suffer, then he must be heard as he is entitled to be heard.[373]

338. The issue of whether or not the plaintiff has *locus standi* will be determined from the writ of summons and statement of claim, because it is the aggregate of facts in the statement of claim that determines the right of the claimant to sue and claim the reliefs he is seeking. In *Abraham Adesanya v. The President of the Federal Republic of Nigeria & Anor*[374] the court held that where a party lacks *locus standi* to bring an action, the court lacks jurisdiction to enter the party's suit. The rigidity surrounding the issue of *locus standi* has been greatly relaxed in recent times. For example, under the Fundamental Rights (Enforcement Procedure) Rules 2009 the categories of persons and institutions that have *locus standi* to file fundamental rights suits have been enlarged as individuals and non-government organizations now have the standing to institute actions to enforce the rights of others.[375] Objections based on *locus standi* must be raised timeously usually before the defendant files his defence. It can also be raised as a point of law in the defence. In such an instance, the court will determine the issue first before continuing the trial.

339. Another issue that will determine whether an action will be admitted is whether the parties in the action have legal capacities to sue and be sued. For example, persons under legal disability lack the capacity to institute or defend any proceedings by reason of age, insanity, unsoundness of mind or otherwise.[376] For them, to sue or be sued, they have to do so through their guardians or a guardian appointed for that purpose.[377] Natural persons can sue and be sued in their proper or legal names while alive. Married couples are to sue in their personal capacities as individuals and jointly as Mr and Mrs XYZ. In *Lion of Africa Insurance Co. Ltd v. Mr and Mrs Esan*,[378] the court held that it was not proper for a married couple to

372. (2017) 18 NWLR (Pt 1597) 175 (SC).
373. *Inakoju v. Adeleke* (2007) 7 NWLR (Pt 1025) 423 at 601–602 (SC).
374. (1981) 5 SC 112.
375. Preambular para. 3(e) of the Fundamental Rights (Enforcement Procedure) Rules 2009.
376. Order 1(5) Abuja; Order 1 Rule 2(3) Lagos.
377. Order 13 Rule 11 HCCPR Abuja; Order 15 Rule 9 HCCPR Lagos.
378. (1999) 8 NWLR (Pt 614) 197 (CA).

sue as Mr and Mrs Esan rather it should be Mr Esan as the first claimant and Mrs Esan as the second claimant. Artificial persons can sue and be sued in their registered, corporate or designated names as long as they remain a corporate personality. For example, a company registered under Part A of Companies and Allied Matters Act[379] as Zenith Bank Plc must sue or be sued as such. An entity incorporated under Part C of Companies and Allied Matters Act sues or is sued through its Registered Trustees. For example, Living Faith Church worldwide will sue and be sued as the Incorporated Trustees of Living Faith Church worldwide.

340. There are also bodies conferred with the power to sue and be sued by statutes. For example, the Nigerian National Petroleum Company is established by an Act of the National Assembly and conferred with power to sue and be sued in the name 'Nigerian National Petroleum Corporation'. Non-corporate statutory bodies created under the Constitution/Statutes/Laws and conferred with certain powers although not expressly endowed with the attributes of a corporate personality can sue and be sued in proceedings for declaration or prerogative orders in their names. Firms or partnerships may sue or be sued in the name of the partnership or in their individual names. Where they sue in the firm's name, the plaintiff or their legal practitioner should, on demand in writing by or on behalf of any defendant, declare in writing the names and addresses of the partners. Trustees, executors or administrators may sue and be sued on behalf of or as representing the property or estate of which they are trustee or representatives without joining the beneficiary. Associations of persons who do not possess a personality different and distinct from their members generally sue or are sued through representatives. However, the individual members can sue and be sued in their names. Where such associations enters into a contract the individuals that signed the contractual agreement are the proper persons to sue and be sued in respect of any cause of action arising thereof. The governments of the Federation or State are corporate entities and can sue and be sued. They properly sue or are sued through their respective Attorneys General.

341. The HCCPR allows for the admittance of actions filed by a few individuals on behalf of a group of persons whose interests have been affected. The group of persons affected may not be easily identifiable or found. They are called representative actions and class action. A representative action is one where the group of people represented is identifiable. In class action the members of the group remember may not be identifiable and even if they are may not be easily found. The categories of proceedings that can come under class actions are limited. They include proceedings for:[380]

(1) the administration of an estate; or
(2) property subject to a trust; or
(3) land devolved under other interest as family or community property; or
(4) the construction of any written instrument, including a statute; or

379. Companies and Allied Matters Act Cap C20 LFN 2004.
380. Order 13 Rule 15 HCCPR Abuja; Order 15 Rule 13 HCCPR Lagos.

(5) torts or any other class action.[381]

§3. Vexatious Litigation

342. Litigation is said to be vexatious, where it is calculated only to annoy the defendant. A vexatious litigation amounts to an abuse of court process. This can happen where a party institutes two actions against the same person on the same subject matter both asking for the same relief. The second action can be said to be vexatious and calculated to irritate and annoy the adversary. Vexatious litigation comes under the generic group of abuse of court process. Where matters involving the same parties and on the same claims are raised contemporaneously in two or more court, it is needful and in the interest of justice that all the matters be heard in one court. The rationale behind this principle is that this will avoid a situation where contradictory decisions are made on the same issues by different courts of co-ordinate jurisdiction. The court has held that it is an abuse of court process for a litigant to use the judicial process to the annoyance and irritation of the other party.[382]

381. This only applies under the HCCPR Abuja.
382. *P.D.P. v. Sheriff* (2017) 15 NWLR (Pt 1588) 219 (SC).

Chapter 2. Claims and Defences

§1. Definition

343. A claim has been defined as 'the aggregate of operative facts giving rise to a right enforceable by a court'.[383] Defences, on the other hand, have been defined as 'a defendant's stated reason why the plaintiff has no valid case'.[384] The claimant claims are stated in the statement of claim in the HCs and particulars of claim in the Magistrates' and Districts Courts while the defendant's defence is stated in the statement of defence. Generally, in every action initiated in a court, it is the claimant that has a claim. The defendant's reliefs are essentially that the court holds that the claimant's claim be refused. However, in the event that a defendant in an action counterclaims, then such a defendant also has a claim before the court.

344. The parties are responsible for the reliefs they are seeking and a court cannot on its own motion change the object of the reliefs sought. Additionally, a court cannot grant reliefs in excess of what the parties are claiming but can grant below it. For example, a claimant who claims NGN 50 million special damages but succeeds in proving only NGN 10 million will be awarded NGN 10 million. Besides, with respect to general damages whatever is awarded in favour of the claimant is at the court's discretion though usually below what was claimed. A claimant may, however, be allowed to amend the statement of claim to change the relief claimed if there is evidence already before the court that supports the substituted reliefs claimed. It is possible that the evidence necessitating a change of the reliefs claimed came in the process of the court asking witnesses questions to clear ambiguities or clarify points, which had been left obscure by a witness. The court is empowered to ask questions and even order production of documents for the purpose of clarifying any point or clearing ambiguities.[385] But this is limited to facts declared by the Evidence Act to be relevant and duly proved.

345. The parties are responsible for providing the facts on which the claim or defence is based. The job of the court is to apply the law to facts proved before the court.

§2. Distinctions

I. Main Claim and Ancillary Claim

346. The main claim in an action is the principal relief the claimant is seeking, and it is what confers jurisdiction on the court while an ancillary claim is a claim

383. B.A. Garner (ed.), *Black's Law Dictionary* 264 (8th ed., West 2004).
384. *Ibid* at 451.
385. Section 246 of the Evidence Act 2011.

that is dependent on the main claim. Where a court has jurisdiction to entertain a main claim it will in most cases have jurisdiction to entertain the ancillary relief but the reverse is not the case.

II. Defence on the Merit and Procedural Exceptions

347. A defence on the merit is one that essentially answers the claim of the claimant. Where a defendant discloses a defence on the merit, the matter is allowed to go on trial and cannot be tried summarily. On the other hand, a defence on procedural exception seeks to prevent the claim from being heard. A procedural exception when successfully raised can lead to the action being delayed or being dismissed. This is dependent on the effect of the exception. Exceptions such as non-competence of the suit (examples of what can lead to an action being incompetent includes issues such as non-service of a pre-action notice, ineffective service of the originating processes and a suit not disclosing a reasonable cause of action), non-joinder or misjoinder of a party leads to delay in the trial of the claim. Whereas, procedural exceptions such as limitation of action, res judicata, lack of locus standing and immunity will bring to an end the proceedings.

Chapter 3. Sanctions on Procedural Irregularities

348. The Rules of court prescribe the procedures that parties are to follow in prosecuting or defending actions in a court of law. Where any of the parties in an action fails to adhere to the laid down procedures, that party is liable to certain sanctions. The procedural irregularities and sanctions that can be imposed will now be discussed along the lines of formal requirements and time limits to take certain procedural steps.

§1. Formal Requirements

349. The Rules of court provide for certain formalities with regard to particular procedural steps to be taken. Where these are not adhered to, it can lead to imposition of sanctions.

I. Filing a Suit in a Wrong Judicial Division

350. Where a claimant files the action in a wrong judicial division, the matter will continue to be tried in that judicial division except the Chief Judge directs otherwise.[386] In other words, where the Chief Judge is minded to transfer the case to the appropriate judicial division where it ought to have filed, the claimant will suffer the delay occasioned by the transfer and the court may award cost against the claimant in favour of the defendant. The issue of cost being awarded against the claimant in favour of the defendant is backed up by the principle that cost follows the event.

II. Filing a Suit Using the Wrong Mode of Commencement

351. Where a suit ought to have been commenced by a writ of summons and the claimant commenced it by way of originating summons, it will not render the suit a nullity, but it will be regarded as an irregularity. The court may order the striking out of the wrong mode of commencement and order that the claimant bring the matter using the appropriate mode. In addition, it may lead to the court awarding costs against the erring party.

III. Improper Endorsement in a Writ of Summons

352. There are endorsements that the rules require that the claimant must make in a writ of summons. Where the claimant fails to properly endorse the writ, it may lead to the writ being set aside. Where the improper endorsement is with regard to

386. Order 3 Rule 6 HCCPR Abuja; Order 4 Rule 3 HCCPR Lagos.

the claim of the claimant it may render the writ a nullity. For example, it has been held that where the endorsement of the claim is on an attached or separate piece of paper, it was improper and a fundamental defect that makes the writ liable to be struck out.[387] But the application to strike it out must be made timeously.[388]

IV. Failure to File along with Originating Processes the Accompanying Documents

353. The frontloading system practised by the two jurisdictions under review in this work (with respect to the HC) requires that a claimant when commencing an action attaches to the originating processes, certain documents. Where a claimant is commencing an action with a writ of summons, the claimant is required to file along with the writ, the statement of claim, statement on oath of the witnesses of the claimant, copies of the documents the claimant will be relying upon during trial and certificate of pre-action counselling (where the suit is filed in the HC in Abuja) or Pre-action Protocol Form 01 with necessary documents (where the action is filed in the HC in Lagos). The claimant shall provide copies of these accompanying documents for the use of the court and has as many copies as the number of defendants to be served. Failure to follow this procedure comes with sanctions. In Abuja, the writ shall not be accepted for filing by the registry of the court.[389] In Lagos, such non-compliance shall nullify the suit.[390] In the National Industrial Court of Nigeria, non-compliance with any of the rules may be treated as an irregularity and the court may give any direction as it thinks fit.[391]

V. Failure to Serve Originating Processes on the Defendant

354. Failure to serve originating processes in an action on the defendant is a fundamental defect that robes the court of jurisdiction. Originating processes are to be served personally on the defendant and failure to do this renders the service void. For the claimant to serve the originating processes by any means other than personal service, the claimant must seek the leave of the court. Where this is not done, any purported service other than personal service is no service. A court of law cannot exercise jurisdiction over a matter when the defendant has not been served. Consequently, the court will strike out the matter.

387. *Alatede v. Falode* (1966) ALL NLR 101 (SC), *Nwoye v. Road Construction ltd* (1966) NMLR 254 (HC Midwestern State).
388. *Sonuga v. Anadein* (1967) NMLR 77 (SC).
389. Order 2 Rule 4 HCCPR Abuja.
390. Order 5 Rule 1(2)(3) and Order 7 Rule 1(1) HCCPR Lagos.
391. Order 5 Rule 1 National Industrial Court of Nigeria Civil Procedure Rules 2016.

VI. Failure to Comply with the Provisions of the SCPA on Service of an Originating Process Outside Jurisdiction

355. The SCPA regulates service of a court process outside the jurisdiction of the state of issue. By section 97 of the SCPA, no leave is required to serve such an originating process but there must be endorsed on the process, the following:

This writ is to be served outside the -----State and in ------State.

In addition, section 99 of the SCPA provides that the defendant who has served outside jurisdiction must be given not less than thirty days within which to answer to the case against him. What this means is that the period endorsed on the writ for the defendant to enter appearance and defend the suit must not be less than thirty days for a defendant who is outside the jurisdiction. In Lagos, the rules require a defendant generally to enter appearance within forty-two days and as such this requirement in section 99 of the SCPA is satisfied. However, in the Federal Capital Territory, Abuja, a defendant has fourteen days within which to enter appearance to defend the suit against him. So where the defendant is outside jurisdiction, it is very important that thirty days is inserted in the writ in place of fourteen days. Failure to do this will lead to the service be set aside.

VII. Failure to Comply with Certificate of Pre-action Counselling / Pre-action Protocols

356. Under the Abuja rules, counsels to parties are required to counsel their clients as to the relative strength or weakness of their case and inform them of the opportunities available for alternative resolution of the case and the possibilities for reconciliation between the parties. Counsel is required to make an undertaking in a certificate of pre-action counselling that in the event that the action turns out to be frivolous counsel shall be personally liable to pay the cost of the proceedings.[392] In addition, the originating process without the certificate of pre-action certificate shall not be accepted for filing.

357. Under the Lagos Rules, failure to accompany the originating process with a Pre-action Protocol Form 01 with the accompanying document will make the process not be accepted for filing and will nullify the proceedings. The HC of Lagos State (Expeditious Disposal of Civil Cases) Practice Direction No. 2 of 2019: Pre-action Protocol makes provision for a Pre-action Protocol bundle which is made up of the documents accompanying the Pre-action Protocol Form 01. Essentially, the documents are the documentation of every step taken as part of the Pre-action Protocol, the documents and communications made between the parties in the course of it. Failure to file along with an originating process the Pre-action Protocol Form 01 and the accompanying documents in Lagos will make the originating to be rejected for filing. Where the defendant shows unpreparedness in participating in the

392. Order 2 Rule 8 HCCPR Abuja and Civil Form 6 of the schedule to the rules.

Pre-action Protocol process, the claimant may proceed to litigation and obtain a judgment against the defendant. Where a party fails or refuses to comply with settlement procedure under the Pre-action Protocol or directives of court referring parties to a form of ADR, but rather the party insists on trial, the court shall impose a minimum cost of NGN 100,000 deducted or added to monetary award in final judgment. Alternatively, the court may ask the winning party to pay the costs of the losing party from the time of the settlement offer to when judgment was given. This applies in the event that what the court awarded after the trial is not in excess of the offer of settlement initially offered.[393]

VIII. Failure to Follow the Rules of Drafting Pleadings

358. Where a party fails to adhere to the formalities and rules of drafting pleadings as contained in the Rules of court, it can lead to the pleadings being struck out. For the formalities and rules of drafting pleadings, *see* paragraph 452 below.

IX. Failure of Defendant to Enter Appearance or File Pleadings

359. In Lagos jurisdiction, first, a defendant is required to enter appearance within forty-two days of receipt of the writ of summons and accompanying documents. The defendant enters appearance by filing in the registry of the court the original and as many copies of completed and signed memorandum of appearance for the use of the court and for service on the other parties.[394] Where the defendant fails to comply with this requirement, he is liable to a penalty of NGN 1,000 for each day of default.[395] In the Federal Capital Territory, Abuja, the defendant is required to enter appearance (by filing a memorandum of appearance in Form 12) within fourteen days of the service of the writ of summons and other processes on the defendant. Failure to comply with this will make the defendant in addition to paying NGN 200 for each day of default, liable to the cost occasioned by any application to extend the time to enter appearance, including the cost of any order made on the application.[396] Second, the defendant is required to state in the memorandum of appearance an address for service within Lagos (the same is applicable under the Abuja rules). Where the defendant appears by counsel, the legal practitioner shall state his full names, chambers' address within Lagos, telephone numbers and email address. Where a legal practitioner who appears for the defendant is an agent of another legal practitioner, he shall state his full name, full address of chambers, telephone numbers, and email address and the full names, full address of chambers, telephone numbers and email address of the principal legal practitioner. Where the

393. Order 53 Rule 2 HCCPR Lagos.
394. This is as in Form 11 (with such modification or variations as circumstances may require) of the schedule to the HCCPR Lagos State). *See* Order 11 Rule 1(1) HCCPR Lagos.
395. *See* Order 11 Rule 5 HCCPR Lagos.
396. Order 56 Rule 10 HCCPR Federal Capital Territory.

memorandum does not contain an address for service or the address given is illusory, fictitious or misleading, the appearance may be set aside by a judge upon the application of the claimant by way of motion on notice.[397] In addition, under the Lagos and the Federal Capital Territory, HCCPR Abuja, where a defendant fails to enter appearance, the claimant is subject to the nature of the claim entitled to apply for judgment. This is called judgment in default of appearance. This is discussed in paragraphs 489–491 below.

X. Failure to Apply for or Participate in Case Management Conference / Pretrial Conference

360. Where the claimant or the claimant's counsel fail to apply for Case Management Conference / Pretrial Conference, the defendant may do so or apply for an order to dismiss the action.[398] Where the claimant fails to participate or participate in good faith in the Conference, the judge shall dismiss the claim. Where it is the defendant that fails to participate the judge will enter judgment for the claimant.[399] However, any judgment given may be set aside on an application made within seven of the said judgment or such other period as the Pretrial Judge may allow not exceeding the Pretrial Conference period. The application shall be accompanied by an undertaking to participate effectively in the Conference.

XI. Failure to Answer Interrogatories

361. Where a party obtains an order to administer interrogatories on the other party, a legal practitioner on whom the order is served who neglects to bring it to the notice of his client shall be liable to pay the cost at the discretion of the judge.[400] In Lagos, the order served on the counsel shall be sufficient service to found an application for citation of the party for disobedience of the order.[401]

§2. Time Limits

362. The law, rules of court or an order of court appoints a time for the doing of an act. For example, a claimant who seeks to commence an action must do so within the time stipulated in the limitation laws. The defendant on receipt of the claimant's originating process and accompanying document is required to enter appearance within a specific period. In the HC in Lagos, the defendant enters appearance within forty-two days of being served with the claimant's writ of summons and accompanying processes. In the HC of the Federal Capital Territory, Abuja, the defendant

397. Order 11 Rule 3 HCCPR Lagos. Similar provisions are found in Order 9 Rule 2 HCCPR Abuja.
398. Order 27 Rule 1(3) HCCPR Lagos; Order 27 Rule 10(3) HCCPR Abuja.
399. Order 27 Rule 5 HCCPR Lagos; Order 27 Rule 16 HCCPR Abuja.
400. Order 28 Rule 12 HCCPR Abuja.
401. Order 29 Rule 9 HCCPR Lagos.

enters appearance within fourteen days after receipt of the claimant's originating processes. At the Federal HC, the defendant enters appearance within thirty days upon being served with the originating processes. At the National Industrial Court of Nigeria, the defendant shall within fourteen days of being served with the originating process enter appearance.[402]

363. With respect to time to file pleadings in Abuja the statement of claim shall be filed along with writ of summons while the statement of defence is filed within twenty-one days of service of statement of claim on the defendant. A defendant who intends to counterclaim still has to do so within the time to file the defence. The document is titled defence and counterclaim. A claimant who intends to reply to the defendant's statement of claim has within fourteen days of the service of statement of defence on the claimant to do so.[403] Where a counterclaim is pleaded, a reply to it shall be subject to the rules applicable to defence. This means the claimant has twenty-one days to file the defence to counterclaim. In Lagos, the statement of claim is required to be filed along with the writ of summons while the statement of defence is filed within forty-two days of service of claimants originating process and accompanying documents on the defendant. Where the claimant intends to reply to the statement of defence, this is done within fourteen days of the service of the statement of defence on the claimant. Where there is a counterclaim it is subject to the same rules applicable to defence. That is the claimant has forty-two days to file defence to counterclaim.

364. At the National Industrial Court of Nigeria, a defendant is required to file a response to the statement of facts or complaints of the claimant within fourteen days of being served with the statement of claim.[404]

Computation of Time

365. The Interpretation Act 2004 and the various HCCPR make provisions for how time for doing an act is computed.[405] Where time is limited for the doing of an act, the period of time is reckoned as excluding the day on which the order is made or on which the event occurs. Where the last day of the period is a public holiday, the time shall continue until the end of the next day following which is not a public holiday. Where the act is required to be done within a period not exceeding six days, holidays shall be left out of account in computing the period. A holiday means a Sunday or a public holiday. Service of court processes and documents shall be done between the hours of 6 a.m. and 6 p.m. Service effected after 6 p.m. is deemed to have been done the following day but service effected after 6 p.m. on Saturday is deemed to have been effected the following Monday.

402. Order 9 Rule 1 National Industrial Court Rules 2016.
403. Order 15 Rule 1 HCCPR Abuja.
404. *Ibid.* at Order 12 Rule 1(2).
405. Section 15 Interpretation Act Cap 123 LFN 2004; Order 49 Rules 1–3 HCCPR Abuja; Order 48 Rules 1–3 HCCPR Lagos.

Sanctions for Failing to Comply with Time Limits

366. A party who fails to file a required pleading within the time can bring an application for extension of time to file the pleading and the court may extend the time as it deems fit.[406] However, there is a penalty for such default. In the HC in Abuja, it is NGN 200 for each day of default while in Lagos, it is NGN 1,000.[407]

Failure to Amend Pleadings Within the Time Ordered to Do So

367. Where a court grants an application to amend a party's pleadings, the order usually directs the party to effect the amendment within a specific period. Where the order does not specify the period, the Rules of court make provisions for when such amendment should be done. In the HC of Lagos and the Federal Capital Territory, Abuja, the rules provide that in the absence of the court ordering a period for the amendment to be effected, it shall be amended within seven days from the date the order to amend is given.[408] Under the National Industrial Court of Nigeria Civil Procedure Rules, the period is fourteen days.[409] Under the Abuja Rules, failure to amend within the period stated by the rules makes the defaulting party liable to pay an additional NGN 100 for each day of default while in Lagos it is NGN 1,000 for each day of default.[410] Under the National Industrial Court Civil Procedure Rules, the defaulting party shall pay NGN 200 for the first fourteen days of default, after that the penalty shall be NGN 300.

Failure to Adhere to Time Limits in Pre-action Protocols

368. Failure to comply with the time stipulations in the Pre-action Protocol shall not affect the validity of the documents filed but a daily default of NGN 1,000 shall accrue as cost in favour of the counterparty deducted or added to monetary award as applicable in the final judgment. However, a counterparty in the interest of settlement may waive the applicability of these default fees.

406. Order 48 Rule 4 HCCPR Lagos; Order 49 Rule 4 HCCPR Abuja.
407. Order 48 Rule 4 HCCPR Lagos; Order 49 Rule 5 HCCPR Abuja.
408. Order 26 Rule 4 HCCPR Lagos; Order 25 HCCPR Abuja.
409. Order 26 Rule 6 National Industrial Court of Nigeria Rules 2016.
410. Order 25 Rule 4 HCCPR Abuja; Order 26 Rule 4 Lagos.

Part IV. Proceedings

Chapter 1. Pretrial Proceedings

369. In actions commenced by a writ of summons, after the closure of pleadings, certain procedural steps are required before the trial begins. Under the current jurisprudence in civil procedure in Nigeria, these steps are taken during the Case Management Conference / Pretrial Conference. Pretrial conference is also part of the pretrial proceedings in election petition proceedings.

§1. Striking Out Pleadings

370. After the closure of the pleading and before trial, any of the parties in an action can apply to the court to strike out the pleadings or any endorsement of any writ in the action of the opposing party.

I. Likely Grounds for Striking Out Pleadings

371. A party can apply that the pleadings of the opposing party be struck for any of the following reasons:

(1) Where the pleading or endorsement of any writ discloses no reasonable cause of action or no defence is disclosed. A statement of claim is said to disclose no reasonable cause of action where it is such that nobody can understand the claim the defendant is required to respond to. It is a case that is unsustainable or unarguable or incontestably bad.
(2) Where the pleading is frivolous, vexatious, embarrassing or scandalous. A pleading is scandalous where it alleges matters that are indecent or offensive for the mere purpose of abusing or prejudicing the opposing party. It is embarrassing if it is presented in an unintelligible form for the party to which it is served.
(3) Where the pleadings may prejudice, embarrass or delay the fair trial of the action.
(4) Where the pleading is an abuse of court process.

372. A pleading is said to be an abuse of court process where its purpose is merely to annoy the opposing party. A frivolous, vexatious pleading is an abuse of court process. In *Tony-Anthony Holdings Ltd v. C.B.A.*,[411] the Court of Appeal of Nigeria adopted the definition in the case of *Offor v. Leaders &Co Ltd.*,[412] held that:

> The definition of abuse of process of the court is quite trite and age hallowed. It simply means a proceedings lacking in 'bona fides', frivolous, vexatious or oppressive. It is also said to mean misuse of legal process. An example of such is re-litigation of issues previously settled, compromised or decided in a matter. The issue of abuse of court process is also an issue of jurisdiction (and) it is settled that once a court is satisfied that any proceeding before it is an abuse of court process, it is empowered and it behoves it to dismiss such a proceeding.

II. Procedure for Striking Out Pleadings

373. The party seeking the striking out of a pleading may bring an application at any stage of the proceedings to the court by way of motion on notice or summons clearly stating the grounds relied on. It is supported with an affidavit and a written address. On hearing the application, the court may strike out the offensive pleading or grant leave to amend it or order that the action be stayed or dismissed or enter judgment as the case may be. This is provided for under Order 17 Rules 15 and 17 Lagos and Order 23 Rules 2(3) Abuja HCCPR.

§2. Consolidation and Deconsolidation of Actions

374. Consolidation of action connotes a situation where there are several suits on the same issues which can be properly tried and determined at the same time, and there is a need to bring all of them in one court for the purpose of convenience. The SC has held that:

> It is permissible to consolidate suits or applications for the speedy resolution of the issues that might impede the main suit if the applications and suits are handled separately. To get to the decision to order consolidation, the court must be satisfied that there are common questions of law or facts arising in both or all the causes or matters; or that the rights to reliefs which are claimed arise from the same transaction; or for some other reasons it is desirable to make an order of consolidation under the rules of court. Therefore consolidation of suits or applications is generally for expediency and convenience … to avoid multiplicity of actions and to economize time and cost.[413]

Consolidation will be ordered by the court where two or more actions are pending in a court or in different courts in the following instances:

---

411. (2013) AFWLR (Pt 698) 944 (CA).
412. (2007) 7 NWLR (Pt 1032) 1 (CA).
413. *Eye v. F.R.N.* (2018) 7 NWLR (Pt 1619) 496 (SC).

(1) the actions are between the same claimant and the same defendant;
(2) the actions are between the same claimant and different defendants;
(3) the actions are between different claimants and the same defendant; or
(4) the actions are between different claimants and different defendants.

375. The procedure for consolidation of several actions before the same court requires the party seeking consolidation to apply to the court by way of motion on notice supported with an affidavit and a written address. Where the actions are before different courts, the applicant would have to apply to the Chief Judge for transfer of the actions before different courts to one of the courts that has one or more of the actions pending before it. After the order of transfer has been made, the applicant will then apply for the consolidation of all the actions in that court.

376. It is to be noted that when the claimant instituted different actions against different defendants, the actions will not be consolidated without the consent of all parties unless the issues to be tried are identical.

377. An order consolidating several actions shall be drawn up and recorded in the cause book. The cost for drawing up the order shall be borne by the applicant.

378. The fact that different actions have been consolidated does not take away the individual identities of each of the consolidated suits. Consolidated suits still retain their distinct identities and remain different suits for the purpose of the trial. However, though they are separate and distinct, they are tried simultaneously in the same proceeding. Consolidation of suits does not render evidence accepted in one suit to as a matter of fact be accepted in another. The claimants in each suit must prove their case independently of the other. Each of the consolidated suits is considered on its merit and judgment and costs are separately entered in each case. The Court of Appeal endorsed these positions on consolidation of actions in the case of *The Vessel MV Sirius-B v. M.S.& S.C.I. Ltd.* when it held that:

> The law is that consolidated suits still retain their identity and still remain different suits for all intents and purposes of trial ... each of the consolidated suit is considered on its merits and the suits consolidated do not wear a single garment but rather they wear their original or individual garments.[414]

Consolidation of actions is provided for under Order 41 Rule 8 and Order 41 Rule 7 of the Abuja and Lagos HCCPR respectively.

§3. Discovery

379. Discovery can be of facts or of documents. Discovery of facts is referred to as interrogatories and that of document as inspection. It is provided for under Order 28 and 29 of the Abuja and Lagos HCCPR respectively.

414. (2017) 10 NWLR (Pt 1572) 135 at 165 (CA).

I. Interrogatories

380. A party who wants to get the opposing party to disclose or admit certain facts before trial administers interrogatories. It serves the purpose of supporting the case of the interrogating party and weakening the case of the other party. It also places on record facts that the party answering the interrogatories cannot deny. This is achieved by putting written questions in the form of interrogatories to the other party. Such interrogatories when delivered shall have a note at the end of it stating which interrogatories each person is required to answer. Questions in interrogatories must relate to the issues in the matter before the court. They are delivered within seven days after the closure of pleadings and form part of the Case Management Conference (in Abuja, the Pretrial Conference).

381. Interrogatories are as in Form 20 and Form 19 of the Abuja and Lagos HCCPR respectively. Answers to interrogatories are made in affidavit form to be filed within the time stated in the rules which is seven days or as allowed by the judge. The form of the affidavit is stated in the rules (Form 20 Lagos and Form 22 Abuja) and two copies are filed. Where the party answering has any objection to any of the interrogatories, he states this in the affidavit. There are admissible and inadmissible interrogatories:

(1) Admissible interrogatories:
   (a) where they relate to facts directly in issue or related to facts in issue;
   (b) where the answers to them will support the case of the party administering it or harm the case of the other party.
(2) Inadmissible interrogatories:
   (a) question as to credit;
   (b) where it relates to contents of a document;
   (c) fishing interrogatories: this means questions that do not relate to matters in the pleadings filed;
   (d) questions to discover evidence that will be used during trial;
   (e) oppressive interrogatories. These are interrogatories that put undue burden on the other party that is disproportionate with any advantage that it may serve.

382. The party answering can object to an interrogatory on the ground that it is scandalous, it is not administered in good faith, it is not sufficiently material at the stage they are asked or the party enjoys privilege from answering. For example, under section 192 of the Evidence Act 2011, subject to the exceptions, a legal practitioner is not permitted without the express consent of his client to disclose communications/documents made to him in the course and for the purpose of his employment. The exceptions to this provision have been discussed in paragraph 250 above.

II. Inspection of Document

383. This is a procedure where a party can in writing request the other party to disclose before trial material documents in the opponent's possession, custody or control for him to inspect and make copies if necessary. The request for discovery shall be served within seven days of closure of pleadings and shall form part of the agenda for Pretrial Conference (in Lagos, Case Management Conference). The party on whom it is served shall answer completely and truthfully within seven days of being served or such time as the court may allow. The answer is in form of an affidavit as in Form 23 (Abuja) and Form 21 (Lagos) and shall be accompanied by copies of documents referred to. The affidavit shall specify which, if any, of the listed documents the party objects to producing and the grounds for the objections.

III. Consequences of Non-compliance with Order of Interrogatories and Discovery of Documents

384. Where a party fails to comply with an order of interrogatories or inspection any of the following sanctions may be imposed by the court:

(1) The defaulting party may be liable to attachment for disobedience to the order. This is provided for under Order 29 Rule 9 HCCPR Lagos.
(2) The court may on application grant an order requiring the party to answer or to answer further.
(3) A legal practitioner upon whom an order against any party for interrogatories is served who neglects without reasonable excuse to give notice to his client shall be liable to pay cost at the discretion of the court (in Lagos he shall be liable to attachment) (Order 28 Rule 12 and Order 29 Rule 10 Abuja and Lagos HCCPR respectively).

§4. Settlement of Issues

385. This is the process by which the real issues for determination in a case are isolated so that the proceedings are focused on them. It is necessary where there is some form of imprecision or obscurity with regard to the issues emerging from the pleadings. It is provided for under Order 30 Rule 1 HCCPR Lagos and Order 27 Rules 1–6 HCCPR Abuja. It is done within seven days of the conclusion of pleadings and forms part of the agenda of the Pretrial conference in Abuja and fourteen days after closure of pleadings in Lagos and it is taken during the Case Management Conference.

§5. CASE MANAGEMENT / PRETRIAL CONFERENCE

386. These are case management mechanisms provided for under the Lagos and Abuja HCCPR. In Lagos, it is referred to as Case Management Conference, while in Abuja it is called the Pretrial Conference. The procedure in the two jurisdictions is similar with some variations.

By Order 27 HCCPR Lagos, a claimant applies for Case Management Conference within fourteen days after closure of pleadings by applying for the issuance of a Case Management Conference Notice. Where the claimant fails to do so, the defendant may do so or apply for an order to dismiss the action.

Upon application for the notice by the claimant, the judge shall cause to be issued to the parties and their counsel a Case Management Conference Notice in Form 17 and a Case Management Information Sheet in Form 18.

In Abuja, the claimant applies for the Pretrial Conference within seven days after closure of pleadings by applying for issuance of a Pretrial Conference Notice, and the court shall then issue to the parties and their legal practitioners a Pretrial Conference Notice as in Form 19 accompanied by a Pretrial Information Sheet as in Form 20.

I. Purpose of Case Management Conference / Pretrial Conference

387. Generally the purpose of the Case Management Conference / Pretrial Conference is to aid quick dispensation of justice. Specifically, the rules provide four reasons for this Conference. First, it is to dispose of matters that must be dealt with by interlocutory applications. Second, it is to give directions as to the future course of action that will ensure just, speedy and economical disposal of cases. Third, it is to promote the use of ADR to resolve cases, and lastly, to fix trial dates (the fourth purpose is applicable only under the HCCPR Abuja).

II. Matters Dealt with at Case Management / Pretrial Conference

388. At a Case Management/Pretrial Conference the following matters are handled:

(1) formulations and settlement of issues;
(2) amendments and further and better particulars;
(3) the admission of facts and other evidences by consent of parties;
(4) control and scheduling of discovery, inspection and production of documents;
(5) settlement of documents to be admitted as exhibits at the trial;
(6) narrowing the field of dispute between expert witnesses by their participation at Case Management Conference or in any other manner;
(7) hearing and determination of applications and objections on points of law;
(8) giving orders or directions for separate trial of a claim, counterclaim or third-party claim or of any particular issue in the case;
(9) settlement of issues, inquiries and accounts under the Rules;

(10) securing statement of special case of law or facts under the Rules;
(11) determining the form and substance of the Case Management Order;
(12) making referrals to the Lagos Multi-Door Courthouse (LMDC) or other relevant ADR bodies (applicable only under the Lagos HCCPR);
(13) implementing any ADR Order made under the referrals to the LMDC or other relevant ADR bodies (applicable only under the Lagos HCCPR); and
(14) such other matters that may facilitate the just and speedy disposal of the action.

389. In Lagos, the Case Management Conference with respect to any case shall be completed within three months of its commencement unless extended by the judge on the application of either party in the case. The Case Management Conference shall be held from day to day as far as practicable. After the conclusion of a Case Management Conference, the judge shall issue a report that shall guide the subsequent course of the proceedings unless modified by the trial judge.

390. In Abuja, the Pretrial Conference or series of Pretrial Conferences with respect to any case shall be completed within thirty days of its commencement except extended by the judge. After a Pretrial Conference or series of Pretrial Conferences, the judge shall issue a report that shall guide the subsequent course of the proceedings unless modified by the trial judge.

III. Effect of Non-participation in a Case Management / Pretrial Conference

391. Where a party or his counsel fails to attend the Case Management Conference, fails to obey a scheduling order, is substantially unprepared to participate in the Case Management Conference or fails to participate in good faith, the judge shall dismiss the action where it is the claimant that is in default. Where it is the defendant that is in default the judge shall enter judgment against him where appropriate. In Abuja, the judge shall enter final judgment against the defendant. Any judgment given here can be set aside upon an application accompanied by an undertaking to participate effectively in the Case Management Conference made within seven days of judgment or within such other period as the judge may allow. In Abuja, such long period, as the judge may allow for making the application to set aside such judgment, shall not exceed the Pretrial Conference period.

392. In Lagos, where a case is deemed suitable for ADR after screening by the Registrar on the filing of the originating process or the matter is referred to ADR during the Case Management Conference, the ADR Judge shall in case of recalcitrant parties give directions on filing of the statement of parties (claimant files within fourteen days of the order of the ADR Judge and the defendant files his response within fourteen days of service of claimant's statement) and other necessary documents. Where the parties fail to comply with these directives and/or orders of the ADR Judge or fail to participate in the ADR proceedings, the Judge shall in the case of the claimant dismiss the case. Where it is the defendant that is in default, the court shall enter judgment against him where appropriate. Any judgment given here can be set aside upon an application accompanied by an undertaking to participate effectively in the ADR process made within seven days of judgment or within such other period as the ADR Judge may allow.

393. In Abuja, where parties in an action in court consent to a settlement of disputes, the court or judge shall by an enrolment order as in Form 15 refer the matter to the Abuja Multi-door Courthouse (AMDC) for resolution of the disputes within twenty-one days except otherwise ordered by the court. Where it is the court that gave the referral, the court or judge shall by an enrolment order as in Form 15 refer the case to the AMDC for resolution within fourteen days except the judge orders otherwise.[415] Upon acceptance for filing, matters are screened for suitability for ADR. Where a case is deemed suitable for ADR, it can also be referred to the AMDC. Where the court or judge makes the referral or the matter was referred to the AMDC after screening upon filing, the judge may give appropriate directives to parties as to the filing of the statement of issues and other necessary issues. The claimant is required to file the claimant's statement of case with fourteen days of the order of the judge while the defendant shall file the defendant's response within fourteen of receipt of the claimant's statement of case. The parties are required to file notice of compliance with the judge's directives within twenty days of the giving of the directives. Failure to file this notice attracts a penalty of NGN 200 for each day of default. A party who wishes to apply for an extension of time to file the notice of compliance shall attach to the application evidence of payment of the penalty.

IV. Reconciliation Meetings in Matrimonial Proceedings

394. Under the Matrimonial Causes Act, counsel in a matrimonial matter and a court hearing such a case are enjoined to encourage and possibly effect reconciliation between the parties. Such reconciliation meetings between the parties, their counsel and the judge handling the matter can take place at the pretrial stage or even at the trial stage. When it happens at the trial stage, the court necessarily adjourns the case to allow for the exploration of possible reconciliation between the parties. To show how seriously this reconciliation attempt is the Matrimonial Causes Act requires that where a counsel commences a divorce petition on behalf of a petitioner or files an answer on behalf of a respondent, the processes filed shall not be effective except the counsel files along with them a certificate relating to reconciliation in Form 3 or 3A of the Schedule to Matrimonial Causes Rules.[416]

415. Order 19 Rule 2 HCCPR Abuja.
416. Order II Rule 2 of the Matrimonial Causes Rules Cap M7 LFN 2004.

Chapter 2. Proceedings in the First Instance

§1. Adversary Proceedings

395. The general norm is that all civil proceedings in Nigeria are adversarial. Trials are conducted with both the claimant and the defendant participating by putting forward their respective claims. This adversarial nature is present both in proceedings that are proceeded upon on purely written procedure and those that have both written and oral features. There are however situations where though all the parties in an action are entitled to participate in a proceeding, a party fails to participate. In such situations, the court is empowered to go ahead with the trial. Depending on the nature of the claim, the court may on application by a claimant give judgment or set the matter down for trial. This is discussed in paragraphs 488–491 below. In other situations, the court can hear a party without the other party in the action being put on notice. This is however mainly for interim reliefs or situations where the interest of the other party is ordinarily not affected.

I. Ordinary Proceedings

A. *Introduction of the Claim*

396. The claimant in an action before the court introduces the claim by filing the originating process in the registry of the court and payment of prescribed fees made. A designated officer accesses the processes, and the party filing is required to pay the prescribed fees into the court's account. The production of evidence of payment will enable the designated officer to endorse evidence of filing on the processes. Some Rules of court like that of the Federal HC and the HC of the Federal Capital Territory, Abuja allow for electronic filing.[417] During the COVID-19 pandemic, electronic filing can be deployed in most courts, through Practice Directions put in place by the various head of courts. Under electronic filing, the documents to be filed are scanned or converted to an appropriate PDF format and forwarded to the registry of the court through designated email addresses or WhatsApp. Counsel filing them shall sign and seal them and the documents must contain the email address and phone numbers of the counsel or the contact person filing it in the case of a party that is not represented by counsel. A designated officer assesses the fees payable and communicates by email, text messages or WhatsApp. Payment of filing fees is made by electronic transfers into the court's bank accounts. The electronic receipt shall be scanned for verification and shall be deemed filed when payment is verified by the court's registry.[418] The type of originating process that the claimant deploys in commencing an action is determined by the nature of the claim. Under the Federal HC, the HC of states and the HC of the Federal Capital Territory, Abuja,

417. Order 58 of the Federal High Court Rules 2019 and Order 3 Rule 8 of the HCCPR Abuja 2018 respectively.
418. Paragraphs 6–8 of the Lagos State Judiciary Remote Hearing of Cases (COVID-19 Pandemic Period) Practice Direction 2020.

there are four modes of commencing an action. First is the writ of summons that is the most commonly used. It is used for contentious matters.[419] Specifically, a writ of summons can be used in actions for relief for any civil wrong, damages for breach of duty, damages for personal injuries or death of any person, claim based on an allegation of fraud and claim for the declaration by an interested person. In practice, where a party is not sure of which mode of commencement to deploy in a given situation, it is advisable to go by way of a writ of summons.

397. The writ of summons is as in Form 1 to the HCCPR.[420] Counsel to the claimant where such is represented prepares the writ, and it must comply substantially with the prescription in the HCCPR. For example, it must contain the heading of the suit, parties, address of defendant within jurisdiction, the nature of the claim, name and address of claimant's counsel within jurisdiction and address of claimant within jurisdiction.

398. Where a writ of summons is used in commencing an action, the claimant accompanies the writ with a statement of claim, the list of witnesses to be called at the trial, written statement on oath of witnesses (except statements of witnesses who are to be subpoenaed) copies of documents to be relied on at the trial and Pre-action Protocol Form 1 with accompanying documents (for Lagos) or Certificate of Pre-action Counselling in Form 6 (for Abuja).[421] (The defendant is required within forty-two days of receipt of the writ in Lagos to enter appearance and file the defendant's defence while in Abuja, the defendant has within fourteen days to enter appearance and twenty-one days to file defence.) The defendant enters appearance by filing a memorandum of appearance as in Form 12 of the Schedule to the Abuja Rules while it is Form 11 under the Lagos Rules. In filing the defence, a defendant under the Abuja rules is required to file a statement of defence, the list of witnesses to be called at the trial, written statement on oath of witnesses (except statements of witnesses who are to be subpoenaed) and copies of documentary evidence.[422]

399. In Lagos, the defendant is required to file a statement of defence, list and copies of all documents and list of witnesses and their deposition.[423] On receiving the defendant's processes, the claimant may where needful file a reply to the statement of defence. The defendant may instead of just a statement of defence file a statement of defence and set-off or statement of defence and counterclaim. Where this is the case, the statement of defence will be titled: Statement of Defence and Set-off or Statement of Defence and Counterclaim. The facts supporting the set-off or counterclaim come after the facts in the statement of defence under a subheading set-off or counterclaim as the case may be. A defendant will file a statement of defence and set-off where the defendant has a monetary claim against the claimant also. It is a monetary claim by the defendant against the claimant that the defendant

419. *See* Order 3 Rule 1 Lagos; Order 2 Rules 1 and 2 Abuja; *Doherty v. Doherty* (1968) NMLR 241 (SC).
420. Form 1 of the Schedule to the HCCPR of Lagos and Abuja.
421. *See* Order 3 Rule 2(1) Lagos and Order 2 Rule 2(2) Abuja.
422. Order 17 Rule 1 Lagos.
423. Order 19 Rule 1 HCCPR Lagos.

pleads in his defence against an equally monetary claim of the claimant. A set-off is a cross-claim and succeeds only where the claimant's claim succeeds. Consequently, where the claimant's claim is dismissed, the cross-claim will fail. Where the defendant succeeds in the set-off, it reduces the claimant's claim by the amount of the set-off. Where the amount of set-off exceeds the plaintiff's claim, the court may enter judgment for the balance in favour of the defendant.[424] But in *FBN v. I.A.S.C.A. Ltd*,[425] the court held that a set-off should not exceed the plaintiff's claim and that where a set-off does, it is better that the defendant files a counterclaim. On the other hand, the defendant will file a statement of defence and counterclaim where the defendant has a separate action against the claimant that can be conveniently tried together with the claimant's claim. It is a cross-action that is raised in the defendant's statement of defence against the plaintiff. It does not need to be a monetary claim. It is possible to include some persons who were not parties in the main action in the counterclaim. However, the cause of action in the counterclaim must have arisen at the time of filing the main action. A counterclaim survives the main action. Even where the main action is withdrawn or fails, the counterclaim can continue and succeed. In practice, where the parties in the main action are the same in the counterclaim, the numbering of the averments in the counterclaim is a continuation of the numbering of the statement of defence. However, where the parties are different, then the numbering in the counterclaim will begin afresh.

400. The claimant in response to the defendant's statement of defence may where the statement of defence raises new issues file a reply to the statement of defence. Where it is a statement of defence and set-off or counterclaim that was filed and served on the claimant, then what will be filed is headed 'Reply and Defence to Counterclaim or Set-off'. Pleadings are deemed closed when the time to file a further pleading has lapsed, and the party who has the responsibility to file has failed to file. From the commencement of the action up to the point of closure of pleadings, the procedure has been written. However, at the closure of pleadings when parties are said to have joined issues, pretrial proceedings will take place in a Case Management/Pretrial Conference. At the conclusion of pleadings, the claimant shall within fourteen days[426] or seven days[427] apply for the issuance of Case Management Conference Notice or Pretrial Conference Notice respectively.

401. Another mode of commencing an action in the HCs is originating motion. It is used where a law prescribes it as the method to commence a particular action.[428] An example of a matter that is commenced by originating a motion is an application for judicial review.

402. Third, there is the filing of a petition as a means of commencing certain actions. It is used where a statute prescribes that it should be used to commence a

424. *See* Order 19 Rule 12 HCCPR Lagos and Order 17 Rule 12 Abuja HCCPR.
425. (2015) 3 NWLR (Pt 1445) 1 (CA).
426. Order 27 Rule 1 Lagos.
427. Order 27 Rule 10 Abuja.
428. Order 2 Rules 1 and 6 Abuja HCCPR; *KOSAP v. Kofa Trading Co* (1996) 2 SCNJ 325.

particular type of action. Examples of matters that are commenced by petition include election petition, matrimonial causes and winding up of company proceedings.

403. Lastly, there is the originating summons. It is used for non-contentious matters such as interpretation of statutes or construction of a written instrument.[429] In Lagos, an originating summons shall be accompanied by an affidavit setting out the facts relied on, all the exhibits to be relied on, a written address in support of the application and a Pre-action Protocol Form 01 with necessary documents.[430] In Abuja, the processes accompanying an originating summons is the same except for the Pre-action Protocol Form 01. What is filed in Abuja is the Certificate of Pre-action Counselling. The claimant shall provide as many copies of the processes as there are defendants.[431]

404. The language of the courts in Nigeria is English.[432] As such, all processes filed in the court and the proceedings of the court are conducted in English. Where a party does not understand English, the party will have to get an interpreter at the party's expense. Also, documents or statements taken in a language other than English will have to be translated into English, and both the original copy of the document and the translated copy will be produced in court.

1. Notice

405. Upon filing of the claimant's action in court, the originating process together with the accompanying processes is required to be served on the defendant. This is termed service of the court processes. Service is the process of bringing the existence of the suit to the notice of the defendant. Failure to serve is a fundamental defect where service is required. In *Otobaimere v. Akporehe*,[433] the court held that:

> Generally, the issue of service of court process or any other document emanating from a court is so fundamental that a failure in compliance therewith is capable of rendering the proceedings or any step taken in the proceedings null and void.

406. Service of originating process is required to be personal. Except the court upon application of the claimant grants leave to serve an originating process by substituted means, service must be personal or it will be otherwise invalid and the court will lack the jurisdiction to go on with the matter. Service of court processes within

429. Order 5 Rules 4 and 5 Lagos and Order 2 Rule 3 Abuja.
430. Order 5 Rule 5 HCCPR Lagos.
431. Under the Abuja rules, failure to accompany the originating summons with the required processes and providing as many copies as there are defendant will cause the originating summons not to be accepted for filing. This is stated in Order 2 Rule 3(7) HCCPR Abuja.
432. *See Olorunwa v. Akindun* (2016) LPELR-40866 (CA).
433. (2004) 1 NWLR (Pt 894) 591 (CA).

jurisdiction is guided by the Rules of court.[434] Where the service is to be done aside jurisdiction (i.e., outside a state or outside the Federal Capital Territory, Abuja), it is regulated by the SCPA 2004. The Rules of court also make provision for service of a court process outside Nigeria. *See* paragraphs 416–422 below.

a. Service Within Jurisdiction

Personal Service

407. Personal service on an individual is by delivering to the person to be served a copy of the processes. Personal service on a corporation, body corporate or registered company under the Abuja Rules is served subject to the enactment establishing the corporation, by delivery the process at the head office or any other place of business within the jurisdiction of the court. The procedure is the same under the Lagos Rules except that the processes can be left at the registered, principal, advertised office or place of business of the corporation within jurisdiction. The provisions of the rules with regard to personal service on companies and corporate bodies and corporation have been given judicial backing.[435]

408. However, the rules provide that no personal service of originating process is required where the defendant has authorized his counsel in writing to accept service and such counsel enters appearance.[436] The provision in Lagos contains an additional condition that the written authority given to the counsel should be attached to the memorandum of appearance filed by the defendant.

409. Service on a guardian of a person under legal disability is good service though the court may order otherwise. But service on a minor over 16 years who is living independently or doing business is good service. The court may order that personal service on a person under legal disability shall be deemed good and sufficient service.[437] Service on a defendant who is a prisoner is by serving the head or other officer in charge of the prisons where the defendant is kept. Service on partners who are sued as such is by service on any of the partners at the place of business within jurisdiction or upon any person having control or management of the firm. Where the defendant is a foreign corporation or company within the meaning of section 54 of the Companies and Allied Matters Act 2004, with an office within jurisdiction and the cause of action arose within jurisdiction service of processes requiring personal service may be served on the principal officer, representative or by leaving it at the place of business of such foreign corporation or company within jurisdiction.

---

434. Order 7 of the HCCPR Abuja and Order 9 of the HCCPR Lagos.
435. *Bello v. NBN* (1992) 6 NWLR (Pt 246) 206 (CA); *Mark v. Eke* (2004) 5 NWLR (Pt 865) 54 (SC).
436. Order 9 Rule 3 HCCPR Lagos and Order 7 Rule 3 HCCPR Abuja.
437. *See* Order 7 Rule 5 HCCPR Abuja and Order 9 Rule 6 HCCPR Lagos.

410. In Abuja where parties are represented by counsel, advance copies of processes other than originating process may be served by email. While in Lagos, service may be made on such a legal practitioner or on a person under his control. It should be noted that in Abuja the court may serve hearing notices through email and/or SMS except as otherwise directed by the judge.[438] Some Rules of Court like the FHC Rules 2019 and the HCCPR of the Federal Capital Territory, Abuja 2018 allows for service of court processes electronically.[439] The Practice Direction for court sitting and virtual proceeding during the COVID-19 pandemics provides that service of court processes may be effected by email, WhatsApp or as otherwise directed by the court and such service shall constitute proper service.[440]

Substituted Service

411. Where it appears that it is impracticable to serve the defendant personally with or without attempts at personal service, the court may on application by motion ex parte supported with an affidavit and written address order substituted service. Examples of substituted means of service provided for in the Abuja Rules include delivery of the document to some adult inmate at the usual or last known place of above or business of the person to be served, delivery to an agent of the person to be served, advertisement in the Federal Gazette or in some newspaper circulating within jurisdiction, by notice put up at the principal courthouse or some other place of public resort in the judicial division where the proceedings are initiated or at the usual or last known place of abode or business of the person to be served, email or any scientific device now know or later developed, and courier service. However, before service can be done by email, it must have been contemplated by the parties in a written agreement or subsequently agreed by counsel in the course of the proceedings.[441] The Lagos Rules provide that the judge may make such order for substituted service as may seem just including service by electronic means. The addition of the words 'including service by electronic means' is unwarranted as any means of service as may seem just already includes electronic service. Except perhaps the purpose is to emphasize electronic service. In Lagos therefore, any means which the court thinks will bring the processes to the notice of the defendant may be ordered by the judge. Where the court makes an order of substituted service indicating a mode of service, the party has no right to abridge or amend it to suit the party's convenience. The court has held that the order for substituted service can only be altered if personal service is eventually made.[442]

---

438. Order 7 Rule 17 HCCPR Abuja.
439. Order 58 and Order 3 Rule 5 respectively.
440. Paragraphs 10 and 11 of the Lagos State Judiciary Remote Hearing of Cases (COVID-19 Pandemic Period) Practice Direction 2020.
441. Order 7 Rule 11(2)(e)(11) HCCPR Abuja.
442. *Otobaimere v. Akporehe supra* at 614–615.

Who May Serve Court Processes

412. There are official process servers in various courts in Nigeria. They are public servants whose job is to effect service of court processes. The office of the Sheriff who is the Chief Registrar of the HC oversees the service of court processes. Other officers in the Sheriff department include the Deputy Sheriff, Bailiffs, Special Marshall or other officers of the court. The Rules of court also make provision for the Chief Judge of the state to appoint other persons to effect service of court processes. In that light, law chambers, courier companies or any other person appointed and registered by the Chief Judge can effect service of court processes in Lagos State by Order 9 Rule 1 Lagos. In Abuja, in addition to these categories of persons, the Chief Judge of the Federal Capital Territory, Abuja may also appoint any person to serve processes or by electronic means mutually agreed to serve processes.

413. Service of processes shall be effected between the hours of 6 a.m. and 6 p.m. Under the Abuja rules, where service is effected after 6 p.m., it is deemed to have been effected on the next service day. Service shall not be effected on a Sunday or public holiday save exceptional circumstances as ordered by the court.[443] The process server shall after serving any process promptly depose to an affidavit.

Proof of Service

414. This is the means of proving that service has been effected. It is usually by an affidavit of service deposed to by the process server stating the fact, date, time, place and mode of service, description of process served, and exhibits the acknowledgement of service.[444] Under the Abuja rules, proof of service by email shall be evidenced by an affidavit with a printout of an email notifier attached.[445] An affidavit of service is prima facie proof of service of a court process.[446]

415. A person challenging the service of an originating process on him must depose to a counter-affidavit denying the service, and the affidavit shall contain facts to rebut the averments in the affidavit of service. This was the decision of the court in *Mgbenwelu v. Olumba*.[447] The Registrar shall keep a register in such form as the Chief Judge may direct for recording services of processes by any process server indicating the name of the claimant and the defendant, the method of service and the manner used to ascertain that the right person was served. Where there is failure to serve, this fact shall also be recorded in the register.

443. Order 7 Rule 15 HCCPR Abuja and Order 9 Rule 14 HCCPR Lagos.
444. Order 7 Rule 13(1) HCCPR Abuja and Order 9 Rule 15 HCCPR Lagos.
445. Order 7 Rule 13(2) HCCPR Abuja.
446. Order 7 Rule 13(3) HCCPR Abuja and Order 9 Rule 15(3) Lagos.
447. (2017) 5 NWLR (Pt 1558) 169 (SC).

b. Service Outside State of Issue

416. Service of a writ of summons or other originating processes outside jurisdiction is regulated by the SCPA 2004, and this has earlier been discussed in paragraph 354 above.

c. Service Outside Nigeria

417. This is provided for under the rules.[448] The court may allow any process in an action filed in Nigeria to be served outside Nigeria where:

(1) the whole subject matter of the claim is land situated within jurisdiction; or
(2) any act, deed, will, contract, obligation or liability affecting land or hereditaments situated within jurisdiction, is sought to be construed, rectified, set aside or enforced; or
(3) any relief is sought against any person domiciled or ordinarily resident within jurisdiction; or
(4) the claim is for administration of the personal estate of any deceased person, who at the time of his death was domiciled within jurisdiction or for the execution (as to property situate within jurisdiction) of the trusts of any written instrument, which ought to be executed according to the law in force in the state where the originating process is filed; or
(5) the claim is brought against a defendant to enforce, rescind, dissolve, annul or otherwise affect a contract or to recover damages or other reliefs in respect of a contract:
    (a) made within jurisdiction; or
    (b) made by or through an agent residing or carrying on business out of jurisdiction; and
    (c) which by its terms or by implication is to be governed by the applicable law in the state where the action is filed or the parties have agreed that the court shall have jurisdiction to entertain any claim in respect of such contract;
(6) a claim is brought against the defendant in respect of contract for breach committed within jurisdiction notwithstanding that such was preceded or accompanied by a breach out of jurisdiction which rendered performance of the contract which ought to have been performed within jurisdiction impossible;
(7) the claim is founded on a tort committed within jurisdiction; or
(8) an injunction is sought in respect of anything to be done, or any nuisance to be prevented or removed within jurisdiction whether or not damages are claimed; or
(9) any person out of jurisdiction is a necessary or proper party to an action properly brought against any person duly served within jurisdiction; or
(10) the claim is by a mortgagee or mortgagor in relation to a mortgaged property situates within jurisdiction, seeking any of the following reliefs:
    (a) sale, foreclosure, delivery of possession by the mortgagor;

448. Order 10 HCCPR Lagos and Order 8 HCCPR Abuja.

(b) redemption, reconveyance, delivery of possession by the mortgagee but does not seek (except as permitted under (5) above) any judgment or order for payment of any monies due under the mortgage;

(11) the proceedings relate to a person under legal disability; or

(12) the proceedings relate to probate matters; or

(13) any proceedings under any law or Rule of court has been instituted by any originating process.

Procedure for Service of Court Process Outside Nigeria

418. Service of court processes outside is within the domain of diplomatic relations between countries, which is handled by the Ministry of Foreign Affairs in Nigeria. However, the Rules of court provide for the procedure to hand over the court processes to the Ministry of Foreign affairs, which effect the service in the foreign country. The procedure for serving a court process outside Nigeria depends on whether the country where the process is to be served has a convention with Nigeria regarding service of court processes. It should be noted that parties are at liberty in their contract agreement to determine the mode of service. Where parties have by their contract agreement stipulated how processes should be served such mode will be considered good service. The procedure, therefore, is as follows.

(1) Where Nigeria Has No Convention with the Country Where the Document Is to Be Served

419. Where a court process is to be served in a foreign country with which Nigeria has no convention in that regard, the party intending to serve will need the leave of court. Where leave is granted for a process to be served outside Nigeria in any foreign country with which no convention in that behalf has been made, the process shall be sealed with the seal of the court for service outside Nigeria and transmitted to the Solicitor-General of the Federation by the Chief Registrar with a copy translated into the language of that country (if not in English) and with a request for its further transmission to the appropriate authority. The request is as in Form 7 of the HCCPR Lagos (Form 8 for Abuja). The party requesting the service shall file a praecipe in Form 8 of the HCCPR Lagos (it is Form 9 in Abuja).

420. A certificate, declaration, affidavit or other notification of due service transmitted through diplomatic channels by a court or other appropriate authority of the foreign country to the court shall be deemed as sufficient proof of service. Where such certificate indicates that there was a failure to serve, the court may on an ex parte application grant an order of substituted service that shall be effected by transmitting the sealed order, process and its copy to the Solicitor-General of the Federation together with a request in Form 9 with such modifications or variations as circumstances may require. A claimant may instead of this procedure serve the originating process by courier with the leave of a judge.

421. Where lands, funds, choses in action, rights or property within jurisdiction are sought to be dealt with, the court may without assuming jurisdiction over any person outside jurisdiction, cause such person to be informed of the nature or existence of the proceedings.

(2) Where Nigeria Has a Convention with the Country Where the Document Is to Be Served

422. Where Nigeria has a convention with the foreign country where a process is to be served, the party desiring a process to be served shall file in the registry of the court a request in Form 10 (in Abuja it is Form 11) stating the medium through which the document is desired to be served either directly through diplomatic channels or through the judicial authority of the foreign country. The request shall be certified by or on behalf of the person making the request and is accompanied with the original document to be served together with a translated copy in the language of the foreign country (if it is not English), a copy of the document with the translation for every person to be served and further copies as the convention may require (subject to the provisions of the convention where the person to be served is a Nigerian, translation and copies of the document need not accompany the request). The documents will be sealed with the seal of the court for service outside jurisdiction and forwarded by the Chief Registrar to the Permanent Secretary, Federal Ministry of Foreign Affairs for onward transmission to the foreign country. An official certificate transmitted through a Nigerian diplomatic agent to the court establishing the fact and the date of the service of the document shall be deemed to be sufficient proof of service within the requirement of these rules.

423. It must be noted that in appropriate cases, the court, in granting leave to serve a process out of jurisdiction, may upon request direct that courier shall be used by the party who seeks to effect service.[449]

d. Service of a Foreign Process in Nigeria

424. Where a civil proceeding is pending before a court or tribunal of a foreign country, there may be a need to serve processes of that foreign court on a party in Nigeria. The procedure for serving such processes depends on whether Nigeria has a convention in that regard with that foreign country.

Where Nigeria Has No Convention with the Foreign Country Whose Process Is to Be Served in Nigeria

425. A letter of request from the foreign court or tribunal for service on the person or citation in such matter is transmitted to the court by the AG of the state where the process is to be served indicating or suggesting that the processes be served. The letter of request shall be accompanied with two copies of the process or citation in

---

449. Order 8 Rule 4(2) HCCPR Abuja and Order 10 Rule 4(2) HCCPR Lagos.

English and two translated copies to be served. A process server shall serve the process unless the court directs otherwise. The service shall be by delivering to or leaving with the person to be served a copy of the process or citation and a translated copy in accordance with the rules and practice of the court. After effecting the service, the process server shall file an affidavit of service which shall include particulars of charges for the cost of effecting the service. The affidavit is transmitted to the Chief Registrar with a copy of the process served annex to the affidavit. The Chief Registrar of the court is empowered to examine the particulars of charges and may approve or vary it. The Chief Judge of the state shall then forward the letter of request for service, the approved amount for service, the evidence of service and a certificate appended to it to the AG of the concerned state.

Where Nigeria Has a Convention with the Foreign Country Whose Process Is to Be Served in Nigeria

426. Subject to any special provisions in the convention, where the Chief Judge of a state receives a request for service of any process or document on any person within jurisdiction, the process server shall deliver the original or a copy along with a copy of its translation to the party to be served. The process server shall submit the particulars of the costs and expenses of the service to the Chief Registrar who shall certify the amount payable for service. The Chief Registrar shall then transmit to the appropriate foreign authority a certificate establishing the fact and date of service, or indicate reasons for failure to serve and notify the authority of the amount certified as cost and expenses of service.

It must be noted that where appropriate, a court may make an order of substituted or other service of a foreign process.

2. Registration by the Court

427. Cases are filed in the registry of the court. In most jurisdictions in Nigeria, the court's registry is decentralized. This means there is a registry in each judicial division of the HC and each magisterial district in each state. The HC of the Federal Capital Territory, Abuja until recently had a central registry at the main HC Complex situated in Maitama in the heart of the Federal Capital Territory, Abuja. Cases are filed at this central registry, and the Chief Judge of the HC of the Federal Capital Territory, Abuja assigns the cases to different HCs located within the Federal Capital Territory, Abuja. But currently, the cases can now be filed at the different judicial divisions.

428. When a case is accepted for filing (for a case to be accepted for filing, the provisions of the relevant Rules of court must have been complied with; for example, in a matter commenced by writ of summons in the HC of the Federal Capital Territory, Abuja, the writ must be accompanied with a statement of claim, list of witnesses to be called at the trial, written statements on oath of witnesses, except a subpoenaed witness, copies of every document to be relied on at the trial and a certificate of pre-action counselling before it will be accepted for filling) and the prescribed filing fees are paid, the registrar shall indicate the date and time of presentation for filing on the originating process and shall after sealing the process open a file for it.[450] The registrar shall state in the file the number of copies of the processes filed; endorse on the file the suit number assigned to the case that comprises of the abbreviation of the judicial division, a chronological number and the year of filing; and the parties and date of filing. The registrar shall also enter into the cause book the suit number, the parties and date of filing.

429. When a case has been assigned to a particular judge, the registrar of that judge shall bring this to the notice of the judge who shall then enter a date for hearing. This date is entered into the case file and the court's diary of that particular court. On the date the matter comes up for hearing, the case will be slated on the cause list of that court for that day.

3. Summary Judgment

430. Summary judgment in civil litigation in Nigeria means a judgment given in favour of a party without a full trial of the action. Summary judgment serves the purpose of dealing with clear-cut cases without having to go through the whole rigour of a full trial. It is not a function of urgency or time constraint but rather cases where it is clear that the defendant has no defence to the claim. The court has held that it is used for straightforward cases where the claimant believes that the defendant has no defence to the action.[451] A summary judgment is a judgment on the merits. With few exceptions (*see* paragraph 438) the same court that gave a summary judgment cannot set it aside. Setting aside such judgment can only be achieved on appeal. This is as opposed to a judgment in default of appearance or pleading which is not a judgment on the merit and can be set aside by the same court under certain conditions as will be discussed in paragraphs 488–491 below.

a. Types of Summary Judgment

431. There are several types of summary judgment under the various HCCPR in Nigeria. Even at the Magistrates' Court there is summary judgment procedure called summary summons under the Magistrates' Court Civil Procedure Rules of Lagos State and default summons under the District Court Rules of the Federal Capital Territory, Abuja. The different summary judgment procedures under the HCCPR are as follows.

---

450. Order 6 Rule 3 HCCPR Abuja and Order 8 Rule 3 HCCPR Lagos.
451. *Sodipo v. Lemminkaenem* (1986) 1 NWLR 20 (CA).

(i) Summary Judgment under the Undefended List Procedure

432. This procedure applies in all the jurisdictions in Nigeria except Lagos. Under the HCCPR Abuja, the procedure is available only in respect of claims to recover a debt or liquidated money demand. A liquidated money demand means an amount that is capable of mathematical computation or precision. The claimant who intends to commence an action under the undefended list applies for the issuance of a writ of summons in Form 1 (which means taking out a writ of summons), and this is supported with an affidavit setting forth the grounds upon which the claim is based. The affidavit shall also state that in the deponent's belief, the defendant has no defence to the action.

433. The judge in chambers examines the writ and the supporting affidavit and if satisfied that there are good grounds for believing that there is no defence to the claim will enter the suit for hearing under the undefended list and mark the writ of summons accordingly. The court then enters a return date on the writ. When an action under the undefended list comes up for the first time, it is for hearing. This was the position held by the court in *Ben Thomas Hotels v. Sebi Furnitures*.[452] A copy of the marked writ and the supporting affidavit is served to the defendant who has two options available to him.

434. The defendant may concede the claim or may wish to defend the action. If the defendant opts for the first option the rules do not require the defendant to do anything. On the date fixed for hearing, the court may give judgment for the claimant on the strength of the claimant's writ and affidavit and the fact that the defendant has no intention to defend the claim. However, where the defendant intends to defend the action, the rules require that the defendant file a written notice of intention to defend together with a counter affidavit disclosing a defence on the merit.[453] The notice of intention to defend is as in Form 145 of the appendix to the HCCPR Abuja and the defendant is to file it before five days to the day fixed for hearing. However, it has been held that where the defendant fails to file within time, he can bring an application for extension of time within which to file his notice of intention to defend.[454] For the court to be satisfied that there is a defence on the merit the defendant, counter affidavit must disclose a prima facie defence. This was the position of the court in *Agro Millers Ltd v. CMB*.[455] The court at this stage is not concerned with whether the defence will ultimately succeed but whether the facts averred can support a prima facie defence on the merit. Where a defence is disclosed the case is transferred to the general cause list. But where none is disclosed judgment is entered for the claimant.

435. A judgment obtained under the undefended list procedure is a judgment on the merit that can only be set aside on appeal. Even where the defendant did not file

---

452. (1989) 5 NWLR (Pt 123) 523 (SC).
453. Order 35 Rule 3 HCCPR Abuja.
454. *Bulet v. Adamu* (1997) 3 NWLR (Pt 493) 348 (CA).
455. (1997) 10 NWLR (Pt 525) 469 (CA).

notice of intention to defend it is still a judgment on the merit. The court has held that once there is proof that the defendant was served, though he failed to appear or file an intention to defend, the judgment given is a final judgment.[456] There are, however, situations where a judgment obtained under the undefended list can be set aside by the same court that made it. First, where the court finds that there was no service of the writ on the defendant, it can set aside the judgment. This was the position held in *Ben Thomas v. Sebi Furniture*.[457] Second, where the court that gave the judgment was incompetent to handle the matter. Lastly, where the court finds that the judgment was obtained by fraud.

(ii) Summary Judgment under Order 11 HCCPR Abuja and Order 13 HCCPR Lagos

436. This procedure applies under the HCCPR of Lagos and Abuja, and it applies to all types of claims (liquidated and unliquidated). The claimant must believe that the defendant does not have a defence to the claim to come under this procedure. To bring an action under this procedure the claimant shall file with the writ of summons a statement of claim, list of documents to be relied upon (in Abuja it is the exhibits), depositions of witnesses, application for summary judgment (which is by way of motion on notice), affidavits in support of motion stating grounds for the claimant's believe that there is defence to his claim and written brief in respect thereof.

437. The claimant shall deliver to the Registrar as many copies of these documents as there are defendants, and this is served on the defendant in the same manner originating processes are served. Upon been served, where the defendant has no defence to the claim the defendant is not required to do anything. Where defendant intends to defend the defendant shall within the time prescribed for defence (forty-two days in Lagos, in Abuja it is twenty-one days from the date of receipt of the claimant processes) file a statement of defence, depositions of the defendant's witnesses, list and copies of documents to be used in the defence (in Abuja, the exhibits to be used in the defence), a counter affidavit and a written brief in reply to the application for summary judgment.[458]

438. After all relevant documents have been filed at the hearing of the application for summary judgment, the judge considers whether the defendant has a good defence. If the judge finds in favour of the defendant the judge may grant leave to the defendant to defend the action. If otherwise the judge may enter judgment in favour of the claimant and it is a judgment on the merit and cannot be set aside by the same court as held in *Iron Product Ltd v. Sentinel Assurance Co Ltd*.[459] Where the defendant has a good defence to only a part of the claim the court will enter judgment for the part where he has no good defence and grant leave to defend the

---

456. *UAC Technical v. Anglo Canadian Cement Ltd* (1966) NMLR 349 (HC Lagos).
457. *Supra.*
458. Order 11 Rule 4 HCCPR Abuja and Order 13 Rule 4 HCCPR Lagos.
459. (1992) 4 NWLR (Pt 238) (CA).

part where the defend has a good defence. Where there are several defendants and it appears to the judge that any of them as a good defence and ought to be allowed to defend while the others do not, the former may be allowed to defend and judgment entered against the latter. Where a defendant files his statement of defence but fails to appear at the hearing, the court is entitled to look at all the documents filed and proceed to determine whether or not the defendant has a good defence.

439. The effect of judgment obtained under this procedure is that where the court considers the statement of defence and other accompanying documents of the defendant and enters judgment for the claimant, it is a judgment on the merit and cannot be set aside by the same court. Where the defendant does not file statement of defence and the accompanying documents and the court gives judgment on the strength of the claimant's case, it is considered as a default judgment and can be set aside by the same court as held in *UTC v. Pamotei.*[460] However, from the provisions of the rules, a default judgment can only be set aside on grounds of fraud, non-service or lack of jurisdiction upon such terms as the court may think fit.[461]

(iii) Summary Judgment on Admission

440. A party in an action may admit facts averred by the other party in their pleadings or at any stage of the proceedings. The court may on application, at a Pre-trial Conference (in Lagos at the Case Management Conference) or at any other stage of the proceedings where admissions of facts have been made, either on the pleadings or otherwise, make such order or grant judgment in favour of any party with regard to such admission as a party may be entitled to, without waiting for the determination of any other question between the parties.[462]

(iv) Summary Order for Account

441. Where in an originating process a claimant seeks an account in the first instance, or where the claim involves taking an account, if the defendant either fails to appear or after appearance fails to satisfy the court that there is a preliminary question to be tried, the court shall on application make an order for the proper accounts with all necessary inquiries and directions. An application for accounts shall be supported by an affidavit filed on a claimant's behalf, stating concisely the grounds of his claim to an account. The application may be made any time after the time prescribed for defence.[463]

460. (1989) 3 SCNJ 79.
461. Order 21 Rule 12 HCCPR Abuja and Order 22 Rule 12 HCCPR Lagos.
462. Order 20 Rule 4 HCCPR Abuja and Order 21 Rule 4 HCCPR Lagos.
463. Order 12 HCCPR Abuja and Order 14 HCCPR Lagos.

(v) Summary Proceedings for Possession of Landed Property Occupied by Squatters or Without the Owner's Consent

442. Under this procedure provided for in Order 53 HCCPR Abuja and Order 57 HCCPR Lagos, persons occupying landed property as squatters can be summarily ejected. Landed property under this procedure refers to land with or without a building on it. However, the order made under this procedure does not apply to any of the following categories of persons occupying premises namely a tenant, a tenant holding over after the termination of his tenancy, a licensee of the owner or person entitled to possession, or a person who had the consent of the predecessor-in-title of the person who is entitled to possession.

443. The claimant applies for this order of court by way of an originating summons as in Form 38 in Lagos and Form 47 in Abuja. The application is supported by an affidavit stating the claimant's interest in the land, the circumstances in which the land has been occupied without licence or consent and in which his claim to possession arises and the fact that he does not know the name of any person occupying the land who is not named in the summons. The originating summons shall be sealed with the seal of the court from which it is issued. No acknowledgement of service is required. An order of possession under this procedure is as in Form 39 in Lagos and Form 48 in Abuja. No writ of possession shall be issued after three months of giving the order of possession without the leave of the judge, which is obtained by an ex parte application except the court directs otherwise. The order made under this procedure can be set aside or varied by the judge on such terms as the judge deems fit. It is to be noted that any person who is in occupation of the land but is not named as a defendant may apply to be joined as a defendant at any stage of the proceedings in order to be heard on whether an order of possession should be made.

B. *Progress of Proceedings*

1. Preparatory Measures

a. Production of Documents

444. In preparation for trial, a party in a proceeding may request for some documents from the other party. This can be achieved in two ways. The party requiring the document may serve on the other party a notice to produce a document. It becomes needful, where the person giving the notice does not have the original copy of the document and considers the document vital to the party's case and the original is with the adverse party. By section 89(a) of the Evidence Act 2011, secondary evidence of the existence, content or condition of a document may be given where the original is with the person against whom it is sought to be proved or a person legally bound to produce it and when after a notice to produce has been served and such person does not produce it. For a party to rely on this section 89(a) there must be compliance with section 91 of the Evidence Act 2011 to the effect that the person in whose possession the original of the document is must be given a notice to produce it. There are however exceptions to this rule where no notice to produce is required before a party can tender a secondary evidence of such a document. The exceptions are:

(1) When the document to be proved is itself a notice. For example, a notice to quit in recovery of premises cases.
(2) When from the nature of the case, the adverse party must know that the document will be required to be produced.
(3) When it appears or is proved that the adverse party has obtained possession of the original of the document by fraud or force.
(4) When the adverse party or the agent has the original in court.
(5) When the adverse party or the agent has admitted the loss of the document.

445. The notice to produce is usually given in the pleadings of the party requesting it. This is done by making reference to the document in a paragraph of the relevant pleadings and then stating that the other party is thereby given notice to produce the said document. When at the time of trial, the other party has not produced the document in question the party who gave the notice to produce is free to tender secondary evidence of the said document.

446. A party who requires a document may also apply for inspection of documents requiring the opposing party to produce certain documents for the inspection of the party who made the application.

447. All these form part of the pretrial proceedings which essentially take place at the Pretrial / Case Management Conference which have been discussed in paragraphs 385–392 above.

b. Exchange of Pleadings

448. In Nigeria, under the current frontloading system provided for in the HCCPR, the pleadings of the parties are exchanged before pretrial proceeding commences. The claimant files his pleadings at the point of filing the originating process and this is served on the defendant. The defendant who intends to defend the action files his pleading within the time allowed by the rules to do that and serves on the claimant. Where there is a need to file further pleadings the parties do within the period allowed. *See* paragraph 362 above for the time within which parties are to file pleadings subsequent to the Statement of claim, which must mandatorily accompany the writ of summons. Pleadings are deemed closed when no further pleading is allowed to be filed without the leave of court. Pretrial proceeding commences after the closure of pleadings. However, during the pretrial proceedings, parties with the leave of court may file further and better particulars and to that extent, pleadings can still be exchanged during the pretrial stage.

449. Where a party fails to file a pleading within the time prescribed by the rules, leave of court will be required to do so. This is obtained by the party seeking to file the pleading out of time making an application on notice supported by an affidavit and a written address giving good reasons for failing to file within time. Sanctions are imposed for failure to file pleadings within time. *See* paragraph 365 above.

450. All pleadings must first be filed in the registry of the court with the prescribed fees paid before they are served on the parties.

451. The pleadings of parties are required to follow the requirement stated in the Rules of court. The rules of pleadings require that every pleading must contain only material fact. Where a pleading contains irrelevant facts, which make it to be incomprehensible to the court, and the opposing party, it may be struck out. Every pleading should contain facts and not law, legal argument or conclusion. Parties are not allowed to make arguments in their pleadings. The pleadings should only contain facts. When evidence has been led in line with the fact, a party can argue based on them in the final written address. In addition, pleadings should not contain a legal conclusion. It is the court's prerogative to draw conclusions. Also, pleadings should contain only facts and not evidence. As such where a party seeks to rely on a document during the trial, all the party needs to do is to plead facts that point to the existence of such document. However, this area of the law is not so settled. This is because there is sometimes a thin line between facts and evidence. The guiding principle here is where a party is not sure whether a piece of information constitutes fact or evidence, it is better to plead it. As a result, there is no known sanction for pleading evidence in a pleading. Also, facts must be pleaded positively, precisely, distinctly and briefly. Pleadings must be precise and brief. Where a pleading is drafted clumsily, it can hinder its comprehension and may be struck out.

452. Pleadings are required to contain reliefs. Where a party fails to include reliefs in his pleading it is fatal to the case of the party. This is especially so in the case of the claimant, as the statement of claim supersedes the writ of summons. A claimant who fails to include reliefs in his statement of claim is deemed not to be seeking any relief and as such the pleading is incompetent.

453. There are also formal requirements that parties in an action must adhere to when filing their pleadings or applications. Suits/applications filed in a court must be headed in the cause and in the matter. They must carry the suit numbers and the parties and must be dated and signed by the party filing or their counsel. Specifically, with regard to pleadings they must be headed in the title of the court in which the action is filed, showing clearly the parties to the suit, suit number and where necessary the capacities in which the parties are suing or being sued. They must state the description of the pleading, that is statement of claim, statement of defence, statement of defence and set-off, statement of defence and counterclaim, reply to statement of defence, reply to statement of defence and setoff, or reply to statement of defence and counterclaim. The pleading must be divided into paragraphs and numbered successively with each paragraph containing a separate allegation of fact as much as possible. Facts must be stated in a chronological manner and pronouns are to be avoided as they create ambiguity. There must be consistency in nomenclature used in the pleading and in the allegation of fact. No new ground of claim or allegation of fact inconsistent with an earlier allegation is allowed. Expressions of dates, sums and numbers should be in figures. In Abuja, they may also be expressed in words. In practice, they are expressed in figures and additionally expressed in words. A pleading must be dated and signed by the legal practitioner settling it or by the parties where they are not represented by counsel. Pleadings must contain address for service on the other party, and they are required to be printed or typewritten on durable quality paper.

c. Setting the Matter Down for Trial

454. After the close of the Pretrial / Case Management Conference or in the absence of such after the closure of pleadings, the matter is put in the court's case docket and comes up for the first time for mention. Counsel to the parties will appear in court and formally take a hearing date for trial in the matter.

2. Purely Written Procedure

455. There are actions that are proceeded upon purely on the basis of the documents before the court. Actions commenced by originating summons for example are adjudicated upon purely on the basis of the documents filed. The claimant would have in commencing an action by originating summons filed with it an affidavit setting out the facts relied upon, all the exhibits to be relied upon, a written address in support of the application and a certificate of Pre-action Counselling (under the Abuja Rules) or Pre-action Protocol Form 01 with the necessary document (under the Lagos Rules). The defendant who intends to defend the action will enter appearance by filing a memorandum of appearance and is required to respond to the processes filed by the claimant. The defendant will do this by filing a counter affidavit, all the exhibits to be relied upon by the defence and a written address. The court decides the case on the basis of the affidavit evidence before it and does not call for oral evidence. The exception where the court would have to call for oral evidence is where there are conflicts in the affidavit evidence. To resolve the conflicts the court may resort to calling oral evidence. This procedure also applies to actions proceeded upon by originating motions. In the wake of the COVID-19 pandemic, hearings on matters that are generally decided on the basis of affidavit evidence like matters commenced by originating summons or motions can be conducted virtually.[464]

464. *See* para. 9 of the HC of the Federal Capital Territory, Abuja COVID-19 Practice Direction 2020.

3. Determination of the Trial Date

456. At the end of the Pretrial Conference / Case Management Conference, the pretrial judge writes a report that shall guide the subsequent course of proceedings (unless the trial judge modifies it) and hands the case file over to a trial judge. The trial judge directs that hearing notices be issued to the parties. On the said date the matter will be listed for mention, thereupon the parties take a date for hearing subject to the convenience of the court. Under the Abuja Rules (the Pretrial Conference is not mandatory), upon completion of pleadings, where trial date has not been fixed by the trial judge, either party in the action may apply to the Registrar to set the matter down for trial. The Registrar upon such application causes hearing notices to be issued to all the parties in the suit.[465]

4. Trial

457. The parties are entitled to represent themselves in person or through an attorney of their choice. Where counsel represents parties in an action the respective cases of the parties are presented by their counsel to the court. In civil proceedings in Nigeria, once parties are represented in court, the appearance of the parties themselves in court is not mandatory.

458. The effect of appearance or non-appearance of the parties during trial is provided for under Order 33 Rules 1–5 Lagos and Order 32 Rules 1–5 Abuja. On the date fixed for the hearing, where both parties are absent from court (and are not represented by counsel), the court shall unless it sees good reason to the contrary strike out the case. Where the claimant is absent, if the defendant has no counterclaim, the defendant shall be entitled to judgment dismissing the action. Where there is a counterclaim, the defendant proceeds to prove the counterclaim as far as the burden of proof lies on the defendant. Where the defendant is absent, the claimant may prove his case as far as the burden of proof lies on the claimant. Where a matter is struck out during trial for non-appearance of the parties or a party, either party may apply that the matter be restored on the cause list on such terms as the judge may deem fit. Any judgment given during the trial for non-appearance of a party may be set aside by the judge on such terms as the judge may deem fit. An application to relist a matter struck out or to set aside a judgment shall be brought within seven days after the order or judgment is made. It can also be brought within such time as may be extended by the judge.

459. Where both parties are present, on the date fixed for trial, the court will call on the party on whom the burden of proof lies by the nature of the issues or questions between the parties to open its case. This is usually the claimant. The claimant may make an opening statement stating succinctly the case of the claimant and the number of witnesses to be called in support. This is hardly done because Nigeria

465. Order 32 Rule 1 HCCPR Abuja.

does not practice a jury system where an opening statement is needful. The usual practice is that the case of the claimant opens by examination of claimant's witnesses. When the claimant closes its case, the defendant opens his defence and the defence witnesses are examined. Where additional witnesses whose witness depositions where not frontloaded with the originating processes need to be called, the party who needs to call such witnesses shall apply to the judge for leave to call such witnesses. Such application shall be accompanied with the deposition of such witnesses. This does not apply to subpoenaed witnesses who may have to give their testimony orally.

460. The oral examination of all witnesses is preceded by the taking of oaths or affirmations by the witness in the witness box. The Evidence Act 2011 makes it mandatory that oral evidence given in any proceeding must be given upon oath or affirmation administered in accordance with the Oath Act.[466] Despite the mandatory nature of this provision the court has held in *Mkpa v. Mkpa*[467] that failure to comply with it is a mere irregularity and does not affect the decision based on evidence given by a witness who was not sworn.

461. With regard to the procedure for administering oath or affirmation on a witness section 5(1) of the Oath Act[468] provides that where the person taking an oath is a Christian, the person shall hold a copy of the Holy Bible or New Testament in the right hand and says or repeats after the person administering the oath the words prescribed by law or the practice of the court as the case may be. Where the person is a Muslim both hands are placed on the Koran. Where the person is a Jew, a copy of the Old Testament is held in an uplifted hand while saying or repeating the prescribed words. The oath can also be administered in any other manner that is lawful according to any law, customary or otherwise in force in Nigeria. In this light, in practice, when a traditionalist is taking the oath, such a person places both hands on a sword or metal object. The words prescribed by law for the person taking the oath to say or repeat is as follows:

> I (followed by the name of the person taking the oath) do hereby solemnly swear that the evidence I shall give in this case before this court shall be the truth, the whole truth and nothing but the truth. So help me God (Allah for Muslim, Ogun, Sango, etc. for traditionalist) …

Where the person elects to affirm, the form of affirmation is as follows:

> I (followed by the name of the person taking the oath) hereby affirm that the evidence I shall give in this case before this court shall be the truth, the whole truth and nothing but the truth.

---

466. Section 205 of the Evidence Act 2011.
467. (2010) 14 NWLR (Pt 1214) 612 (CA).
468. Cap O1 LFN 2004.

462. There are exceptions to the rule that every person giving oral testimony in any proceeding must do so on oath or affirmation. First, the evidence of a person who declares that taking of any oath whatsoever is unlawful according to the person's religious belief or a person who for want of religious belief ought not to in the opinion of the court give evidence on oath may be received by the court though not given on oath.[469] It is worthy to note, however, that where an oath has been duly administered and taken, the fact that the person to whom it was administered had at the time of taking the oath no religious belief does not affect for any purpose the validity of the oath taken.[470] Second, a child who has not attained the age of 14 years cannot give evidence on oath.[471] The child can only give unsworn testimony. Where such a child who testifies unsworn gives false evidence in such circumstance that he would, if the evidence had been on oath have been guilty of perjury shall be guilty of an offence under section 191 of the Criminal Code and on conviction shall be dealt with accordingly.

463. In addition to the taking of oath before giving oral testimony, any witness brought to testify in any proceedings upon an order of court summoning the witness or by a subpoena shall before giving evidence be cautioned by the court or the Registrar upon the court's direction. The form of the caution is as follows:

> You (Full name of the witness) are hereby cautioned that if you tell a lie in your testimony in this proceeding or willfully mislead this court you are liable to be prosecuted and if found guilty you will be seriously dealt with according to law.

464. Witnesses are examined in chief, cross-examined and re-examined. The examination-in-chief of witnesses in civil proceedings is by leading the witnesses to adopt their witness statement on oath. Where counsel intends to put any document in evidence through the witness, the witness's attention is drawn to the part of the witness statement on oath where facts pointing to the existence of the document were deposed to and leads the witness to identify the document. The counsel can then tender the document in evidence. Counsel then informs the court that the examination-in-chief is over. The witness is then cross-examined by the opposing counsel and where need be re-examined by the claimant counsel. The court will then order the witness to step down. This procedure is adopted for all witnesses except subpoenaed witnesses whose witness statements on oath were not frontloaded. Such witnesses will have to be examined viva voce. After the claimant is through calling witnesses, the claimant will close its case. The court will then call on the defendant to open its calls. Subject to the option chosen by the defendant at the close of the claimants' case, the defendant will equally conduct an examination-in-chief of its witnesses, they will be cross-examined and re-examined where necessary. The

469. Section 208(1) of the Evidence Act 2011.
470. Section 207 *ibid.*
471. Section 209(1) *ibid.*

defendant will then close its case and the matter will be adjourned for parties to file and serve their final written addresses and adopt the addresses on the next adjourned date.

465. A judge presiding over a case can examine witnesses called by the parties. Section 246(1) of the Evidence Act 2011 provides that:

> The court or any person empowered by law to take evidence may, in order to clear ambiguities or to clarify points which have been left obscure in the evidence given by any witness, ask any fact relevant or irrelevant; and may order the production of any document or thing; and neither the parties nor their agents shall be entitled to make any objection to any such question or order or, without the leave of the court, to cross-examine any witness upon any answer given in reply to any such question.

Based on this provision, a judge can put questions to a witness or request a witness to produce a document if the interest justice so demands. However, such questions must be based on facts declared by the Evidence Act 2011 to be relevant and duly proved. The questions or documents must also not be ones that the witness is entitled to refuse to answer or produce or ones considered improper by sections 224 and 225 of the Evidence Act 2011.

466. There are options open to the defendant at close of the claimant's case. The defendant has the option of making a no case submission, resting the defence case on that of the claimant or opening the defendant's defence. First, the defendant will opt for a no case submission where the defendant believes that an important ingredient of the claim of the claimant has not been established by the evidence led by claimant. Second, the defendant can also rest its case on that of the claimant. The defendant exercises this option if the defendant is of the belief that the claimant's case as it stands cannot sustain a judgment in the favour of the claimant. Third, the defendant can choose to open its defence. Where the defendant exercises the first option and is overruled by the court, the defendant can still opt for the third option. However, a defendant who exercises the second option cannot exercise any of the other options.

467. After the close of the defendant's case, the court adjourns the matter for the parties to file and serve their final written addresses. Where a defendant led evidence, such shall within twenty-one days of the close of evidence file and serve the defendant's written address. Where the defendant does not lead evidence, it will be the claimant who shall within twenty-one days of close of evidence file the claimant's written address first. The defendant is said to have not adduced evidence where he did not call any witnesses nor testify for himself nor tendered any document in support of his defence. In a situation where the defendant is the one entitled to file a written address first, the claimant shall within twenty-one days after receipt of the defendant's address fill the claimant's written address. The defendant has a right to reply on points of law, which shall be done within seven days of receipt of the claimant's address. On the date fixed for the adoption of written addresses, the parties adopt their addresses. Parties are allowed time to emphasize and clarify the written address already filed (twenty minutes).[472] Where a party is absent on the day for adoption of written addresses, such a party shall be deemed to have adopted his written address. Each party is required to file two copies of their addresses in court and also serve a copy each on every party in the action.

468. The role of a closing address is to assist the court in arriving at a just decision based on the evidence led and the law. In *Beloxxi & Co. Ltd v. Southtrust Bank*[473] the court held that:

> No matter how brilliant a counsel's address is, it cannot take the place of legal evidence and a judgment cannot be avoided on the basis of non-mention or non-consideration of counsel's address.

The structure of a final written address outlined below as stated in the HCCPR is the same for a written address in support of an application. The difference lies in the content. While for a final written address the claim of the claimant is outlined, for a written address in support of a motion what is outlined is what the motion is for. Also a written address in support of an application will not have issues arising from the evidence rather it will have issues for determination, which are usually the conditions to be satisfied for the grant of such an application. These conditions may be as laid down by statutes or case law. A closing address shall be printed on white opaque A4 size paper and set out in paragraphs numbered seriatim. The structure of a written address is as follows:

- the claim/application;
- a brief statement of the facts with reference to the exhibits attached to the application or tendered at the trial;
- issues for determination arising from the evidence;
- a succinct statement of argument on each issue incorporating the purpose of authorities cited with full citation of each authority; and
- it shall be concluded with a numbered summary of points raised and the party's prayer.

A list of all authorities referred to in the address must be submitted with the address. Where any unreported judgment is relied upon, the certified true copy shall be submitted along with the written address.

5. Opinion by the Ministere Public

469. This is not applicable in Nigeria. What is practised is that sometimes in a matter before it, the court may seek the opinion of very senior lawyers with respect

472. Order 33 Rule 4 HCCPR Abuja; Order 35 Rule 4 HCCPR Lagos.
473. (2012) 2 NWLR (Pt 1285) 605 (CA).

to an issue. The lawyers may be in court when the issue comes up in a case that such lawyers are not involved in. It may also be that the court may invite a senior counsel who was not in court when the issue came up in a case to give their opinion on an issue. It is called amicus curiae. The court is not bound to accept the opinion given but may allow itself to be guided by it.

C. Judgment

1. Deliberation

470. The judgment of a court is a binding, authentic, official and judicial determination of the court in respect of claims and in an action before it. The court after close of evidence and final addresses of the parties delivers its judgment. A court may deliver its judgment immediately after the parties have made their final addresses or it may adjourn proceedings to another date or it may reserve judgment to another. It is the *ratio decidendi* or *rationes decidendi* of the case as opposed to passing remarks of the judge that constitutes the judgment of the court. The *ratio decidendi* is the decision of the court on the issues for determination before it. In an appellate court, for example, the Court of Appeal of Nigeria where three justices of the court preside over an appeal, one of the justices writes the leading judgment. The others are required to write their concurring or dissenting judgments. However, it is the leading judgment that constitutes the authority for which the case stands. The SC has held that:

> All other expressions contained in the concurring judgment, particularly those not addressed in the leading judgment are obiter dictum or dicta. Obiter dictum in the leading judgment as well as in the concurring judgments may be of persuasive effect in other occasions.[474]

471. The 1999 Nigerian Constn permits at the level of the SC and the Court of Appeal of Nigeria, a situation where all the justices who heard a cause or matter need not be present when judgment is to be delivered.[475] For the purpose of delivering its judgment, the SC and the Court of Appeal of Nigeria is duly constituted if at least one justice of the court sits for the purpose. The opinion of a justice who heard the cause or matter may be pronounced or read by any other justice who may not have been present at the hearing. When a justice who heard the cause or matter is still a justice of the court at the time of the delivery of judgment, though absent, the opinion of the justice will be read. Where such a justice has ceased from been a justice of that court either by retirement, resignation, dismissal, elevation or death, the justices opinion on the case can only be pronounced. This position has judicial backing in the case of *Shitta-Bey v. A.G. Federation.*[476] At the HCs however, there is no constitutional or statutory provision for a judge's judgment to be delivered by

474. *Abacha v. Fawehinmi* (2000) LPELR-14 at 115–117 (SC).
475. Section 294(2) of the 1999 Nigerian Constn.
476. (1998) 7 SCNJ 264.

another judge in civil proceedings. However, in *A.G. Federation v. ANPP*, the Court of Appeal of Nigeria held that a judgment written and signed by a judge of the Federal HC but delivered by another judge of the same court was valid.[477]

472. At the trial courts because in most cases only one judge preside over a matter (at the National Industrial Court of Nigeria more than one judge may preside over a matter by the direction of the President of the Court) and Nigeria does not practice the jury system of administration of justice, there are no deliberations. The judge alone analyses the facts of the case, the evidence admitted with respect of those facts and applies it to the relevant laws and makes a finding, giving reasons for the finding. The judge then goes ahead to give the judgment of the court. However, at the appellate courts[478] where more than one justice/judge presides over an appeal, there are deliberations on the case by all the justices/judges. This is usually done in the form of conference room deliberations. The decision of the court is determined by the opinion of the majority of the justices/judges.[479]

2. Different Types of Judgments

a. Final Judgment

473. A final judgment is one that finally disposes of the rights and liabilities of the parties and brings the action to an end with the judge becoming *functus officious*. Examples include a decision of a court that it does not have jurisdiction, consent judgment, judgment on constitutional reference, judgment on leave to the plaintiff to discontinue an action, dismissal of action, adjudication on a claim on the merit, etc. A final judgment is appealed against as of right within three months of the delivery of the judgment.[480]

b. Interlocutory Judgment

474. An interlocutory judgment is one that determines only an issue before the court without finally determining the rights and liabilities of the parties.[481] For example, an order of striking out of a suit but with leave to relist, order for consolidation, decision on any of the constituent issues in a suit, etc. An interlocutory judgment requires the leave of court to appeal against it except the appeal is on points of law only, and it is appealed against within fourteen days.

477. (2003) 15 NWLR (Pt 844) 600 (CA).
478. Such as the SC, Court of Appeal of Nigeria, Customary Court of Appeal and Sharia Court of Appeal.
479. Section 294(3) of the 1999 Nigerian Constn.
480. Section 24(2)(a) Court of Appeal Act Cap C36 LFN 2004.
481. *Western Steel Works Ltd v. Iron & Steel Western Union* (1986) 3 NWLR (Pt 30) 617 (SC).

c. Consent Judgment

475. This is a judgment made consequent upon the voluntary agreement of parties in a dispute on all issues in a claim. The agreement is reached in an out-of-court settlement, and the terms of the settlement are then filed in court and made the judgment of the court. It is a final judgment but as opposed to the position with final judgments generally, a consent judgment requires the leave of court before it can be appealed against.[482]

d. Default Judgment

476. This is a judgment made as a result of the default of the defendant. The default Judgment could be in default of the defendant appearing in court or failing to file pleadings. Since it is not a judgment on the merit, it can be set aside or varied by the same court or a court of co-ordinate jurisdiction. The Lagos and Abuja Rules list three grounds for setting aside a default judgment. They are fraud, non-service and lack of jurisdiction. The SC in *Williams v. Hope Rising Voluntary Funds Society*[483] laid down five considerations for granting or refusing an application to set aside a default judgment namely:

(1) The reason for the failure of the applicant to appear at the trial.
(2) Whether there had been undue delay in bringing the application such as will prejudice the respondent.
(3) Whether the respondent would be prejudiced or embarrassed upon an order for rehearing being made such that it would be inequitable to permit the case to be reopened.
(4) Whether the applicant's case is manifestly unsupportable.
(5) Whether the applicant's conduct throughout the proceedings from service of the writ upon him to the date of judgment has been such as to make the application worthy of sympathetic consideration.

e. An Order of Non-suit

477. Where satisfactory evidence is not given entitling the claimant or defendant to judgment, the judge may suo motu or on application non-suit the claim of a claimant. An order of non-suit is one that neither dismisses nor grants the claimant's claim. It is ordered where neither the claimant nor the defendant is entitled to judgment and no wrong or injustice will be occasioned to the defendant by the order.[484] The claimant can come back and file the case again and estoppel per rem judicata cannot be raised. Where a court is of the view that an action should be non-suited, the parties' legal practitioner, shall have the right to make submissions about the propriety or otherwise of making the order.

482. Section 241(2)(b) of the 1999 Nigerian Constn.
483. (1982) 1-2 SC 145.
484. Order 38(1) HCCPR Lagos and Order 38 HCCPR Abuja.

f. Dismissal Order

478. This is made where the claim of the claimant has not been proved and making an order of non-suit will occasion injustice to the defendant. A dismissal order is different from a non-suit because it puts an end to a suit, the only option open to the claimant is to appeal whereas an order of non-suit keeps the case alive and the claimant can bring the action again in the same court. An order of dismissal is distinct from an order of striking out because while a dismissal order is made after the matter is heard on the merit and can only be appealed against, a striking out order is made when the matter has not been heard on the merit and can be relisted again.

3. Formal Aspects of a Judgment

479. For a judgment to be valid, it must possess certain features. The 1999 Nigerian Constn provides for some of these features while others are by the Rules of court or judicial decisions of courts. The 1999 Nigerian Constn of Nigeria provides that the judgment of a superior court of record must be in writing[485] and must be delivered in open court.[486] There is however an exception provided in the 1999 Nigerian Constn where the proceedings as well as the judgment of a court can be held in camera. These are where it is in the interest of defence, public safety, public order, public morality, the welfare of persons who have not attained the age of 18 years, the protection of the private lives of the parties, or to such extent as it may consider necessary by reason of special circumstances in which publicity would be contrary to the interest of justice. In any proceedings before a court or tribunal, where it is needful that the proceedings be held in camera and a Minister of the Federal Republic of Nigeria or a Commissioner of a state satisfies the court of this fact, the court or tribunal shall make arrangements for the evidence relating to that matter to be taken in private and shall take such other actions that may be necessary or expedient to prevent disclosure of the matter.[487] In the wake of the COVID-19 pandemic, judgments of courts in some jurisdictions and courts can be delivered virtually.[488]

480. The 1999 Nigerian Constn also stipulates that the judgment should be delivered within ninety days after the conclusion of the evidence and final addresses and all parties in the matter are entitled to authenticated copies of the judgment

---

485. Section 294(1) of the 1999 Nigerian Constn. The requirement that a judgment be in writing is also applicable to the inferior court of record.
486. Section 36(3) of the 1999 Nigerian Constn. The HCCPR also provide that the judgment of the HC be delivered in open court. This is provided for under Order 39 Rule 1 HCCPR Lagos and Order 39 Rule 1 HCCPR Abuja.
487. Section 36(4) of the 1999 Nigerian Constn; s. 243 Evidence Act 2011. The exceptions to delivery of judgment in open court provided in s. 36(4) of the 1999 Nigerian Constn pertains to criminal trial but there is no reason why it cannot be extended to civil matters.
488. *See* para. 25 of the Lagos State Judiciary Remote Hearing of Cases (COVID-19 Pandemic Period) Practice Direction 2020, para. 9 of the HC of the Federal Capital Territory, Abuja COVID-19 Practice Direction 2020.

within seven days of its delivery.[489] A judgment delivered after ninety days is nevertheless valid except the non-compliance has occasioned a miscarriage of justice.[490] The party seeking the nullification of the judgment on this ground must show that injuries had been suffered traceable to the court's failure to deliver the judgment within time. The presiding Justice of the Court of Appeal shall report the fact of the non-compliance of the judgment with section 294(1) of the 1999 Nigerian Constn to the NJC.[491] Sometimes after a court has adjourned for judgment, the judge may in the course of writing the judgment discover an issue that needs to be addressed by the parties. The judge would direct that hearing notices be issued to the parties. At the hearing the court would ask the parties to address it on the issue. The effect of a situation such as this is that the ninety days within which to deliver the judgment will now start running from the last address by the parties. However, the court has held that re-adoption of written addresses by counsel does not reopen the computation of the period within which judgment is to be delivered.[492]

481. A judgment must be signed and dated by the judge as at the date the judgment is pronounced by the judge and shall take effect from that date except if the judge orders otherwise.[493] It should contain the claim of the claimant, a summary of the facts of the case, the evidence of the parties including the documentary evidence admitted in the case, and the issues for determination, the resolution of the issues of fact or law, the conclusion or general inference from the facts and the law as resolved, the verdict, terminal and consequential orders. The evidence in the case must be properly evaluated in the judgment. In *Mogaji v. Odofin*,[494] the court held that: 'Judgment must state issues or questions to be decided, essential facts and evidence, contain resolution of the issues of fact or law and the general inference from the facts and the law as resolved.' The decision of the court must be confined to the issues before it and the claims sought. The court can however make consequential orders that must have a direct and natural bearing on the decision.

4. Notice and Service

482. The 1999 Nigerian Constn provides that the court furnishes all parties in an action with duly authenticated copies of the judgment of the court within seven days of the delivery of it.[495] In practice, it is the party in whose favour the judgment is given that applies for it to be served on the other party upon payment of necessary fees. In Nigeria, it is discourteous to a court for counsel not to appear in court on the date of judgment. As such, the need for notification of the judgment to the parties becomes superfluous. Once the judgment of a court is delivered, it binds all parties in the action.

---

489. Section 294(1) of the 1999 Nigerian Constn.
490. Section 294(5) *ibid.*
491. Section 294(6) *ibid.*
492. *Idowu & Ors v. Segun Okoya Investment Ltd* (2017) LPELR-43580 (CA).
493. Order 39 Rule 2 HCCPR Lagos and Order 39 Rule 2 HCCPR Abuja.
494. (1978) 3 SC 91.
495. Section 294(1) of the 1999 Nigerian Constn.

5. Res Judicata

483. Res judicata is a Latin expression, which means a thing or matter settled by judgment. A final judgment of a court of competent jurisdiction in Nigeria on the merits constitutes res judicata with respect to the decision on the issues between the parties. The court has held that:

> The rule is that a final judgment rendered by a court of competent jurisdiction on the merits is conclusive as to the rights of the parties and their privies, and as to them, constitutes an absolute bar to a subsequent action involving the same claims, demand or cause of action.[496]

By effect, res judicata means the same issues and between the same parties cannot be re-litigated upon again as the parties are estopped from so doing. The estoppel created by a successful plea of res judicata bar a person from asserting the same rights or claim that contravenes what one has said or done before or what has been legally established as true and robs the court where the plea is raised of jurisdiction. For the principle of estoppel per rem judicata to apply, the following conditions must be met:

(1) the parties/privies must be the same in both the previous and present proceedings;
(2) the claim or the issues in dispute in both proceedings must be substantially the same;
(3) the res or subject matter of the litigation in the two cases must be the same; and
(4) the decision relied on for the plea must be a valid and subsisting one and must have been given by a court of competent jurisdiction.

484. The principle of res judicata is based on two rules of public policy, which is that there should be an end to litigation and no one ought to be proceeded against twice on the same issues if there had been a final decision on them by a competent court.

6. Interpretation and Rectification of Judgments

485. Once a judge delivers the final judgment in a case, the judge ceases to be seized of the matter and he becomes *functus officio* with regard to that case. The judge may however make such ancillary orders like order for instalment of payment, stay of execution and injunction pending appeal. In *Unipetrol (Nig) Plc v. Adireje (W/A) Ltd* the Court of Appeal of Nigeria per Sanusi JCA held that:

496. *Tony-Anthony Holdings Ltd v. C.B.A* (2013) AFWLR (Pt 698) 944 at 963 (CA).

> It is settled law that once a trial court has delivered judgment, the court's authority over the case expires. The judge thereupon becomes *functus officio* except to deal with issue such as stay of execution of that judgment he delivered or on order for installment of payment of judgment debt.[497]

The judge cannot after delivery of judgment in a case alter the decision or supplement it. Where there are mistakes, errors in the judgment, the judge can do nothing about it, and the parties can only seek review before an appellate court. However, there are situations where the same judge that gave a judgment can make corrections on it. The various HCCPR make provision for it.[498] Under the HCCPR Abuja, a judge can *suo motu* or upon application correct errors arising from accidental slips or clerical mistakes in judgment or orders without an appeal being filed. Under the Lagos Rules, a judge can only make such corrections upon an application made to the court.

486. It is the job of the court to give interpretation to its judgment. This is done at the instance of the parties. Either of the parties can apply to the court for the interpretation of the judgment. The import is usually to enable the parties to clearly know their respective rights and liabilities arising from the judgment.

7. Penalty in Case of Non-compliance

487. A judgment of a court is to be obeyed, as the court does not give judgment in futility. Where the judgment is a money judgment and the judgment debtor does not obey it willingly, the judgment creditor can apply for the enforcement of the judgment. For judgments other than money judgments, and any person refuses or neglects to obey it, the court can order that such a person be committed to prison and detained in custody until he has obeyed the order of the court.[499] This is usually achieved by the person seeking for the order to be obeyed filling and filing a notice in Form 48 of the First Schedule to the SCPA which is a notice of consequences of disobedience to order of court. This will be served on the disobedient person. Where the person fails to obey, on application by the party seeking the order to be obeyed, the registrar of the court shall issue a notice in Form 49 of the First Schedule to the SCPA which request the disobedient party to come and show cause why an order of committal should not be made against him. Where the disobedient person does not obey, on the date stated in the notice, after satisfying itself that the person was served, the court may order that he be committed to prison and a warrant of committal issued.

488. It is pertinent to note that when the court awards cost against a party as a result of a party's action (such as not being prepared to go on with trial and

497. (2004) AFWLR (Pt 231) 1238 at 1296 (CA).
498. Order 25 Rule 7 HCCPR Abuja and Order 26 Rule 7 HCCPR Lagos.
499. Section 72 SCPA 2004.

applying for an adjournment), which affects the other parties in an action, it is to be obeyed like the judgment of the court. As such where the party fails to pay the cost, the party in whose favour the judgment is given can move the court to refuse the other party any further audience in the case until the order of the court is obeyed. The party also has the option of enforcing the award of cost like any other monetary judgment of the court. Costs, when ordered, become payable within seven days of the order. Failure to make such payment attracts the sum of NGN 100 daily. The daily penalty is paid to the court. In addition to this daily penalty, the court may deny the defaulting party or his legal practitioner further audience in the proceedings.[500]

§2. Default Proceedings

489. Default proceedings arise in situations where a claimant gets judgment as a result of the defendant's failure to comply with procedural rules. A court of law in Nigeria can give judgment in default of the appearance of the defendant or in default of the defendant filing pleadings. The rules of the various HCs make provision for it.[501]

490. Where a defendant fails to appear in a case or fails to file his defence, the claimant may apply to a judge for a judgment with respect to the claim on the originating process. Under the HCCPR, a claimant can only make such an application if the claim is one of the following:

(a) a liquidated money demand;
(b) claim for pecuniary damages or for detention of goods with or without a claim for pecuniary damages;
(c) claim for pecuniary damages or for detention of goods with or without a claim for pecuniary damages including a liquidated demand;
(d) claim for recovery of land.

491. Judgment entered into under this provision is called a judgment in default of appearance and may be set aside by the same court that gave it on an application by the defendant to set it aside or vary it on terms. The application to set aside the judgment shall be made within a reasonable time showing evidence of payment of penalty, a good defence to the claim and a reasonable cause for the default. The application is by way of motion on notice supported with an affidavit and a written address. The court has to satisfy itself of the reason given by the applicant for the default and whether there has been undue delay in making the application or not. Also, the court will consider whether the party in whose favour the default

500. Order 56 Rule 9 HCCPR Abuja and Order 53 Rule 10 HCCPR Lagos.
501. Order 12 HCCPR Lagos and Order 10 HCCPR Abuja.

judgment was given will be prejudiced and/or embarrassed or not by an order setting it aside. Moreover, the court must be satisfied of the fact of whether or not the applicant's case has merit or not and whether the applicant's conduct throughout the proceedings is worthy to be given sympathetic consideration. These conditions were laid down by the court in *Williams v. Hope Rising*.[502]

492. It must be noted, however, that by a later provision of the rules, a judgment gotten in this circumstance, though a default judgment, can only be set aside on grounds of fraud, non-service or lack of jurisdiction. This is contained in Order 21 Rule 12 HCCPR Abuja that provides:

> Any judgment by default whether under this Order or this Rule shall be final and remain valid and may only be set aside upon application to the court on grounds of fraud, non-service or lack of jurisdiction upon terms as the court may think fit.

The rules of interpretation of statutes are to the effect that a latter provision of a legislation that is at variance with an earlier provision is deemed to modify the earlier one and should prevail over the earlier provision.

In Abuja, a defendant is required to file his statement of defence and the accompanying documents within twenty-one days of the service of the writ of summons on the defendant while in Lagos it is forty-two days from the service of the writ of summons.[503] Where a defendant defaults in filing pleadings within the time allowed, the claimant is entitled to apply for judgment which is a default judgment and the same provisions discussed under default of appearance in paragraph 490 above applies.

§3. Ex Parte Proceedings

493. These are proceedings in which the other party is not a part of and is not put on notice as to the existence of such proceedings. The general rule is that every party in an action is entitled to a fair hearing. This requires all parties in an action be heard. This is a constitutional guarantee. *See* paragraphs 56–58 above for discussions on this and instances when ex parte proceedings are allowed under the law.

The various Rules of court provide that generally all applications made before the court should be on notice to all parties.[504] The following are proceedings that are allowed to be ex parte because of their nature and the objectives they seek to achieve.

502. (1982) 1-2 SC 145.
503. Order 15 Rule 1(2) HCCPR Abuja and Order 17 Rule 1(2) Lagos.
504. Order 43 Rule 1(1) HCCPR Lagos and Order 43 Rule 1 HCCPR Abuja.

I. Anton Pillar Order Proceedings

494. This is a proceeding where an applicant seeks a special type of injunction employed in ensuring that pending the trial of a suit the defendant does not destroy material evidence in his possession that could be prejudicial at the trial. The proceeding has its roots in the English case of *Anton Pillar K.G. v. Manufacturing process Ltd*[505] and is adopted under the various HCCPR.[506]

By section 25 of the Copyrights Act an application for an Anton Pillar order must be made to the Federal HC as copyright matters are within the exclusive jurisdiction of the Federal HC.[507] The order empowers the applicant to enter the premises of the respondent to search and seize goods or documents in possession of the respondent.

For the court to grant this order, certain conditions must be satisfied as stated by the English court in the *Anton Pillar K.G. v. Manufacturing process Ltd*. These conditions are:

(a) The plaintiff must have an extremely strong prima facie case.
(b) The potential or actual damage to his interest must be very serious.
(c) There must be clear evidence that the defendant has in his possession the said incriminating evidence, and there is reasonable fear of him destroying them.
(d) Plaintiff must give satisfactory undertaking as to damages.

495. The application for an Anton Pillar order is by way of a motion ex parte supported with an affidavit and a written address. The proceedings are usually taken by the courts not only ex parte but also in camera due to the nature of the orders sought.

II. Mareva Injunction

496. This is a special type of injunction that attaches temporarily the property or asset (which is not the subject matter of the dispute) of a defendant who the claimant has reasonable cause to believe intends to dissipate such property or asset to frustrate any possible Judgment in favour of the claimant. *See* paragraphs 609–610 below for further discussion on this.

505. (1976) CH 55. *See* s. 25(1) Copyrights Act Cap C28 LFN 2004.
506. Order 42 Rule 4 HCCPR Abuja and Lagos.
507. *See* s. 25(1) Cap C28 LFN 2004. By s. 251(1)(f) of the 1999 Nigerian Constn as amended matters arising from copyrights, patents, designs, trademarks, and passing-off, industrial designs and merchandise marks, business names, commercial and industrial monopolies, combines and trusts, standards of goods and commodities and industrial standards are under the exclusive jurisdiction of the Federal HC.

III. Third-Party Proceedings

497. This is a proceeding initiated by a defendant in an action. It is applicable in situations where the defendant believes that someone who is not a party in the proceedings may bear eventual liability either in whole or in part and as such should be made a party in the action. The purpose of the third-party proceeding is to avoid multiplicity of actions. Since the third party will bear the liability that may be awarded against the defendant, instead of having to bring a separate suit to recover the liability from the third, joining the third party in the existing will effectively avoid the need for a separate suit. Examples where a third-party proceeding would be suitable are cases of defendants with comprehensive insurance cover such as insurance cover over cars. In an action for damages against a defendant in an accident case involving the insured car, the defendant knowing that they are entitled to indemnity from the insurance company will apply to join the insurance company as a third party. The application for a third-party proceeding is by way of a motion ex parte supported with an affidavit stating the grounds for believing that such a third party may bear eventual liability and a written address. The judge may upon such application allow any person to be joined as a third party by the defendant. The order joining the third party and the existing processes shall be served on the third party within the time prescribed for filing defence. This proceeding is provided for under Order 15 Rules 19–22 HCCPR Lagos and Order 13 Rules 21–24 HCCPR Abuja.

498. The third party becomes a party in the action as from the time of service of the order on him and has eight days to enter appearance (thirty days if he is outside jurisdiction, but in Abuja, the rules require the third party to enter appearance not later than thirty-five days from the date of service). A third party having been served who fails to appear or file appropriate pleading is deemed to have admitted the claims and is bound by the judgment of the court in respect to such claims. A party joined as a third party in any proceeding may in turn join any other person as a third party. *See* Order 13 Rule 24 HCCPR Abuja.

499. In addition to the ex parte proceedings described above, there are interlocutory applications that the rules allow to be made by motion ex parte. This is usually as a result of cases where the rules provide that such applications are to be made ex parte or in situations of extreme urgency or where the interest of the other party is not affected. Examples of applications that are made ex parte are application for an order of interim injunction, application for an order of substituted service of court processes and application for leave to apply for any of the prerogative writs.

Chapter 3. Review Proceedings

§1. Appeal

I. Right of Appeal

500. There is no general right of appeal. Right of appeal is conferred by statute (the 1999 Nigerian Constn and the statute creating a court) both on the party seeking to appeal and on the court before which an appeal is lodged.

Section 243(a) of the 1999 Nigerian Constn provides that parties in action have a right of appeal against its judgment and interested parties can appeal against the judgment of a court in a case with the leave of court. A person who was not a party in an action during the trial can be granted leave to appeal against the judgment where such a person satisfies the court that his interest has been sufficiently affected by the decision of the court.

501. In Nigeria, all the superior courts of record having civil jurisdiction have appellate jurisdiction confer on them. Some inferior courts of record also have appellate jurisdiction. *See* paragraph 79 above. An appellant must exhaust an available level of appeal before moving on to the next. For example, an appellant cannot appeal from the decision of an HC to the SC. The appellant must first appeal to the Court of Appeal and if not satisfied with the decision of the Court of Appeal, he can make a further appeal to the SC. The SC has held that it is only after the Court of Appeal has exercised its appellate jurisdiction over an appeal from the HC that the jurisdiction on appeal to the SC can inure.

II. Nature of Appeals

502. The right to appeal conferred by the 1999 Nigerian Constn or a statute can be exercised by a party as of right or with leave of a court. A party can exercise the right to appeal as of right if the party does not require the consent of the court before appealing. Where a party will require the leave of court before appealing, the right of appeal is said to be exercisable with the leave of court.

A. Appeals as of Right

503. For appeal from the Court of Appeal of Nigeria to the SC, cases where an appeal can be made as of right are provided for under section 233(2) of the 1999 Nigerian Constn. While for appeal from the HC/Federal HC to the Court of Appeal of Nigeria as of right is provided for under section 241(1) the 1999 Nigerian Constn. Situations of appeals as of right from the inferior courts of record to the HC are determined by the HC Laws and HC Appeals Rules of the various states including the Federal Capital Territory, Abuja.

B. Appeals with Leave

504. Appeals from the Court of Appeal of Nigeria to the SC that does not fall under appeals as of right are made with the leave of the Court of Appeal of Nigeria. For appeals to the Court of Appeal of Nigeria from the HC/Federal HC leave is required to appeal against the decision of the HC in any case not falling under section 241(1) of the 1999 Nigerian Constn.[508] In addition leave of court is required to appeal against a consent judgment of an HC/Federal HC.[509] Situations of appeals with leave from the inferior courts of record to the HC are determined by the HC Laws and HC Appeals Rules of the various states including the Federal Capital Territory, Abuja.

C. Cases Where There Is No Right of Appeal

505. Parties have no right to appeal against an order of an HC granting unconditional leave to defend to a defendant. Also, there is no appeal against an order absolute dissolving a marriage in a divorce proceeding where the aggrieved party had time and opportunity to appeal from the order of decree nisi but neglected to do so.[510]

III. Procedure on Appeal

A. Time Within Which to Appeal

506. The time within which to appeal is a function of the court the appeal is lodged in and whether the appeal is one against an interlocutory or final decision of the court. Appeals from the Magistrates' Courts to the HCs are made within thirty days.[511] Appeals from the final decisions of the HC to the Court of Appeal is made within three months of the decision, while it is fourteen days in appeals against interlocutory decisions.[512] Appeals from the decision of the Court of Appeal of Nigeria to the SC is made within fourteen days for interlocutory appeals and three months for appeals against final decisions.[513]

507. Where leave is required to file an appeal, the application for leave shall be filed in the first instance in the court that gave the judgment being appealed against. The application shall exhibit a certified true copy of the judgment sought to be appealed against (where the application is made before a judge other than the one who gave the judgment) and a copy of the notice of appeal. Where leave to appeal

508. Section 242 of the 1999 Nigerian Constn.
509. Section 241(2)(C) *ibid.*
510. Section 241(2)(a) and (b) *ibid.*
511. This is contained in the HC Laws of the various States and the Federal Capital Territory Abuja.
512. Section 24(2) Court of Appeal Act Cap C36 LFN 2004.
513. Section 27(2)(a) Supreme Court Act (as amended) Cap S15 LFN 2004.

is filed in the HC and refused, another application for leave may be filed in the Court of Appeal within fifteen days of the ruling refusing the leave and the application to the Court of Appeal shall contain in addition a certified true copy of the ruling refusing the application. After leave is obtained, the appeal can then be filed. Where leave is required, a notice of appeal filed without first obtaining leave is a nullity. The application for leave has to be made within the time required to appeal. Where an appellant appealing from the decision of an HC is out of time in appealing, he has to apply to the Court of Appeal for extension of time within which to appeal, as it is only the appellate court that can extend the time to appeal.[514] The application for enlargement of time within which to appeal is by way of motion on notice supported by affidavit setting forth good and substantial reasons for failing to appeal within time. The notice of appeal containing grounds of appeal should be attached to the application.

508. The court will consider factors like whether there is an unreasonable delay in bringing the application; whether the failure was as a result of negligence, inadvertence or carelessness; whether the supporting affidavit discloses good reason for the failure to file within time; and whether the grounds of appeal shows prima facie good cause.

509. Where time to appeal has elapsed and from the nature of the appeal, leave is required to file the appeal (as an appeal filed out of time without obtaining leave of court is invalid), the application for extension of time to appeal will contain what is termed the trinity prayers, which is an order extending the time within which to seek leave to appeal, an order granting leave to appeal, and an order extending the time within which to file appeal. Where the application for extension of time is granted, the order granting it shall be attached to the notice of appeal.

510. Where a party's appeal contains grounds of appeal that fall under those that can be appealed against as of right and those that require leave, the party files only one notice of appeal and seeks leave to argue the grounds that requires leave. This was the position held by the court in *Okeke v. Petmag Ltd.*[515]

511. A notice of appeal is filed in the registry of the court whose decision is being appealed against. The Registrar will cause the notice of appeal to be served on all the parties mentioned therein. The notice of appeal contains the grounds of appeal, an indication of whether it is the whole or part of the judgment that is appealed against, the exact nature of the relief sought and the names and addresses of all parties affected by the appeal. A notice of appeal that does not contain grounds of appeal is incompetent and will be struck out.

512. All grounds in the notice of appeal must arise from the decision being complained against. Where an appellant wants to argue new grounds, such must seek the leave of court. Grounds of appeal may be grounds of law or of facts or of mixed

514. Section 24(4) Court of Appeal Act Cap C36 LFN 2004.
515. (2005) 4 NWLR (Pt 915) 245 (CA).

law and facts and they may allege a misdirection or error in law. Ideally, a ground of appeal should not allege both a misdirection and error in law.[516] But this will not necessarily make such a ground of appeal incompetent.[517]

513. Where grounds of appeal allege misdirection or error in law, the particulars and the nature of the misdirection or error must be clearly stated. A ground of appeal that is vague or general in terms will be struck out.[518] However, a ground of appeal alleging that the judgment was against the weight of evidence can be without stating particulars. This is referred to as the omnibus ground of appeal in civil appeals.

514. A notice of appeal, which is not signed, is defective and the defect cannot be cured by an amendment, as the nullity inherent in the process is incurable.[519]

515. A respondent who is served with the notice of appeal for an appeal from the HC to the Court of Appeal shall within fourteen days after service on him of the Notice of Appeal, file in the court below ten hard copies and an electronic copy of his full and sufficient address for service with the Registrar of the HC.[520] A respondent who fails to comply with this rule shall not be entitled to be served further processes in the appeal.

516. The Registrar of the HC shall compile and transmit to the Registrar of the Court of Appeal the records of proceedings within sixty days of filing the Notice of Appeal. The Registrar of the HC shall within fourteen days invite parties to reconcile the documents to be included in the records. The appellant may by himself compile the records if the registrar fails to comply with the sixty days requirement. This must be done within thirty days. Parties are allowed to file additional records of appeal within fifteen days of service of records. Ordinarily, an appellate court can only assume jurisdiction over an appeal on a complete record of appeal as the court will be incapacitated to adjudicate on the appeal on the merit and fairly where some part of the records are missing. However, the court has held that depending on the circumstance, an appellate court can with the consent of parties (such consent been recorded in the court's record of proceedings) hear an appeal on incomplete records of appeal.[521]

517. An appeal is entered when the records of appeal have been received in the registry of the Court of Appeal within the time prescribed by the Rules or such other time as extended by the court.. From the moment the appeal is entered, the matter ceases to be within the jurisdiction of the lower court and the appellate court is now vested with jurisdiction over the matter. All subsequent applications in respect of the appeal shall be brought before the Court of Appeal.

---

516. This was the position held in *Nwadike v. Ibekwe* (1987) 4 NWLR (Pt 67) 718 (SC).
517. This was the decision of the court in *Aderounmu v. Olowu* (2000) 4 NWLR (Pt 652) 253 (SC).
518. Order 7 Rule 3 Court of Appeal Rules 2021.
519. *Ada v. Hashimu & Ors* (2017) LPELR-42510 (CA).
520. Order 2 Rule 4(1) Court of Appeal Rules 2021.
521. *Atoshi & Ors v. Agbu & Ors* (2018) LPELR-44477 (CA).

518. A Respondent Notice is filed by a respondent in an appeal who has not also appealed against the decision in question but desires to contend at the hearing of the appeal that the decision should be varied either in any event or in the event that the appeal be allowed in whole or in part. The Respondent Notice is also filed where the respondent wants the appellate court to affirm the decision appealed against on grounds other than those relied on by the court in reaching its decision. A respondent who fails to file the Respondent Notice would not, except with the leave of court, be allowed to make these contentions. The Respondent Notice is filed in the case of an interlocutory appeal within fifteen days after the service of the notice of appeal on the respondent and within thirty for a final appeal.[522]

519. Respondent Notice is distinct from a cross-appeal. A cross-appeal is an independent appeal filed against the judgment by the respondent who is dissatisfied with the judgment of the lower court and wishes to contend a distinct point either of law or facts not covered by the main appeal. A cross-appeal is governed by the same rules as the main appeal. While Respondent Notice is dependent on the notice of appeal filed, a cross-appeal is a separate appeal. Also whereas a Respondent Notice is seeking for an affirmation/variation of the decision of the trial court on grounds different from the one contained in the judgment, a cross-appeal is contending that a point of law or facts in the judgment not covered by the notice of appeal should be reviewed or reversed. As a result, a respondent cannot file a cross-appeal and a Respondent Notice at the same time.

520. A respondent who intends to rely on a preliminary objection to the hearing of the appeal shall give the appellant three clear days' notice before hearing setting out the grounds of objection and shall file such notice together with twenty copies of it with the registry within the same time.

521. Every party to an appeal must file a brief of argument. It is a written argument in support of a party's position in the appeal. A brief of argument must contain the issues for determination, relevant facts in the appeal and submissions on points of law arising from the appeal. It serves the purpose of informing the adversary and the court of what to expect at the appeal.[523] The counsel who filed a brief of argument must sign it. The court has held that non-signing of a brief of argument by a legal practitioner is a jurisdictional issue as it makes the processes incompetent.[524] In appeals from the HC to the Court of Appeal, the appellant fills the Appellant's brief within forty-five days of receipt of the records of appeal. The respondent is required to file the respondent's brief within thirty days of the receipt of the Appellant's brief and where necessary the appellant within fourteen days of the receipt of the respondent's brief file a reply brief. Where an appellant fails to file his brief of argument within the time prescribed or within the time as extended by court, the respondent may apply for dismissal of the appeal. Where the respondent fails to file his brief of argument, he will not be heard in an oral argument during the hearing

---

522. Order 9 Rule 4 Court of Appeal Rules 2021.
523. Order 19 Court of Appeal Rules 2021.
524. *R.A. Oliyide & Sons Ltd v. O.A.U., Ile-Ife* (2018) 8 NWLR (Pt 1622) 564 at 581 (SC).

of the appeal. An appellant who fails to file a reply brief shall be deemed to have conceded all the new points or issues arising from the respondent's brief.

522. Before the hearing of the appeal, an appellant may withdraw his appeal.[525] If an appeal is withdrawn with the consent of all the parties, this shall be a bar to further proceedings and application made by the respondent with regard to Respondent Notices. In such an instance, any sum deposited by the appellant against cost shall be paid out to the appellant. Where all the parties do not consent to the withdrawal, the appeal shall remain on the list and come up for hearing of any issue as to cost or otherwise remaining outstanding between the parties including any application made by the respondent regarding a Respondent Notice.

§2. Cassation

523. There are no courts of cassation in Nigeria. There is only one SC in Nigeria. It is not a court of cassation.

§3. Extraordinary Appeals

524. Strictly speaking there are no extraordinary appeals in Nigeria. However, some appeals are put on fast track and given expedited hearing and determination. The Court of Appeal Practice Direction 2013 enables the presiding Justices of the Court of Appeal divisions to fast track the hearing and determination of interlocutory applications and appeals from the decision of the HC. This is done by the Presiding Justice of each division of the Court of Appeal in collaboration with the Deputy Chief Registrars of the divisions given priority to interlocutory applications and appeals in the areas of listings, considerations and determination of such.[526]

525. The objectives behind these fast tract hearings are to establish a specialized system of case management at the Court of Appeal, to eliminate unnecessary delays in the conduct of appeals, fast track the hearing and determination of interlocutory appeals, reduce time spent in hearing these appeals, minimize delays or adjournment at the instance of counsel and the court and ensure that hearing is not delayed. In line with these objectives, the time for compiling the records of appeal by the registrar for interlocutory appeal is shortened to seven days after the filing of the notice of appeal and also required to summon the parties to settle the documents to be included in the records of appeal within seven days. Where the registrar fails or neglects to do this, it becomes mandatory for the appellant to compile the records of appeal within seven days after the registrar's failure. The appellant shall within fourteen days of receipt of the records of appeal file the appellant's brief. The respondent in turn has ten days after receipt of the appellant's brief, to file the

525. Order 11 Rule 1 Court of Appeal Rules 2021.
526. Paragraph 3 of the Court of Appeal Practice Direction 2013.

respondent's brief. Where necessary, the appellant shall file the reply brief within five days of the service on him of the respondent's brief.

Also appeals from the decision of the LPDC go straight to the SC, and the appellant does not need leave to appeal against the decision of the Committee.

Part V. Incidents

526. Under Nigerian civil procedure, there are issues that are dealt with either before or during the pendency of an action. They include interlocutory applications, withdrawal and discontinuance of an action, and challenge of judges.

Chapter 1. Interlocutory Applications

§1. Meaning of Interlocutory Application

527. These are provisional, interim or intervening applications made usually between the commencement and end of a suit to decide some points or matter but not a final decision of the whole controversy. An interlocutory application can also be made after judgment has been given in an action such as an application for instalment of payment of the judgment debt.

528. The purpose of interlocutory applications is either to cure defects in a substantive suit, obtain some temporary relief especially when time is of essence, nip an action in the bud, or to fulfil a condition precedent to the commencement of a substantive suit.

529. Examples of interlocutory applications are applications for substituted service, extension of time to file pleadings, leave to sue in a representative capacity, application for substitution of a party in an action, interim or interlocutory injunctions, striking out of a suit for non-compliance with the Rules of court or lack of jurisdiction, application for joinder of a party or striking out the name of a party wrongly joined, application to amend a party's pleadings, application for third-party notice, application for adjournment, etc.

§2. Some Specific Interlocutory Applications and Principles for Their Grant or Refusal

I. Interim Injunction

530. This is an injunction applied for ex parte and granted to preserve the status quo/*res* pending the hearing of an application on notice for interlocutory injunction. No application for interim injunction will be granted unless it is accompanied with a motion on notice for an interlocutory injunction. It is usually granted for a specific short time. The HCCPR in Lagos and Abuja makes provision for an interim injunction to last for seven days.[527]

II. Interlocutory Injunction

531. This is an injunction granted to preserve the status quo/*res* pending the determination of the substantive suit. The court has held that the object of this injunction is to protect the applicant against injury by violation of his right for

527. Order 43 Rule 3 HCCPR Lagos and Order 43 Rule 3(1) Abuja.

which he could not be adequately compensated in damages recoverable in the action if the uncertainty is resolved in his favour at the trial.[528]

532. In considering an application for injunction, the court will look at factors such as whether the applicant has a legal right to be protected, whether there are substantial issues to be tried, the possibility of damages not been adequate compensation for the applicant with regard to the anticipated loss, whether the balance of convenience is in favour of the applicant, whether the applicant has undertaken to indemnify the respondent in the event that the order of injunction ought not to have been granted, and the conduct of the applicant.

Where the application is for interim injunction, an additional factor of whether a situation of extreme urgency is presented is also considered.

Procedure for Making Interlocutory Applications

533. Interlocutory applications are made by way of motions. In exceptional cases, they can be made orally. For example, applications for adjournment can be made orally. Until recently, an application for adjournment can also be made by simply sending a letter of adjournment to the court. However, in the case of *The Registered Trustees of the Presbyterian Church of Nigeria v. John Asuquo Etim,*[529] the SC held that a letter of adjournment is a formal document and should be filed and filing fees paid for at the registry of a court before it can be properly submitted before the court. Motions are either made on notice or ex parte. Ordinarily, motions are to be made on notice. Motions can however be made ex parte in the following situations:

(1) when the prayer sought for affects only the interest of the applicant;
(2) when a law or rule stipulates so; and
(3) when time is of the essence. With regard to urgent application, the HCCPR provides that no such application will be heard unless the applicant files with a motion on notice of the application.[530]

See earlier discussions on this in paragraphs 56–58 above. Motions are filed with supporting affidavit deposed to by the applicant or someone else seized of the facts and has the applicant's consent and authority to so do. The affidavit should contain the facts the applicant seeks to rely on for the grant of the applicant. A party can only rely on facts contained in his affidavit. To rely on facts outside the affidavit requires the leave of court. Applicant may not file affidavit where he intends to rely on points of law only or on materials already before the court. Motions must also be accompanied with a written address containing arguments in support of the reliefs

---

528. *Kotoye v. CBN* (1989) 1 NWLR (Pt 98) 419 (SC), *Obeya Memorial Hospital v. AGF* (1987) 7 SC (Pt 1) 52.
529. (2017) 13 NWLR (Pt 1581) 1 (SC).
530. Order 43 Rule 3(1) HCCPR Abuja and Order 43 Rule 3(2) HCCPR Lagos.

sought.[531] In Lagos, every application shall be served within five days of filing otherwise the judge may strike it out.[532] Where a respondent intends to oppose the application, he must file within seven days his affidavit countering the facts averred in the affidavit in support of the motion. The respondent need not do this where he intends to rely on points of law only or on facts already before the court. The respondent also files a written address in opposition to the application. The applicant may, on being served with the respondent's processes file and serve within seven days a reply on points of law and may also file a further affidavit[533] or Reply affidavit.[534] There must be at least two clear days between the service of a motion on notice and the day for hearing.[535]

534. Where there are two applications before the court for hearing, the court will first hear the one that will lead to substantial justice. The court will hear the constructive application (the one that seeks to correct an error to allow the case to go on) first before taking the one that seeks to terminate the case. For example, where there is an application for default judgment by a claimant and an application for extension of time to enter appearance and file defence by the defendant before a court, the court will hear the application of the defendant first. Where the defendant's application is granted, the claimant's motion becomes needless and would be withdrawn and struck out. This position is supported by the decision of the court in *NALSA & Team Associates v. NNPC.*[536]

---

531. *See* Order 43 Rule 1(2) HCCPR Lagos and Order 43 Rule 1 HCCPR Abuja.
532. Order 43 Rule 1(3) HCCPR Lagos.
533. The Lagos HCCPR refers to the additional affidavit filed by the applicant as a Further affidavit.
534. The Abuja HCCPR refers to the additional affidavit filed by the applicant as a Reply affidavit.
535. Order 43 Rule 5 HCCPR Lagos and Order 43 Rule 6 HCCPR Abuja.
536. (1991) 11 SCNJ 51.

Chapter 2. Withdrawal or Discontinuance of Action

§1. Withdrawal or Discontinuance Before Defence

535. Where a defendant in an action has not served his statement of defence and the claimant intends to withdraw the action, the HCCPR requires that the claimant may by notice in writing duly filed and served, withdraw or discontinue wholly or in part the claim, either against any or all of the defendants. Under the HCCPR Abuja, it also includes a situation where the defence has been filed and served on the claimant but before the claimant takes any further proceedings in the action.[537] The claimant in such a case is liable to pay such defendants' cost of the action. Where the action was not wholly withdrawn, the claimant is liable to pay the cost of the matter so withdrawn or discontinued. That a matter was withdrawn or discontinued cannot be a defence to any subsequent claim.[538]

§2. Withdrawal or Discontinuance after Defence

536. Where a defendant has filed and served on the claimant his defence, a claimant can still withdraw or discontinue the action or any part of it. This has to be done before taking any further steps in the proceedings. It is done with the leave of court, and the judge will strike out the action upon such terms and conditions as the judge may order. The effect of a withdrawal at this stage is that the claimant shall not be able to make any subsequent claim on the same or substantially the same facts until the terms imposed by the judge have been fully complied with.[539]

537. The HCCPR of Abuja provides that the same principles are applicable where a defendant applies that the whole or any part of the grounds of the defendant's defence or counterclaim be withdrawn or struck out.[540]

§3. Withdrawal or Discontinuance by Consent

538. Where a matter is ready for trial, it may be withdrawn by either party in the action upon producing to the Registrar of the court, consent to withdraw in writing signed by the parties. Consequent upon this, the judge shall strike out the matter without the necessity of the parties or their counsel attending court. This procedure for withdrawal is only provided for under the HCCPR of Lagos.[541]

537. Order 24 Rule 1(1) HCCPR Abuja.
538. Order 25 Rule 1 HCCPR Lagos and Order 24 Rule 1 HCCPR Abuja.
539. Order 25 Rule 2(2) HCCPR Lagos and Order 24 Rule 1(4) HCCPR Abuja.
540. Order 24 Rule 1(5) HCCPR Abuja.
541. Order 25 Rule 3 HCCPR Lagos.

§4. Withdrawal or Discontinuance at Trial

539. Where trial has already commenced before the claimant withdraws the action or a part of it with the leave of court, the judge may dismiss the claim wholly or in part or make such order as the judge deems fit.

Chapter 3. Challenge of Judges

540. The principle of fair hearing is fundamental to all court proceedings, and the lack of it will vitiate any proceedings so held. A breach of fair hearing leads to the inevitable conclusion that the end result of the proceedings cannot be fair, as an unfair method cannot produce a fair result. The SC speaking on the issue of allegation of bias against a judge held that:

> In considering whether there was real likelihood of bias, the court does not look at the mind of the Justice himself or at the mind of the chairman of the tribunal, or whoever it may be who sits in a judicial capacity. It does not look to see if there was a real likelihood that he would, or did in fact favour one side at the expense of the other. The court looks at the impression, which would be given to other people. Even if he was impartial as could be, nevertheless, if right-minded persons would think that, in the circumstances, there was real likelihood of bias, on his part, then he should not sit. And if he does sit, his decision cannot stand.[542]

541. Bias in its ordinary meaning is an opinion or feeling in favour of one side in a dispute resulting in the likelihood that the court so influenced will be unable to hold an even scale. Where reasonable people would think that in the circumstance of a case there was real likelihood of bias, then the decision of such a judge cannot stand. The basis of this principle is that justice must be rooted in confidence, which is destroyed when right-minded people go away with the impression that the judge was biased. The courts have held that:

> To allege bias or disqualify a judge from performing his judicial function on ground of interest (other than pecuniary or proprietary interest) in the subject matter of the proceedings, a real likelihood of bias must be made to appear not only from the material ascertained by the party complaining but from such further facts as he might readily have ascertained and easily verified in the course of the proceedings.[543]

542. There is no specific law saying this is how to proceed when a party believes that a judicial officer's impartiality is in question with regard to a given case. The practice is for the counsel or the party to apply to the court either orally or by a motion requesting that the judge transfers the matter to another judge or sends it back to the registry for reassignment to another judge. This is a judicial procedure in handling such an issue. Where the judge whose impartiality is called to question refuses to step aside from the case after hearing the application, the party can write

---

542. *Akingbola v. F.R.N.* (2018) 14 NWLR (Pt 1640) 395 at 414 (SC). In this case, the SC was reiterating its earlier position in *Abiola v. F.R.N.* (1995) 7 NWLR (Pt 405) 1 at 24 (SC).
543. *Aondoaka v. Obot* (2016) 6 NWLR (Pt 1508) 280 at 322–323 (CA).

a letter to the Chief Judge of the state or the Chief Judge of the Federal Capital Territory, Abuja for an administrative action transferring the matter. The Chief Judge of the state will transfer the matter to another court where he finds the application meritorious.

543. Where a judge is a party to a suit or unable, for personal interest or any other sufficient reason, to adjudicate on a matter, the Chief Judge shall direct some other judge to hear the matter.[544]

544. In addition, it has earlier been discussed that the code of conduct for judicial officers puts an obligation on a judge to step aside from presiding over a matter if his impartially would be in doubt. *See* paragraph 147 above.

---

544. Section 10 District Court Act of the Federal Capital Territory, Abuja *supra*.

Part VI. Legal Aid and Legal Costs

Chapter 1. Legal Aid

545. Legal assistance is available to persons who cannot afford to pay for legal representation. The Legal Aid Act[545] makes provision for assistance to indigent persons to enable them to access justice. The Legal Aid Act establishes the Legal Aid Council (LAC) that is mandated to establish an office in each of the states of the Federation of Nigeria, headed by an officer of appropriate rank whose task is to provide legal aid services in the state.

§1. Categories of Legal Aid Provided by the LAC

546. Legal aid, advice and access to justice is provided for in three broad areas namely:

(1) The Criminal Defence Services;
(2) Advice and Assistance in civil matters including legal representation in court; and
(3) Community Legal Services.

The rendering of these services is subject to the merit and indigence test. This means for the LAC to take on any case, such a case must pass both tests. Since the LAC's ability to carry out its functions is largely dependent on the availability of funds that is universally recognized as a scarce resource cases are sieved on the basis of the merit of the case and the financial status of the individual for whom legal aid is contemplated. On the issue of merit, cases that fall within the areas of services provided by the LAC are further subjected to the ability of the persons requiring such assistance showing to the satisfaction of the Director-General of the LAC or any person authorized by the LAC that there are reasonable grounds for requiring legal aid to take such actions, or defending such actions, or being a party in such actions. Legal aid may be refused where it appears to the Director-General of the LAC or any person authorized by the LAC that it is unreasonable that a person be given legal aid in the particular circumstance of the case.[546]

545. Legal Aid Act 2011.
546. Section 8(6) Legal Aid Act 2011.

547. A unit known as the Civil Litigation Services Unit is established by the LAC for the purpose of assisting indigent persons to access advice, assistance and representation in court where the interest of justice demands to enable such persons to secure, defend, enforce, protect or otherwise exercise any right, obligation, duty, privilege, interest or service that they are entitled to under Nigerian legal system. The assistance rendered to indigent persons also extends to issues of breach or denial of any of their rights, obligations, duties, privileges or services.

548. The legal aid provided is in the form of assistance usually provided by private legal practitioners in steps preliminary or incidental to commencing proceedings in court, legal representation before any court of persons qualified for legal aid, and such additional aid as may be prescribed. The LAC is also mandated to establish, maintain and develop a service known as Community Legal Service for the purpose of promoting individual services particularly, ensuring that individuals have access to services that effectively meet their needs. Community Legal Services are services that may include non-court advisory services, public awareness service, mediation, and other counselling services required generally.[547] However, for the purpose of providing legal aid and advice the Legal Aid Act specifically provide that Community Legal Service means:[548]

(a) the provision of general information about the law and legal system and the availability of legal services;
(b) the provision of assistance in preventing or settling or otherwise resolving disputes about legal rights and duties;
(c) the provision of assistance in enforcing decisions by which such disputes are resolved;
(d) the provision of assistance in financial support and rendering; and
(e) the provision of assistance with regard to claims against public authorities, private organizations and individuals.

549. The Director-General of the LAC reserves the right to set the limit of assistance provided under the Community Legal Service. Every person authorized by the LAC to exercise the functions of the Community Legal Services are under obligation to ensure they exercise these functions in such a manner that promote improvement in the quality of services provided for the benefit of those who need them. They must also see to it that the services provided in respect of any matter are appropriate having regard to its nature and importance. Moreover, they must aim to achieve swift and fair resolution of disputes in order to avoid the necessity of a protracted court proceeding.

547. Section 24 Legal Aid Act 2011.
548. Section 8(7) Legal Aid Act 2011.

§2. Persons Eligible for Legal Aid

550. The Legal Aid Act provides that only persons whose income does not exceed the minimum wage in Nigeria are entitled to legal aid. Currently, the National minimum monthly wage in Nigeria is NGN 30,000.[549] However, the Governing Board, which is a component of the LAC, may in exceptional cases grant legal aid services to a person whose earnings exceeds the minimum wage provided that the LAC will have the right to recover the expenses incurred in giving legal aid to such a person by retaining an amount equal to 10% of damages awarded in the case in the person's favour and the costs warded to such a person.[550] In addition, the Governing Board may approve the giving of legal aid services on a contributory basis to a person whose income is as high as more than ten times the national minimum wage on two conditions.

551. First, the LAC will have the right to recover the expenses incurred in giving legal aid to such a person by retaining an amount equal to 10% of damages awarded in the case in the person's favour and the costs warded to such a person. Second, the person shall be entitled to a refund of his contributions from the cost awarded in his favour in the case. The contribution shall not exceed the appropriate sum calculated in the manner prescribed for that purpose. In determining a person's earning for the purpose of ascertaining eligibility for legal aid, the person's income, his personal and real property shall be taken into account.[551] But prescribed commitments of such a person shall be deducted from his resources to ascertain his means.[552] A person seeking legal aid or advice commits an offence where such a person knowingly or recklessly in giving any information required under the Legal Aid Act makes a false statement in a material particular. On summary conviction, the person shall be liable to a fine of NGN 50,000 or a term of imprisonment not exceeding six months or both.[553]

552. By section 14 of the Legal Aid Act, the staff of the LAC shall maintain panels of legal practitioners willing to act for persons receiving legal aid. The legal practitioners may represent the legal aid recipients on a pro bono basis or otherwise. There may be separate panels for different purposes, different courts and different districts as the LAC may deem fit. A legal practitioner is entitled to have his name on the appropriate panel or panels unless the designated staff of the LAC has a reason for excluding such a legal practitioner. Such reasons include previous conduct of such a legal practitioner when acting for or selected to represent a person receiving legal aid or it may be tied to the general conduct of such a legal practitioner. In addition, it is only legal practitioners who have paid their annual practising fees that can be appointed by the LAC to act for persons receiving legal aid. A legal practitioner whose name is excluded from the panel and is aggrieved can refer

549. National Minimum Wage Act 2019.
550. Section 10(2) Legal Aid Act 2011.
551. *See* ss 11 and 23 *ibid.*
552. Section 10(2) *ibid.*
553. Section 21 Legal Aid Act 2011.

the matter to the Director-General of the LAC and if not satisfied with the outcome of the referral can appeal to the Governing Board of the LAC. A legal practitioner or another service provider who acts for a person receiving assistance from the LAC shall be paid for the services rendered from a legal aid fund. Acting for a person who is receiving legal aid includes acting indirectly for such a person such as acting as an agent for his legal practitioner.[554] The amount payable shall be as such determined by the LAC. Thereafter such legal practitioner shall not be entitled to payments charge from the person receiving legal aid nor can the legal practitioner recover any amounts from such a person by way of costs in respect of work assigned to him by the LAC or by way of disbursement incurred on behalf of that person in connection with the work except the Governing Council approves.

553. To safeguard this provision, the Legal Aid Act provides that any agreement in writing or not and whether made before or after the commencement of the Act or that has the effect of excluding, restricting or modifying the operation of this provision is void to the extent of the exclusion.[555] Legal practitioners who are undergoing the compulsory one-year National Youth Service Corps can if the LAC so direct act for persons receiving legal aid, but the LAC shall not pay them any professional fees and such legal practitioner shall only be entitled to stipend and travelling allowance.[556] The LAC can also partner with or engage the services of non-government organizations and law clinics in rendering legal aid or assistance to persons entitled to legal aid under the Legal Aid Act in a manner consistent with its mandate. In this light, the LAC shall keep a register on non-government organizations and law clinics that are engaged in the provision of legal aid or assistance. Also, the LAC may grant licences to persons who have undergone a prescribed course in paralegal services to render such services in appropriate situations.[557] The Legal Aid Act describes a paralegal as a person though not admitted to the Nigerian Bar to practise law performs substantially legal tasks under the direction and supervision of a legal practitioner.[558] It is pertinent to state that the LAC shall not be liable in any way to pay costs awarded against a person granted legal aid. A person granted legal aid services is exempted from payment of fees in court such as payments of filing fees.[559]

§3. Legal Aid and Pro Bono Services by Lawyers

554. Legal aid to indigent Nigerians is so important to society and the legal profession in particular that handling a required number of cases on a pro bono basis is one of the conditions for having been conferred with the distinguished rank of Senior Advocate of Nigeria. Section 18 of the Legal Aid Act provides that:

554. Section 15(4) *ibid.*
555. Section 15(2) *ibid.*
556. Section 16 *ibid.*
557. Section 17(3) *ibid.*
558. Section 24 *ibid.*
559. Section 11 *ibid.*

A legal practitioner who applies to be appointed to the rank of Senior Advocate of Nigeria shall be required to show evidence of diligent conduct of not less than three pro bono cases in the legal year immediately preceding his application.

555. A legal practitioner who institutes or conducts a case for a person entitled to legal aid under the Legal Aid Act on a pro bono basis must register such with LAC who shall keep a record of it and monitor the progress of the case. It is professional misconduct for a legal practitioner handling a matter on a pro bono basis to neglect or abandon it.[560] The RPC in Nigeria specifically prohibits a legal practitioner assigned to defend an indigent prisoner from withdrawing from the matter except for substantial reasons, but such legal practitioner must deploy his best efforts in defending such accused person.[561]

§4. Proceedings in *Forma Pauperis*

556. The HCCPR of Lagos and Abuja makes provision for persons not covered by the Legal Aid Act to sue *in forma pauperis*. The Court (in Lagos, it is the Chief Judge) may allow a person to sue or defend *in forma pauperis* where the court is satisfied that the person's means will not enable the person to engage the services of a legal practitioner in the prosecution or defence of a case and there is reasonable ground for suing or defending in the circumstance.[562]

557. A person seeking to sue under this procedure shall forward a written application to the Chief Judge accompanied by an affidavit signed and sworn to by the applicant stating that by reason of poverty, the applicant is unable to afford the services of a legal practitioner. Where the Chief Judge is of the view that the application has merit, the Chief Judge shall appoint a legal practitioner to represent the applicant and such legal practitioner so appointed shall not dispense of his services without the leave of the Chief Judge. The applicant or the legal practitioner shall not discontinue, settle or compromise the action without the leave of court.

558. Court fees payable by a person allowed to sue or defend *in forma pauperis* may be remitted wholly or in part as the court deems fit. Also, such a person shall not be liable to pay or receive cost except the court otherwise direct. Except where the Chief Judge permits, the legal practitioner shall not accept any payment from the applicant or any person connected to the applicant or the action taken or defend as this will lead to a revocation of the order appointing the legal practitioner. Where the legal practitioner discovers that the applicant has means beyond that disclosed in the affidavit, he is obliged to bring this fact in writing to the attention of the registrar. The Chief Judge (in Lagos, it is the Chief Registrar) is empowered to revoke the order granting the application and where that happens, the applicant shall not be

560. Section 18(3) Legal Aid Act 2011.
561. Rule 38 RPC 2007.
562. Order 54 Rule 2 HCCPR Abuja and Order 51 Rule 2 HCCPR Lagos.

entitled to the benefit of suing or defending *in forma pauperis* in the case to which the application relates except there is an order to the contrary.

559. Every other order, notice or application on behalf of the applicant is signed by the legal practitioner except an application for the discharge of the legal practitioner.

560. The court may order payment for the legal practitioner appointed under this procedure from monies recovered by the applicant or may charge in favour of the legal practitioner any property recovered by the applicant such sums as it deems fit.

561. The order granting the application to sue *in forma pauperis* does not extend to appeal *in forma pauperis* except by leave of the HC or the Court of Appeal. Where such leave is granted the procedure described in paragraphs 556–559 will apply *mutatis mutandis* to all the proceedings on the appeal.[563]

563. Order 54 Rule 9 HCCPR Abuja and Order 51 Rule 2 HCCPR Lagos.

Chapter 2. Legal Costs

562. Legal cost refers to the cost of accessing and getting justice in any given situation using the administration of justice system. This cost includes the cost of enlisting the services of a lawyer and court fees. Cost follows events unless there are circumstances warranting the contrary. The award of cost involves judicial discretion, which is exercised based on certain principles and premised on the pleadings of the parties and the evidence adduced in support. Legal cost cannot cure all financial loss sustained in litigation but is meant to compensate a party for the expenses incurred in prosecuting or defending an action.

563. A party who did not receive legal assistance as discussed in paragraphs 549–550 and 555 above will have to personally pay the cost of prosecuting or defending a case. A claimant who intends to claim litigation cost can claim it specifically in his originating process and pleadings and adduce evidence to prove the claim.

564. Order 53 Rule 1 of the HCCPR Lagos provides for the principle to be observed in fixing cost.[564] Essentially from the provisions, a party who is in the right is to be indemnified for the necessary expenses incurred in the course of the proceedings and compensated for the time and effort in coming to court. The expenses to be considered include cost of legal representation and assistance of the successful party to the extent determined as reasonable by the judge, travel and other expenses of parties and witnesses to the extent adjured as reasonable by the judge, and such other expenses as the judge determines in the circumstances as the cost that ought to be recovered. Where the court orders that cost be paid, the amount to be paid where practicable is determined summarily by the judge at the time of delivering the judgment or making the order otherwise the judge shall refer it to an assessment officer.

565. Where an offer of settlement was earlier made in relation to the Pre-action Protocol or in the course of a case management conference or during an ADR platform, and it was rejected by the party who eventually succeeds in the action, but the award made by the court is not in excess of the settlement offer, the successful party shall pay the costs of the losing party from the time of the settlement offer to the date the judgment was delivered.[565]

566. Where in the circumstances of the case, the judge in his discretion decides not to award costs, the judgment of the court will usually contain an order that the parties are to bear their respective costs.

---

564. Similar, but not as elaborate, provisions are contained in Order 56 Rule 1(3)(4)(5) of the HCCPR Abuja.
565. Order 53 Rule 2 HCCPR Lagos. The HC of Lagos State (Expeditious Disposal of Civil Cases) Practice Direction No. 2 of 2019 on Pre-action Protocol also contains alternative cost to be borne by such a winning party. The Practice Direction empowers the court to impose a minimum of NGN 100,000, which shall be deducted or added to monetary reliefs awarded in the final judgment.

Part VII. Evidence

Chapter 1. Burden of Proof

567. Burden of proof means the duty a party bears to adduce evidence to establish a case. By section 131 of the Evidence Act 2011 any person who desires any court to give judgment as to any legal right or liability dependent on facts which he asserts shall prove that those facts exist. In civil cases, the burden of proof is on the person against whom the judgment of the court will be given if no evidence were produced on either side regard been given to any presumption that may arise in the pleadings. This person is usually the claimant who is the one that filed a claim and will lose if no evidence at all is led. Where the claimant adduces evidence that ought reasonably to satisfy the court that the facts sought to be proved is established, the burden will now shift to the defendant who will now be the person to lose in the case if no further evidence is adduced.

568. There are two types of burden of proof. First, there is the legal burden of proof, which is the burden that rests on the party who institutes an action in court. This burden rests at all times on the claimant and does not shift. Second, there is evidential burden of proof, which is the burden on a party to adduce evidence at any point in the trial. This burden rests first on the claimant and where he has led satisfactory evidence, it shifts to the defendant and so on. This general position that the legal burden of proof rests on the claimant can change based on the pleadings. For example in a claim based on negligence arising from an accident, where the claimant pleads *res ipsa loquitur*, the legal burden of proof is on the defendant to prove that the accident did not occur as a result of his negligent act.

569. Standard of proof means the quantum of proof required in order for a party on who the burden of proof lies to successfully discharge the burden. In civil cases in Nigeria, the standard of proof generally is on the balance of probability or preponderance of evidence. However, there are exceptions to this position. They include the standard of proof required to prove special damages, which is that special damages must be proved strictly. Also, allegations of crime in a civil action like fraud, electoral offences like ballot stuffing, snatching, etc. require proof beyond reasonable doubt. The SC iterated this position in the case of *Akeredolu v. Mimiko*.[566] Where in a civil suit, there are allegations of crime in the pleading, the court will have to adopt the doctrine of severance of pleadings to the effect that the

566. (2014) 1 NWLR (Pt 1388) 402 (SC).

court separates the facts to be established by balance of probability from the facts requiring proof beyond reasonable doubt. Where the facts requiring proof beyond reasonable doubt outweighs the ones requiring proof on a balance of probability, then the predominant standard of proof will be proof beyond reasonable despite the fact that it is a civil case and vice versa. In addition, in matrimonial cases, the standard of proof is to the reasonable satisfaction of the court.

570. Only facts in dispute need to be proved. Also, no fact of which the court shall take judicial notice needs to be proved. Section 122 of the Evidence Act lists the facts that the court shall take judicial notice of. With respect to matters listed in the section and all matters of public history, literature, science or art the court may resort to appropriate books or documents of reference to aid it. However, if called upon by any person to take judicial notice of any fact, a court may refuse to do so unless and until such person produces any such book or document, as it may consider necessary to enable it to do so. In any civil proceeding, no facts need to be proved which the parties or their agents have agreed to admit at the hearing or which before the hearing the parties agreed to admit by writing under their hands, or which by any rule or pleadings in force at the time they are deemed to have admitted by the pleadings.[567] However, the court may in its discretion require such facts to be proved otherwise than by such admission. Also, proof shall not be required to prove facts of common knowledge.[568] In this regard, proof shall not be required of a fact the knowledge of which is reasonably open to question and which is common knowledge in the locality in which the proceedings is being held, or generally or capable of verification by reference to a document the authority of which cannot reasonably be questioned.

571. Facts requiring proof at trial shall be proved by deposition and oral examination of witnesses in open court.[569] All agreed documents or other exhibits may be tendered from the Bar or by the party where he is not represented by counsel. Real evidence is tendered during trial and the oral examination of a witness during the witness evidence-in-chief is limited to confirming the witness' deposition and tendering in evidence of disputed documents or other evidence referred to in the deposition. However, a judge will allow a subpoenaed witness to give oral evidence-in-chief without having sworn to a written statement in appropriate cases.[570]

572. The rules regarding burden of proof are fundamental rules as the Evidence Act regulates the conduct of trials in courts of record in Nigeria and parties cannot by agreement derogate from it.

567. Section 123 of the Evidence Act 2011.
568. Section 124 of the Evidence Act 2011.
569. Order 36 Rule 1 HCCPR Lagos and Order 34 Rule 1 HCCPR Abuja.
570. Order 36 Rule 1(4) HCCPR Lagos and Order 34 Rule 1 HCCPR Abuja.

Chapter 2. Admissibility of Evidence

573. The Evidence Act 2011 makes provision for five means of adducing evidence before a court in a matter. They are by documentary evidence, oral evidence, real evidence, affidavit evidence and admissions.

Documentary Evidence

574. The basis of admissibility of a document is relevancy. The document must be relevant to the case before the court as distilled from the pleadings. A party who seeks to tender a document must have pleaded it. As earlier stated in the discussions on pleadings, what the rules of pleadings require is that you plead facts showing the existence of such document and not necessarily pleading the document itself. A party cannot tender a document that was not pleaded unless for a special reason, the court orders otherwise. Generally, a party can only do that where the court has granted an application to amend the pleadings to reflect the document sought to be admitted. In addition to the issue of relevancy with respect to admissibility of a document, section 14 of the Evidence Act 2011 gives the court discretion as to whether to admit or not a document though the document is relevant. The court's discretion is exercised taking into consideration the matters listed in section 15 of the Act in deciding whether the desirability of admitting the document is or is not outweighed by the undesirability of admitting it. As such a document that was not properly obtained or was obtained unlawfully may be rejected by the court though it is relevant if the court is of the view that the desirability of admitting it is outweighed by the undesirability of admitting it.

575. Documentary evidence is admitted either in its primary or secondary form. Primary Evidence of a document means the original document itself produced for the court's inspection.[571] The original of both public and private documents are admissible as primary evidence. In *Kassim v. the State*,[572] the SC held that the original of a public document is admissible laying to rest the earlier controversial position that it is only the certified true copy of a public document that is admissible in evidence. Public documents by section 102 of the Evidence Act 2011 are documents forming the official acts or records of the official acts of the sovereign authority, official bodies or tribunals or public officers, legislative, judicial and executive, whether of Nigeria or elsewhere and public records kept in Nigeria of private documents. Examples of public documents include: Federal Government Gazette, court records, certificate of call to bar of a person in the custody of the Nigerian Law School, etc.

576. Secondary evidence of a document is any copy of the document other than the original. Secondary evidence of a public document is certified true copies of that

571. Section 86 of the Evidence Act 2011.
572. (2017) LPELR-42586 (SC).

document, and it is the only admissible secondary evidence of a public document.[573] As such once a copy of a public document is not certified it is inadmissible. A document inadmissible in law is invalid for all intents and purposes. It cannot form the basis of any competent finding of a court of record. Where it is wrongly admitted, the same court has the power and jurisdiction to expunge it at the judgment since a court can only base its judgment on legally admissible evidence.[574]

577. Secondary evidence of documents other than public documents includes copies made from the original by mechanical or electronic processes which in themselves ensure the accuracy of the copy and copies compared with such copies, copies made from or compared with the original, counterparts of documents as against the parties who did not execute them, and oral accounts of the contents of a document given by some person who has himself seen it.[575] Secondary evidence of a document may be given in the following circumstances:

(a) Where the original is shown or appears to be in the possession or power of the person against whom the document is to be proved or anybody legally bound to produce the document and has not done so after a notice to produce has been given to him.
(b) Where the existence, condition or content of the document have been proved to be admitted in writing by the person against whom it is sought to be proved or his representative in interest.
(c) Where the original has been destroyed or lost.
(d) The original is of such a nature as not to be easily movable.
(e) The original is a document of which a certified true copy is permitted by law.
(f) The original is a public document.
(g) The original consists of numerous accounts or other documents which cannot conveniently be examined in court and the fact to be proved is the general result of the whole collection.
(h) The document is an entry in a banker's book.

578. Where a secondary evidence of a document is to be tendered in an action, counsel in the case must lay the necessary foundation for such document to be admitted. In essence, counsel will guide the witness to explain from the witness box his inability to produce the original.

Admissions

579. Any party in a matter may by notice in his pleading or otherwise in writing admit the truth of any fact or the whole fact stated in the other party's pleadings. A party may by notice filed and served not later than the seven days before the first

573. Sections 90(1)(c) and 105 of the Evidence Act 2011; *Hassan v. EFCC* (2014) 1 NWLR (Pt 1389) 607 (CA).
574. *Nwaogu v. Atuma* (2013) 11 NWLR (Pt 1364) 117 (SC).
575. Section 87 Evidence Act 2011.

Case Management Conference require any other party to admit any specific fact. Where admission of fact has been made, either on the pleadings or otherwise at the Case Management Conference or at any other stage of the proceedings, the judge may upon application by the party in whose favour such admissions are made make such orders or grant judgment pending the determination of any other question between the parties.

Admissibility of Computer Generated Evidence

580. By section 258 of the Evidence Act 2011, a computer means any device for storing and processing information. In the same section, document includes any device by means of which information is recorded, stored or retrievable including computer output. Statements in a document produced by a computer shall be admissible as evidence of any fact stated in it of which direct oral evidence would be admissible if it is shown that the following conditions are satisfied:[576]

(a) The document must have been produced by the computer during a period over which the computer was used regularly to store or process information for the purposes of any activities regularly carried on over the period for profit or not by anybody or body corporate.
(b) Over the said period there was a regular supply of information of the kind contained in the statement or of the kind from which the information so contained is derived to the computer in the ordinary course of those activities.
(c) Throughout the material part of that period the computer was operating properly or even where it was not, the fault in the computer was not such as to affect the production of the document or the accuracy of its content.
(d) The information contained in the statement reproduces or is derived from the information supplied to the computer in the ordinary course of those activities.

581. The SC has held that evidence to satisfy these conditions can be given by a witness orally in court or by tendering a certificate signed by a person occupying a responsible position in relation to the operation of the relevant device or the management of the relevant activities.[577] The court has held that there is no single approach to authentication of electronically produced evidence across board. Instead, the most appropriate form of authenticating electronic evidence will often depend on the nature of the evidence and the circumstances of each particular case. It can be by an authentication certificate or direct oral testimony.[578] The certificate shall in addition to dealing with matters stated in section 84(2) of the Evidence Act 2011, identify the document containing the statement and describe the manner in which it was produced and give such particulars of any device involved in the production of the document as may be appropriate to show that the document was produced by a computer.

576. Section 84 Evidence Act 2011.
577. *See Dickson v. Sylva* (2016) LPELR-41257 (SC).
578. *Brila Energy Ltd v. FRN* (2018) LPELR-43926 (CA).

582. The SC held in *Dickson v. Sylva*[579] that merely getting a document admitted in court is not enough but that the party tendering the document must go ahead to relate to the court the relevance of the document to the case so as to avoid dumping of documents on the court which will make such document to be of no benefit to the party that tendered them. On the issue of who is the proper person to tender a document, the court has held that the maker of a document is the proper person to tender it. Where a document is not tendered by the maker it will affect the weight that the court will attach to it.[580]

Translation of Documents

583. For a document to be admitted in a court in Nigeria, the document must be written in English, that is the language of the court in Nigeria. As such, when a document was originally written in a language other than English, it must be transcribed into English before it can be admitted.

Oral Evidence

584. Facts are proved in court by oral evidence. Under the HCCPR, oral evidence of witness in his evidence-in-chief is limited to confirming his witness statement on oath. In cross-examination and re-examination a witness gives oral evidence. Except where allowed by law, oral evidence shall in all cases be direct and must be the evidence of what a witness saw, heard or perceived.

Hearsay Evidence

585. This is evidence given by a witness of events he did not see, hear or perceive himself. Evidence given by a witness of a statement made by a person who himself is not called as a witness may or may not be hearsay. It is hearsay and inadmissible when the object of the evidence is to prove the truth of the facts asserted by the statements. It is not hearsay when it is proposed to establish by evidence not the truth but the fact that it was made. Section 37 Evidence Act 2011 provides that hearsay evidence is inadmissible except as provided for under the Act. Some of the exceptions are:

(a) Statements whether written or oral made by a person who is dead as to the cause of his death or circumstances of the event which resulted in his death in cases in which the cause of his death is in question would be admissible if at the time of making the statements the maker believed himself to be in danger of approaching death although he may entertain at the time of making in hopes of recovering.
(b) The declaration of a deceased testator as to his testamentary intentions and the content of his will are admissible when his will is lost and there is a question as

579. *Supra.*
580. *Chukwu v. FRN* (2013) 12 NWLR (Pt 1369) 488 (CA).

to the content, or the question is whether an existing will is genuine or was improperly obtained or the question is whether any and which of more existing documents than one constitute his will.

(c) Evidence given by a witness in a judicial proceedings is admissible for the purpose of proving the truth of the facts which it states in a subsequent judicial proceeding or at a later stage in the same proceeding when the witness cannot be called either because the witness is dead, cannot be found, has become incapable of giving evidence or his attendance cannot reasonably be procured. However for this evidence to be admissible the proceedings must be between the same parties, the adverse party must have had the opportunity to cross examine the witness in the first proceedings and the question in issue were substantially the same in the first proceeding as in the second one.

Real Evidence

586. This is evidence consisting of material things other than documents. Where oral evidence refers to the existence or condition of any material thing, the court may require the production of such for its inspection or inspect any movable or immovable property the inspection of which may be material to the proper determination of the question in dispute.[581]

Affidavit Evidence

587. In any civil proceeding, a court may make an order at any stage directing that certain facts be proved by affidavit with or without the attendance of the deponent for cross-examination. For an affidavit to be used in court for any purpose the original must be filed in court, and it is only the original or an office copy of it that shall be recognized by the court.[582] An affidavit is headed in the cause and matter in which it is sworn. It carries the suit number and names of the parties. It is written in numbered paragraphs and contains a mandatory clause called the oath clause that is usually the last paragraph in the affidavit.

588. Facts contained in an affidavit constitute evidence, and the court can properly act on it without calling for oral evidence. Also, documents exhibited in an affidavit constitute evidence. The fact that an affidavit purports to have been sworn in the manner prescribed in by law shall be prima facie evidence the seal or signature of any court, Magistrate or other officer or person mentioned in, or appended or subscribed to any such affidavit and the authority of the court, Judge Magistrate or other officer or person to administer oaths.[583]

---

581. Section 127(1) of the Evidence Act 2011.
582. Section 108 *ibid.*
583. Section 111 *ibid.*

589. Before an affidavit can be admitted in evidence, it must not have been sworn before a person on whose behalf the same is offered or before such a person's legal practitioner or partner or clerk of the legal practitioner. *See* paragraphs 598–599 below for more discussion on affidavit evidence.

Chapter 3. Administration of Evidence

§1. Forced Production of Documents

590. A person whether a party or not in a cause may be summoned to produce a document without being summoned to give evidence or the person may be summoned to both produce a document and give evidence. Where a person who is summoned to produce a document causes such document to be produced in court, the court may dispense with the person's personal attendance.[584] There are situations when there is need to compel a witness to produce a document or testify in court. For example, where the witness is a public servant he will need official permission from his superiors to come and testify in court. The summons or subpoena will serve as notice for him to be granted the release. Also, where the witness is unwilling to come and testify for some reason ranging from fear of harm coming to him or the witness has been compromised, their attendance has to be compelled. This is done through the use of witness summons and subpoenas. A subpoena is generally used in the HC while the witness summons can be used in both the Magistrates' Court and the HC.[585] There are two types of subpoenas. There is the *subpoena ad testificandi,* which is used when you want a witness to come and testify, *the subpoena duces tecum* which is used when you want a witness to come and tender a document only. The court has introduced a third type of subpoena, which is *subpoena ad testificandi duces tecum* and used to compel a witness to come to court to both testify and tender a document.[586]

591. The application for subpoena is by filling the praecipe in Form 26 and Form 28 under the HCCPR of Lagos and Abuja respectively. A subpoena is served personally but can be served by substituted means with the leave of court where personal service cannot be achieved. Refusal to appear after being subpoenaed is contempt of court. A subpoena remains in force from the date of issue until the trial of the action in which it is issued.

592. Any person required to attend court to testify or produce a document is entitled to payment for expenses and loss of time occasioned by his attendance.

593. There is also the procedure where either party in an action can apply for discovery and inspection of documents in the possession of the adverse party. A notice to produce a document can also be given by a party in his pleadings to the opposing party. These have earlier been discussed in paragraph 382 above.

---

584. Section 218 of the Evidence Act 2011.
585. Order 34 Rule 16 HCCPR Abuja and Order 32 Rule 16 HCCPR Lagos.
586. *Lasun v. Awoyemi* (2009) 16 NWLR (Pt 1168) 513 (CA).

§2. DEPOSITIONS BY WITNESSES

594. The deposition of witnesses in a case is frontloaded with the writ of summons in the case of the claimant and with the statement of defence with regard to the defendant. The deposition contains the oral evidence of a witness that he wants to give in court. It does not become evidence before the court until the witness adopted it in court. It must contain all material evidence that a party intends to put through that witness. Where counsel intends to tender documents through the witness, reference to such documents must be made in the deposition. The witness statement is sworn by the witness in the registry of the court before a commissioner of oath.

§3. DEPOSITION BY THE PARTIES THEMSELVES

595. There is no obligation that a party must be a witness in his case. Where counsel represents a party, such a party need not attend the proceedings in court. But where the case of the party requires that the party testify in the case has decided by the party's counsel, the deposition of such a party is also frontloaded with the party's pleadings. The deposition is similar to that of a witness. One difference is that for the deposition of a party it will contain the relief the party is seeking.

§4. EXPERT EVIDENCE

596. The opinion of a witness is generally inadmissible. This is contained in section 67 of the Evidence Act 2011. The evidence of an opinion of a witness on a subject on which he is not held out to be an expert or has not demonstrated his expertise is inadmissible as held in the case of *Baytide Nig Ltd v. Aderinokun*.[587]

However, under sections 68–76 of the Evidence Act 2011 exceptions to this general rule is provided where the opinion of a witness would be admitted. The witnesses would be people specifically skilled (experts) in the field in which they are expressing their opinion through scholastic knowledge or professional attainment or through the acquisition of practical experience in the relevant field.[588] As such a person can be an expert by reason of qualification or experience gathered in the relevant field. The Evidence Act 2011 also permits the evidence of non-experts with respect to opinions on handwriting or finger impression. The areas where the opinions of experts are admissible in evidence are foreign law, customary law or custom, science or art. Where the court has to form an opinion as to these issues, the opinion of experts on that point is admissible.

597. The opinion of a non-expert is admissible on handwriting or finger when the court has to form an opinion as to the person by whom a document was written or signed. The opinion of any person acquainted with the handwriting of the person

587. (2013) 15 NWLR (Pt 1377) 374 (SC).
588. *Okereke v. Umahi* (2016) 11 NWLR (Pt 1524) 438 (SC).

by whom it is supposed to be written or signed that it was or was not written or signed by that person is admissible. Here the person acquainted with the handwriting in question need not be a handwriting expert. What the law requires is that such a person has seen that person write, or has received documents purported to be written by that person in answer to a document written by himself or under his authority and addressed to that person. A witness opinion on a person's handwritten will also be admissible if the person in the ordinary course of business has documents submitted to him purportedly written by that other person. For example, a confidential secretary to a chief executive can be called to give his opinion with regard to a document purportedly written by the chief executive.

598. The opinions and conclusions which an expert proffers before a trial court must be supported by scientific analysis otherwise his evidence would be valueless or worthless.[589] The court is not bound to follow the opinion of an expert especially when such opinions are contradictory and not consistent with normal conduct and human happenings as held in the case of *Oando (Nig) PLC v. Adijere W/A Ltd.*[590] Also if on the proven facts a judge can form his own conclusions without help then the opinions of an expert is unnecessary. The court has the power to determine whether expert evidence is required on an issue or not. In *Brown v. State* the SC held that:

> A trial court has the right to determine whether the issue on which a party purposes to adduce expert evidence is one that requires such degree of skill and knowledge as to be outside the experience of the court … 'an expert opinion is admissible to furnish the court with scientific information which is likely to be outside the experience and knowledge of a judge … if on the proven facts, a judge or jury can form their own conclusions without help, then the opinion of an expert is unnecessary'.[591]

§5. Affidavit

599. An affidavit is a statement of fact made voluntarily and confirmed on oath. It is headed in the cause and matter in which it is sworn. It carries the suit number and names of the parties. It is written in numbered paragraphs and in accordance with the Oath Act contains a mandatory clause called the oath clause that is usually the last paragraph in the affidavit.

Facts contained in an affidavit constitute evidence, and the court can properly act on it without calling for oral evidence. The facts deposed to in an affidavit by the deponent should either be from personal knowledge or from information, which he believes to be true. When such belief is derived from information received from

589. *Supra.*
590. (2013) 15 NWLR (Pt 1377) 374 (SC).
591. (2017) 4 NWLR (Pt 1556) 341 (SC).

another person, the deponent must state the name of his informant with reasonable particulars of the informant and the time, place and circumstance of the information.[592]

600. Documents attached to an affidavit are regarded as exhibits and should be consistent with the facts/depositions averred in the affidavit. It is signed by the deponent, dated and sworn at the registry of the court where the action is filed or the affidavit is sworn before a commissioner for oath. At the Federal HC, HC and Magistrate Court of the Federal Capital Territory (which practice is now common in most jurisdictions in Nigeria) the deponent is required to affix his passport photograph to the affidavit. Where an affidavit is made in support of application in a matter before a court, the respondent in such application who is served with an affidavit will if he intends to oppose the application be required to file his own affidavit commonly referred to as counter affidavit. The counter affidavit must specifically deny averments in the affidavit as held by the SC in *Nwosu v. Imo State Environmental Sanitation Authority*.[593] However, where the respondent who is opposed to an application seeks to rely only on points of law to oppose the application or he seeks to rely on facts already before the court, he need not file a counter affidavit. Where there are conflicts in affidavit evidence the court shall call for oral evidence to resolve the conflict.[594] Where there is documentary evidence attached to any of the affidavit, the court can also resort to it in resolving the conflict. It is pertinent to note that the conflicts referred to here that the court is required to resolve are material conflicts.

§6. Inspection by Judge

601. Sometimes in the course of a trial the need arises for the court to visit either the scene of dispute or the subject matter of litigation. This is usually the case where oral evidence refers to the existence or condition of any material thing other than a document. For example, in disputes bordering on declaration of title to land, boundary dispute, claims arising from nuisance, where evidence points to real evidence on the land like land beacons, physical evidence of the act of nuisance and the like. In such instances, the court may require the production of such material thing for its inspection or the court may inspect any moveable or immovable property the inspection of which may be material to the proper determination of the question in issue. The visit of a court to a place to inspect any movable or immovable property in this regard is commonly termed a court's visit to the locus in quo. The issue of the court's visit to the locus in quo can be raised by the court on its own motion or on application by any of the parties. The purpose of the visit is to give the court a clear picture of the evidence given in court that may not be properly appreciated without an onsite inspection.

592. Section 115(3)(4) of the Evidence Act 2011.
593. (1990) 2 NWLR (Pt 135) 688 (SC).
594. Section 116 of the Evidence Act 2011.

Procedure for the Conduct of a Visit to Locus in Quo

602. When the court has made an order for the court to move to the locus in quo, the manner the inspection is conducted is provided for under the Evidence Act 2011.[595] There are two ways the court may conduct the visit. The court can be adjourned to the place where the subject matter of the inspection may be, and the proceedings of the court shall continue at that place until the court further adjourns back to its original place of sitting or to some other place of sitting. The alternative is that the court can attend the place and make an inspection of the subject matter only, and evidence, if any, of what transpired there is given in court afterwards.

603. Where there is non-compliance with these procedures, the court has held that it would not nullify the proceedings unless the party seeking to nullify the proceedings can show that the non-compliance has occasioned a serious miscarriage of justice.[596]

604. It must be noted that the parties and their representatives are to be present during the visit and must also fully participate therein.

595. Section 127 *ibid.*
596. *Unipetrol (Nig) Plc v. Adireje (W/A) Ltd* (2004) AFWLR (Pt 231) 1238 at 1303 (CA).

Part VIII. Particular Proceedings

Chapter 1. Interpleader Summons Proceedings

605. Relief by way of interpleader may be granted where the person seeking the relief is under liability in respect of a debt and there are two or more persons making adverse claims to it.

It is applied for in the following circumstances:

(a) Where a person is under liability in respect of a debt or money or goods and he expects to be sued in respect of that debt or money by two or more persons making adverse claims to it. For example, Mr A is a tenant of Mr B. Mr B dies leaving two sons both of whom are laying claims to being the new landlord to Mr A whose rent is due. Mr A knows he is indebted but does not know who is entitled to the rent. To avoid paying to a wrong person, he approaches the court through interpleader proceeding for the court to interplead on his behalf with regard to the conflicting claims.

(b) In a situation when a sheriff while executing a court's judgment is faced with a claim to money or goods taken by a person other than the judgment debtor. For example, a Sheriff goes to execute the judgment of a court on a property supposedly belonging to the judgment debtor. But someone other than the judgment debtor comes up to say the property belongs to him. The sheriff can approach the court to interplead for him with regard to the conflicting claims. The court has held that persons other than the Sheriff who are genuinely aggrieved by reason of attachment of their property are not excluded from instituting interpleader proceedings in court.[597]

Procedure for Commencing Interpleader Proceedings

606. Order 47 Rule 1 HCCPR Lagos and Order 48 Rule 1 HCCPR Abuja provide for the procedure for commencing interpleader proceedings, which is by originating summons but when made in a pending suit by interlocutory summons. For the application to be granted, the applicant should by his affidavit in support of the application satisfy the following conditions:

597. *Ogbuchi v. Deputy Sheriff BSHC* (2015) 8 NWLR (Pt 1460) 172 (CA).

(a) the property is in the applicant's possession;
(b) he claims no interest in the subject matter in dispute other than for charges or cost;
(c) he does not collude with any of the claimants; and
(d) he is willing to pay or transfer the subject matter into court or as may be directed by court.

607. Where the applicant is a sheriff or another officer charged with the execution of a court's judgment, the provision of section 34 of the SCPA applies.

608. On hearing the application, the court may, where the question is one of law and the facts are not in dispute, decide the question without directing the trial of an issue or order that a special case be stated for the opinion of the court.

Where the rival claimants having been served failed to appear or appears but failed to comply with any order made after the appearance, the court may make an order declaring such claimant and any other person claiming under the claimant forever barred against the applicant and any other person claiming under the applicant but the order shall not affect the rights of claimants as between themselves.

Chapter 2. Proceedings for Appointment of Representatives for Class Actions

609. This is a type of representative action but different from the regular representative actions in the sense that the group of people in class actions are not ascertainable and can sometimes cover a range of persons whose cause of action may not have arisen. It is captured under the broad spectrum of public interest litigation. There are special cases where the court may appoint representatives to commence a class action under the HCCPR. They are:[598]

(a) administration of an estate;
(b) property subject to a trust;
(c) land held under customary law as family or communal land; or
(d) the construction of any written instrument including a statute.

The HCCPR Abuja makes more extensive provisions. In addition to the above categories of actions suitable for class action, it includes proceedings based on torts or any other class action.[599]

In these cases the court will be satisfied if:

- The person, the class or some members of the class interested cannot be ascertained or readily be ascertained.
- The person, the class or some members of the class interested if ascertained cannot be found.
- Though the above could be found it is expedient for the purpose of efficient procedure that one or more persons be appointed to represent the others.

A judge may make the appointment and the decision given in the proceedings shall be binding on all the persons or class of persons.

In addition, the HCCPR Abuja provides that notice of appointment made by the court and all processes filed in court shall be served on a person(s) so appointed and published in a National Newspaper (Order 13 Rule 15 HCCPR Abuja).

598. Order 13 Rule 15(a)–(d) HCCPR Abuja and Order 15 Rule 13 HCCPR Lagos.
599. Order 13 Rule 15(e) HCCPR Abuja.

Part IX. Seizure for Security and Enforcement of Judgments

Chapter 1. Seizure for Security

§1. Proceedings

I. Mareva Injunction

610. This is a special type of injunction that attaches temporarily the property or asset (which is not the subject matter of the dispute) of a defendant who, the claimant has reasonable cause to believe, intends to dissipate such property or asset to frustrate any possible judgment in favour of the claimant. This procedure also has its roots in the common law as it was established in the English case of *Mareva Compania Naviera S.A. v. International Bulkcarriers.*[600] This principle is applicable in Lagos and Abuja by section 2 of their HCCPR, which provides that in the case of a lacuna in the HCCPR the court shall adopt such procedure, as may do substantial justice between the parties concerned. In the case of *Sotuminu v. Ocean Steamship Nig Ltd.*[601] The court in Nigeria laid down the following conditions for the grant of a Mareva injunction:

(a) the applicant must show that he has a cause of action against the defendant, which is justiciable within jurisdiction;
(b) that there is real and imminent danger of the defendant removing his assets from within jurisdiction;
(c) the applicant must make full disclosure of all relevant facts/full particulars of the assets within jurisdiction must be given;
(d) the balance of convenience must be in favour of the applicant; and
(e) undertaking as to damages.

611. This injunction is applied by way of a motion ex parte supported with an affidavit and a written address. The court may direct the plaintiff to put the defendant on notice to furnish sufficient security in fulfilment of any decree that may be made against him. The affidavit in support of the application should contain the

600. (1980) I AER 213.
601. (1992) 5 NWLR (Pt 239) 1.

specification of the property required to be attached, the estimated value of the property and a declaration that to the applicant's belief and information the defendant is about to dispose of or remove his assets from within jurisdiction.

§2. Judicial Review

612. The respondent whose assets are attached can bring an application for the court to review the order of interim attachment of the assets. The grounds for such application include:

(a) the fact that the applicant has misrepresented facts in obtaining the order; and
(b) the respondent is ready to give security for the action in the event that the applicant is successful.

Chapter 2. Enforcement of Judgments

§1. Enforcement of Domestic Judgments

I. Proceedings

613. This is the process of effecting the orders and decisions of the court. Ordinarily, judgments of court ought to be obeyed voluntarily by parties that such orders are directed at. In practice, some amount of force is usually needed for orders of court to be obeyed. The SCPA regulates enforcement of judgments in Nigeria. Execution of court judgments is under the exclusive legislative list, and as such can only be legislated upon by the National Assembly of Nigeria.[602] Most states in Nigeria have adopted the SCPA as laws in their states.

A. *Methods for Enforcement and Execution of Judgments*

614. The method to be adopted to enforce a particular judgment is a function of the nature of judgment delivered. It may be a money judgment, an order of possession, etc.

Money judgments can be enforced in the following manner.

1. Writ of *Fieri Facias* or Writ of Fifa

615. It is also referred to as writ of execution. It is issued first against the moveable properties of the judgment debtor. However, wearing apparels, bedding of the judgment debtor or his family or his implements of trade to the value of NGN 10 are exempted.[603] The judgment creditor applies for it and pays the necessary filing fees. After the writ is issued, the bailiffs of the court will execute the judgment against the moveable properties of the judgment debtor.

If no moveable property of the judgment debtor can with reasonable diligence be found or such is insufficient to satisfy the judgment debt and cost of execution, the judgment creditor shall by a motion on notice supported with an affidavit apply to the HC (as an inferior court of record cannot issue a writ against the immoveable properties of a judgment debtor) for a writ of execution against the immoveable properties of the judgment debtor.[604]

Order IV Rule 16 of the Judgment Enforcement Rules provides that the affidavit in support of the application must contain the following:

(a) steps already taken to enforce judgment and the effect;
(b) amount left unsatisfied; and

602. Item 57 Part 1 of the Second Schedule to the 1999 Nigerian Constn.
603. Section 25(a) SCPA 2004.
604. Section 44 SCPA 2004.

(c) the fact that no moveable property or such that can satisfy the judgment debt can with reasonable diligence be found.

Upon the hearing of the application, the court may grant it if it appears that the writ of attachment and sale may lawfully issue against such immoveable properties. The procedure for carrying out the execution is contained in Orders IVV and VII of the Judgment Enforcement Rules 2004.

2. Garnishee Proceedings

616. This is another method of enforcing a money judgment. It envisages a situation where a judgment in favour of a judgment creditor has been given but is yet unsatisfied. Where the Judgment creditor is aware that there is someone within the jurisdiction of the court that gave the judgment who is indebted to the judgment debtor. He can apply to court to attach the debt to satisfy the judgment.[605] The debt owed by the third party must be due and payable to the judgment debtor. The application for garnishing proceedings is brought by the judgment creditor making an ex parte application supported by an affidavit and a written address. The affidavit that is as in Form 25 of the First Schedule to the SCPA 2004 (Order VIII Rule 3 of the Judgment Enforcement Rules requires the application for garnishee proceedings to be made by filing Form 25 only) shall state the following:

(a) names, addresses and occupation of the judgment creditor, the judgment debtor and the garnishee;
(b) the fact that judgment has been given and what date;
(c) the fact that judgment has been recovered and is still unsatisfied;
(d) the amount of the judgment that remains unsatisfied; and
(e) the fact that a third party (the garnishee) who is within the state is indebted to the judgment debtor.[606]

617. The judgment creditor shall attach to the application a CTC of the judgment if it was obtained in a court other than the court hearing the garnishee application.[607] The court upon the hearing of the application may make an order nisi asking the garnishing to come and show cause why he should not pay the amount. The order nisi and the affidavit must be served on the garnishee and the judgment debtor at least fourteen days before the hearing. Once the order nisi is made, it effectively attaches the amount with the garnishee. If at the hearing, the garnishee is

605. *UBA Plc v. Magama Nig Ltd* (2013) 16 NWLR (Pt 1379) 36 (CA).
606. Order 46 of the HCCPR Federal Capital Territory Abuja makes provision for garnishee proceedings that is largely similar. However, under this rule the garnishee order nisi shall be served on the garnishee at least fifteen days before hearing (as opposed to fourteen days under the SCPA 2004) and on the judgment debtor at least seven days after the order has been served on the garnishee and at least seven days before hearing (as opposed to fourteen days before hearing under the SCPA 2004). This is no problem with the service on the garnishee, but there appears to be a conflict with the SCPA 2004 with regard to the service on the judgment debtor.
607. Section 83(1) SCPA 2004.

unable to show cause, the order nisi becomes absolute and the garnishee shall be made to pay the amount to the judgment creditor/garnishor.[608] Service of the order nisi on the garnishee attaches the debt, and the garnishee will be in contempt of court if the debt is tampered with while the order is in place.

618. The SC has held in the case of *CBN v. Interstella Communications Ltd*[609] that it is imperative that an application for garnishee proceedings be brought in the jurisdiction where the garnishee resides as that is the purport of section 83 of the SCPA 2004.

619. The Court of Appeal of Nigeria has held in the case of *Zenith Bank Plc v. Omenaka*[610] that the judgment debtor is a mere passive or nominal party in a garnishee proceeding and cannot be heard.

620. An order nisi shall not be made where the money sought to be attached is in the hands of a public officer in his official capacity except consent to such attachment is first obtained from the AGF or AG of state. This is because section 84 of the SCPA 2004 requires the consent of the AG for monies kept by a public official to be attached by garnishee proceedings. However, the Court of Appeal of Nigeria held in the case of *Purification Techniques Nig Ltd v. A.G of Lagos State*[611] that monies held by the AG of Lagos State in the garnishee banks were not under the custody or control of the respondent or a public officer and as such not subject to the limitations in section 84 of the SCPA 2004. The court stated that where money belonging to a public corporation is in a commercial bank, the account could be garnished without the leave of the relevant AG. In a similar light, in the case of *CBN v. Interstella Communications Ltd*[612] the SC held that the CBN by virtue of sections 2(e) and 36 of the Central Bank of Nigeria Act 2007 acts as a banker to the Federal Government and the relationship between them is that of banker customer relationship. And as such the CBN is not a public official in the context of section 84 of the SCPA 2004, so the need to seek the consent of the AGF does not arise.

621. A garnishee bank has no business defending a judgment debtor by attempting to protect the money of the judgment debtor in its custody.

3. Judgment Summons

622. Where a judgment debtor makes a default in payment of any sum recovered against or any instalments under a judgment, the judgment creditor may apply to any court by filing a praecipe in the appropriate form for the issue of a judgment

608. Section 83(2) SCPA 2004.
609. (2018) 7 NWLR (Pt 1618) 294 (SC); *Darsey Digital Press Ltd & Anor v. Ayo & Anor* (2019) 1 NWLR (Pt 1654) 379 (CA).
610. (2016) LPELR-40327 (CA).
611. (2004) 9 NWLR (Pt 879) 665 (CA); *CBN v. Interstella Communications Ltd* (2018) 7 NWLR (Pt 1618) 294 (SC).
612. *Supra.*

summons.[613] The summons require the judgment debtor to appear and be examined on oath as to his means. The court at the conclusion of the investigation may order one or more of the following: the committal to prison of the judgment debtor or the attachment and sale of the judgment debtor's property or payment of the money by instalments or otherwise or a discharge of the judgment debtor from prison.[614]

4. Writ of Sequestration

623. The writ of sequestration is aimed at attaching the moveable and immovable properties of a judgment debtor not for the purpose of selling them but to hold unto them until the judgment debtor purges himself of contempt or until the court directs otherwise. While the attachment subsists, rents and profits collected may be used to pay the judgment debt. It is issued against the property of a judgment debtor for whom an order or warrant of arrest has been issued but the judgment debtor is not and cannot be found or is taken and detained in custody without obeying the judgment of the court.

Execution of a Court's Judgment Granting Possession of Land

624. Judgment for possession of land other than action involving landlord and tenant is enforced by way of writ of possession.[615]

Judgment of Court Ordering Possession of Premises by Landlord

625. An order of court granting possession of premises to a landlord is executed by way of a warrant for possession as provided for under the Recovery of Premises Act.[616]

Judgment for Delivery of Goods

626. Where a judgment orders the delivery of goods to the judgment creditor, such a judgment is executed by taking out a Writ of delivery.[617]

613. Section 55 SCPA 2004.
614. Section 63 SCPA 2004.
615. Order XI Rule 5 Judgment Enforcement Rules 2004.
616. Cap 544 LFN (Abuja) 1990.
617. Order XI Rule 4(1) Judgment Enforcement Rules 2004.

Enforcement of a Court's Judgment Made in One Judicial Division in Another Judicial Division

627. This is done by the Registrar of the court where the judgment is given sending the process for execution with a warrant in Form 11 to the SCPA to the Registrar of the court in the division where it is to be enforced. After enforcement, the executing Registrar fills Form 12 and sends to the Registrar of the court that originally gave the judgment.

Enforcement of Judgment Made in One State in Another State

628. Where a judgment creditor seeks to enforce a judgment delivered by a court in a state in Nigeria, in another state, the SCPA 2004 makes specific procedure for the judgment creditor to follow to achieve this.[618] The judgment creditor applies to the Registrar of the court that gave the judgment for the issuance of a certificate of judgment signed and sealed by the Registrar, and this is taken to the state of execution and registered with the Registrar of a court of similar jurisdiction. The Registrar enters it in the Nigerian Register of Judgments. By section 105(2) SCPA 2004, from the date of registration of such a judgment, the certificate of judgment shall be a record of the court in which it is registered and shall have the same force and effect in all respects as a judgment of that court and such like proceedings may be taken upon the certificate as if that court had given the judgment.

For the judgment to be enforced by the registering court the judgment creditor must file an affidavit in the court stating the following facts:

(1) that the amount for which the process is proposed to be issued is actually due and unpaid; or
(2) that an act ordered to be done remains undone; or
(3) that the person ordered to forbear from doing an act has disobeyed the order.

Where a third party had guaranteed the judgment debt, once the original debtor fails to pay the judgment debt, the guarantor becomes the judgment debtor, and the judgment creditor has the discretion to proceed against the guarantor to execute judgment without having to proceed against the judgment debtor.

II. Judicial Review

629. Where a judgment debtor brings an application for stay of execution pending appeal the court may if it considers the application meritorious, stay the execution of its judgment notwithstanding that a writ of attachment has been issued though not yet executed. The factors the court will consider in reviewing the execution of its judgment are:[619]

---

618. Sections 104–110 SCPA Cap S6 LFN 2004.
619. *Martins v. Nicanner Foods Co Ltd* (1988) 2 NWLR (Pt 74) 83.

(a) The chances of the appeal.
(b) The nature of the subject matter. Whether execution of the judgment will result in the destruction of the subject matter of litigation and as such applicant cannot be returned to status quo if the appeal succeeds.
(c) Whether if the appeal succeeds the applicant will reap the fruit of his appeal.
(d) Where the execution of the judgment will render nugatory any order or orders of the appellate court or foist upon the court a situation of complete helplessness.
(e) Where it is a monetary judgment the possibility of recovering the judgment sum from the judgment creditor.

The court may make an order of stay of the execution of judgment conditionally or unconditionally.

§2. Recognition and Enforcement of Foreign Judgments

I. Rules Applicable in the Absence of a Treaty

630. Where the country where the judgment was obtained from has no reciprocal arrangement with Nigeria for enforcement of judgment, the foreign judgment will be enforced in Nigeria by an action in common law. An action in common law requires bringing an action with the foreign judgment being the subject matter or cause of action. This can be brought under summary judgment procedure, as the claimant can believe that the defendant does not have a defence to the action. The foreign judgment must be final and conclusive and must have been made by a court of competent jurisdiction.

II. International Treatises

631. Nigeria recognizes and enforces judgments obtained in foreign courts in countries with which it has reciprocal enforcement of judgment conventions. Enforcement of such judgments is by registration of such judgment in an HC in Nigeria. The applicable treaties are the Foreign Judgment (Reciprocal Enforcement) Act[620] and the Reciprocal Enforcement of Judgment Act.[621] The Foreign Judgment (Reciprocal Enforcement) Act applies to judgments from countries with which Nigeria has reciprocal arrangement. Currently, no country has been listed. The Reciprocal Enforcement of Judgment Act applies to judgments of courts in the UK and the commonwealth countries. The SC has held in *Grosvenor Casinos Ltd v. Ghassan Halaou*,[622] that due to the fact that the AGF is yet to list the countries with

620. CAP F35 LFN 2004.
621. CAP 175 LFN 1958.
622. (2009) 10 NWLR (Pt 1149) 309 (SC). *See also Witt & Busch Ltd v. Dale Power Systems Ltd* (2001) 8 NWLR (Pt 716) 699 (SC).

which Nigeria has such reciprocal arrangement under the Foreign Judgment (Reciprocal Enforcement) Act, the provisions of the law is yet to come into operation. That leaves the Reciprocal Enforcement of Judgment Act as the only operative law regulating registration of judgments in Nigeria for the time being.

Procedure for Registration of a Foreign Judgment under the Foreign Judgment (Reciprocal Enforcement) Act

632. For a foreign judgment to be registered in Nigeria, the following procedure is followed:

(a) An application for leave to register a foreign judgment must be made by way of a petition ex parte and supported by an affidavit. This must be done within twelve months after the date of the judgment or any longer period as may be allowed by the registering HC.
(b) When an order granting leave to register the judgment is made on notice by the court the order shall be served on the judgment debtor.
(c) Notice in writing of the registration of the judgment must be served on the judgment debtor within a reasonable time after registration.
(d) Upon registration, the foreign judgment can be enforced the same way that a domestic judgment may be enforced.

Procedure for Registration of a Foreign Judgment under Foreign Judgment (Reciprocal Enforcement) Act

633. To register a foreign judgment under this law, the following procedure is taken:

(a) An application by way of a motion on notice to an HC in Nigeria is made within six years after the date of the judgment or where there is an appeal against the judgment, after the date of the last judgment given in the appeal.
(b) On the registration of the judgment by the court, the judgment will have the same force and effect as a judgment given by the court in which the foreign judgment is registered and can be enforced in the same way that a domestic judgment may be enforced.

634. Once a foreign judgment has been registered in an HC in any state in Nigeria, it can be enforced anywhere in Nigeria.[623] A court before whom an application to register a foreign judgment is made is not sitting on appeal over the foreign judgment. The court is required to find out whether or not the applicant complied with the requirement of Nigerian laws on registration of foreign judgments and if the court that gave the judgment had jurisdiction.

---

623. *See In Goodchild (carrying on business as H.C Beeton & co v. Onwuka* (1961) ANLR 163 (HC).

Limitations Involved in Enforcement of Foreign Judgment in Nigeria

635. There are some limitations on the registration of a foreign judgment. They are:

(1) Registration of a foreign judgment must be done within six years of its delivery (under the Foreign Judgment (Reciprocal Enforcement) Act CAP F35 Laws of the Federation of Nigeria (LFN) 2004) or twelve months (under the Reciprocal Enforcement of Judgment Act CAP 175 LFN 1958) after the date of the judgment.
(2) Judgments for recovery of taxes and penalties are not enforceable.
(3) The defendant must have voluntarily appeared/submitted to the jurisdiction of the foreign court during the trial in the foreign country.
(4) The judgment must have been given by a superior court of the country where it was given.
(5) The judgment must not be contrary to Nigeria's public policy.
(6) It must relate to a definite sum.

Part X. Arbitration

Chapter 1. Arbitrability

636. Arbitration is a dispute resolution mechanism involving one or more neutral parties appointed by the agreement of the disputing parties and who gives a binding decision. Certain disputes are better suited for resolution by arbitration as an alternative resolution mechanism to litigation. Disputes such as commercial disputes and labour disputes are suitable for resolution by arbitration. The ACA[624] that regulates arbitration in Nigeria applies to a commercial dispute. The long title to the ACA states as follows:

> An Act to provide a unified legal framework for the fair and efficient settlement of commercial disputes by arbitration and conciliation; and to make applicable the Convention on the Recognition and Enforcement of Arbitral Awards (New York Convention) to any award made in Nigeria or in any contracting State arising out of international commercial arbitration.

637. The First Schedule to the ACA contains the arbitration rules. Article 1 of the rules makes the rules applicable to any arbitration proceedings. However, where there is a conflict between the rules and the ACA, the provisions of the ACA shall prevail.

638. The ACA is of national application in Nigeria subject to the states in Nigeria domesticating it. Many of the states in Nigeria have enacted the ACA as a state law.

624. Arbitration and Conciliation Act Cap A18 LFN 2004.

Chapter 2. Arbitration Agreement and Party Autonomy

639. An arbitration agreement is an agreement in which two or more people agree that present or future disputes between them arising from a relationship between them shall be resolved by arbitration. It is usually part of a contractual agreement between the parties. The law allows parties a wide liberty with respect to the terms contained in the arbitration agreement. The only limitation is that the terms of the agreement must not be contrary to public policy in Nigeria. Every arbitration agreement must be in writing and can be contained in any of the following:[625]

(a) in a document signed by the parties; or
(b) in any means of communication between the parties such as exchange of letters, telex, telegrams, etc. which provide a record of the arbitration agreement; or
(c) in an exchange of points of claim and of defence where the existence of an arbitration agreement is alleged by one of the parties and not denied by the other.

640. It should be noted that any reference in a contract to a document containing an arbitration clause constitutes an arbitration agreement where such contract is in writing and the reference is of such a nature as to make the arbitration clause part of the contract.[626] Generally, an arbitration agreement is irrevocable. The exceptions are where the parties agree that it should be revocable or the arbitration agreement itself contains an intention that it is revocable or it is revoked by the leave of a judge. An arbitration agreement is not rendered invalid at the death of one of the parties. The agreement can be enforced by or against the personal representatives of the deceased party's estate.[627] An arbitration agreement does not oust the jurisdiction of the court. Before a submission to arbitration or an arbitral award is made, any of the parties can file an action in court. However, the other party can apply to the court to stay proceedings before it as the matter was brought to court prematurely having not first resorted to a resolution of the dispute by arbitration. The court is empowered to stay proceedings before it to enable the parties to explore the option of arbitration in resolving the dispute. Section 5(1) and (2) of the ACA provides:

(1) If any party to an arbitration agreement commences any action in any court with respect to any matter which is the subject of an arbitration agreement, any party to the arbitration agreement may, at any time after appearance and before delivering any pleadings or taking any other steps in the proceedings, apply to the court to stay the proceedings.
(2) A court to which an application is made under subsection (1) of this section may, if it is satisfied:

---

625. Section 1(1) ACA 2004.
626. Section 1(2) ACA 2004.
627. Section 3 ACA 2004.

(a) that there is no sufficient reason why the matter should not be referred to arbitration in accordance with the arbitration agreement; and
(b) that the applicant was at the time when the action was commenced and still remains ready and willing to do all things necessary to the proper conduct of the arbitration, make an order of stay of proceedings.

641. A party who seeks to apply for a stay of proceedings based on an arbitration agreement must not have taken any steps in the matter filed in court. It has been held that applying for extension of time to file statement of defence or delivery of statement of defence amounted to taking steps in a proceeding that is tantamount to a party waiving his right to apply for stay of proceedings based on an arbitration agreement.[628]

628. *Mainstreet Bank Capital Ltd v. Nigeria Reinsurance Corporation PLC* (2018) 14 NWLR (Pt 1640) 423 (SC).

Chapter 3. Composition of Arbitral Tribunal

642. The parties to an arbitration agreement have the liberty to determine the number of arbitrators to be appointed under the agreement. However, in the absence of this, and if within fifteen days after the receipt by the respondent of the notice of arbitration the parties fail to agree that there shall only be one arbitrator, the law provides that the number of arbitrators shall be deemed to be three[629] or three arbitrations shall be appointed.[630] Parties to an arbitration agreement are also allowed to specify in the agreement the procedure for the appointment of an arbitrator. This right of the parties is however limited in two instances namely:

(1) Where under an appointment procedure agreed by the parties:
   - a party fails to act as required under the procedure; or
   - the parties or two arbitrators are unable to reach agreement as required under the procedure; or
   - a third party including an institution fails to perform any duty imposed on it under the procedure.

(2) Where any of the three instances outlined above happens, any party may request the court to take the necessary measure unless the appointment procedure agreed upon by the parties provides other means for securing the appointment. The decision of the court is final.

643. Where the parties did not make provision in the arbitration as to the procedure for appointing arbitrators, the procedure to be adopted will depend on the number of arbitrators. Where the arbitrators are three, each party to the arbitration agreement shall appoint one arbitrator and the two thus appointed shall appoint the third. However, if a party fails to appoint one arbitrator within thirty days of receipt of a request to do so by the other party or if the two arbitrators fail to agree on the third arbitrator within thirty days of their appointments the appointment shall be made by the court on the application of any party to the arbitration agreement. The order of the court cannot be appealed against.[631] In the case of an arbitration where the arbitrator is one, where the parties fail to agree on the appointment of the arbitrator, the court shall make the appointment on the application of any party to the arbitration agreement made within thirty days of such disagreement. In any of the situations where the court is empowered to make the appointment of arbitrators, it shall have due regard to the qualifications required by an arbitrator as contained in the arbitration agreement and such other considerations as are likely to secure the appointment of an independent and impartial arbitrator.

644. An arbitrator who is approached for an appointment and knows of any reason or circumstance that can give rise to justifiable doubt as to his impartiality or

629. Section 6 ACA 2004.
630. Article 5 Arbitration Rules First Schedule to the ACA 2004.
631. Section 7 ACA 2004.

independence shall disclose such reason or circumstance to the parties to the arbitral agreement. This duty to disclose subsists even after the arbitrator is appointed and throughout the arbitral proceedings unless the arbitrator has previously disclosed the circumstance to the parties.[632]

The appointment of an arbitrator can be challenged under two grounds namely:[633]

(1) if circumstances exist that give rise to justifiable doubts as to his impartiality or independence; or
(2) if he does not possess the qualification agreed by the parties.

Procedure for Challenging the Appointment of an Arbitrator

645. The parties can in their arbitral agreement state the procedure for challenging the appointment of an arbitrator. Where this is the case, the procedure so stated will be followed. In the absence of an agreed procedure by the parties contained in the arbitral agreement, a party who wishes to challenge the appointment of an arbitrator shall within fifteen days of becoming aware of the constitution of the arbitral panel or becoming aware of the circumstance that can cast justifiable doubts on the impartiality of the arbitrator, send to the arbitral tribunal a written statement of the reasons for the challenge. The arbitral tribunal shall decide on the challenge under the arbitrator whose appointment is challenged withdraws from office or the other party agrees to the challenge.[634]

Termination of the Appointment of an Arbitrator

646. Arbitrators who have been appointed to be part of an arbitral panel can have their mandate terminated if any of the following occurs:[635]

(a) The arbitrator withdraws from office.
(b) The parties agree that the arbitrator's appointment be terminated because of inability of the arbitrator to perform the functions of an arbitrator. It should be noted that withdrawal from office or termination by the parties due to inability of the arbitrator to perform the functions of the office of an arbitrator shall not be construed to mean that there exists any ground or circumstance that can likely give rise to any justifiable doubts as to the arbitrator's impartiality or independence.
(c) Where the arbitrator fails to act without undue delay for any other reason.

632. Section 8(1)(2) *ibid.*
633. Section 8(3) ACA 2004.
634. Section 9 *ibid.*
635. Section 10 *ibid.*

Where an arbitrator's appointment is terminated, a substitute arbitrator shall be appointed by the same procedure that was adopted in appointing the arbitrator whose mandate is terminated.[636]

636. Section 11 *ibid.*

Chapter 4. Interim Measures and Preliminary Awards

647. An arbitral tribunal is empowered by law to make interim orders for the protection of the subject matter of the dispute between the parties. This may be done before or during an arbitral proceeding. A party who requires the tribunal to make such orders is required to make an application requesting that the other party in the proceedings be made to take interim measures of protection as the arbitral tribunal may consider necessary to make in the circumstance with respect to the subject matter of the dispute. A party can also apply that a party be ordered to provide security in connection with the order for interim measure of protection.[637]

637. Section 13 ACA 2004.

Chapter 5. Conduct of Arbitral Proceedings

648. Generally, an arbitral proceeding commences on the date the notice of arbitration is received by the respondent. However, where the parties agree otherwise then the agreement of the parties will stand. The conduct of arbitral proceedings is in accordance with the arbitration rules as set out in the First Schedule to the ACA 2004. Where the arbitration rules do not contain provision in respect of any matter related to a particular arbitral proceeding, the arbitral tribunal may subject to the provisions of the ACA conduct the proceedings in such manner, as it considers appropriate so as to ensure a fair hearing.[638] Proceedings before an arbitral tribunal are regulated by the agreement of the parties and the ACA 2004. The court has held that the provisions of the Evidence Act 2011 do not apply to arbitral proceedings.[639] A notice of arbitration shall contain the following information:[640]

(a) a demand that the dispute be referred to arbitration;
(b) the names and addresses of the parties;
(c) reference to the arbitration clause or the separate arbitration agreement that is invoked;
(d) reference to the contract out of or in relation to which the dispute arose;
(e) the general nature of the claim and an indication of the amount involved, if any;
(f) the relief the claimant is seeking;
(g) a proposal as to the number of arbitrators where the parties had not previously agree on it.

649. Except the parties agree otherwise, the arbitral tribunal shall decide whether the arbitral proceedings shall be conducted by either of the following methods:[641]

(a) holding of oral hearings for the presentation of evidence or arguments; or
(b) on the basis of documents or other materials; or
(c) a combination of oral hearings and on the basis of documents or other materials.

The tribunal shall hold hearings at an appropriate stage of the proceedings on request by any of the parties except the parties have agreed that there will be no hearings.

Every statement, document or other information supplied to the tribunal by a party must be made available to the other party as well. Where documents, statements or other information are supplied to one party by the tribunal, it must also be given to the other party.[642] Also any expert report upon which the tribunal will rely

638. Section 15(2) ACA 2004.
639. *Adamen Publishers (Nig) Ltd v. Abhulimen* (2016) 6 NWLR (Pt 1509) 431 (CA).
640. Article 3(3) Arbitration Rules, First Schedule to the ACA 2004.
641. Section 20(1) ACA 2004.
642. Section 20(3) *ibid.*

for its decisions must be available to the parties.[643] When taking oral evidence from witnesses the tribunal is empowered to administer oath to or take affirmation of the parties and witnesses appearing unless otherwise agreed by the parties.[644]

Power of the Tribunal to Appoint Experts

650. Except the parties by agreement decides otherwise, the arbitral tribunal may appoint one or more experts to report to it on specific issues to be determined by it.[645] In furtherance of this, the tribunal may require a party to give to the expert appointed, any relevant information, or produce or allow access to, any document, goods or other property for inspection. In addition, except the parties agree otherwise, the expert may at the request of any of the parties or where the arbitral tribunal considers it necessary, after delivering his report (oral or written) participate in a hearing where the parties can put questions to the expert and present expert witnesses to testify on their behalf on the point of issue.[646]

651. It is to be noted that an arbitral tribunal shall not decide *ex aequo et bono* or as *amiable compositeur* unless the parties agree otherwise. It shall decide in line with the terms of the contract between the parties taken into account the usages or trade applicable to the transaction.[647]

Notice of Hearings

652. The arbitral tribunal shall give to the parties adequate advance notice of any hearings and meetings of the tribunal held for the purposes of inspection of documents, goods and other party.

Power of the Court to Order Attendance of Witnesses

653. An application by a party, a court or a judge may order that a writ of *subpoena ad testificandum* (used for compelling the attendance of a witness to come and testify in court only) or *subpoena duces tecum* (used in compelling attendance of a witness for the purpose of tendering documents only) shall be issued to compel the attendance before any arbitral tribunal of a witness wherever he may be within Nigeria.[648] However, no person shall be compelled under any such writ to produce any document that he could not be compelled to produce on the trial of an action.[649] It is pertinent to add at this point that online dispute resolution is practised in Nigeria where the parties agree to it and many arbitration hearings are conducted successfully online.

---

643. Section 20(4) *ibid.*
644. Section 20(5) *ibid.*
645. Section 22(1) ACA 2004.
646. Section 22(3) *ibid.*
647. Section 22(3)(4) *ibid.*
648. Section 23(1) *ibid.*
649. Section 20(6) *ibid.*

Power of the Court to Grant Anti-arbitration Injunction

654. The court has the power to grant anti-arbitration injunction. But the court usually approaches an application for such injunction with caution especially when a foreign tribunal will be affected. Such applications are only granted under exceptional circumstances.

Language of the tribunal

655. The language or languages to be used in the tribunal is as determined by the parties. In the absence of the parties' agreement, the arbitral tribunal shall determine the language or languages to be used taking into cognizance the circumstance of the case.[650] The language or languages agreed by the parties or chosen by the tribunal shall be the language used in any written statements by the parties, in any hearings, award, decision or any communication in the arbitral proceedings. The tribunal can also order that any documentary evidence be accompanied with a translation of the documentary evidence into the language used in the arbitral proceedings.

650. Section 18 *ibid.*

Chapter 6. Arbitral Award

656. At the end of arbitral proceedings the tribunal will make an award. The award is the final determination of issues referred to an arbitral tribunal. It is generally a final decision and it is binding and enforceable. The award shall be in writing and signed by the arbitrator or arbitrators as the case may be. Where the arbitral tribunal is made up of more than arbitrator and one or more of them did not sign the award, the signatures of a majority of all the members of the tribunal shall suffice if the reason for the absence of any signature is stated.

Types of Award

657. Awards can be categorized as final interim, partial, agreed, additional, interlocutory or default.[651]

(1) Agreed or consent award:
This is an arbitral award on agreed terms. Where in the course of the arbitral proceedings, the parties settle the dispute, the tribunal shall issue an order for termination of the proceedings and shall where it deems it fit at the request of the parties record the settlement in the form of an arbitral award on agreed terms. An award made in this circumstance has the same status and effect as any other award on the merit of the case.[652]

(2) Final award:
This is an award given after full trial in arbitral proceedings where all the issues submitted for arbitration have been determined. Article 32 of the Arbitration rules states that such award is final and binding on the parties.

(3) Additional award:
Sometimes the arbitral tribunal makes an award but omit to make awards with respect to some claims presented to the arbitral tribunal. On the request of any of the parties the tribunal can make additional awards with respect to those claims that were omitted in the awards.

(4) Interim award:
The issue of the power of an arbitral tribunal to make interim orders had earlier been discussed. *See* paragraph 646 above. Such interim orders may be established in the form of an interim award.

(5) Interlocutory award:
In the course of an arbitral proceeding, the arbitral tribunal may make orders on procedural issues. These are necessarily interlocutory in nature. P.O.

651. David St John Sutton and J. Gill, *Russel on Arbitration* 280 (23rd ed., Sweet & Maxwell 2007); *see* also Arts 32(1), 34(1) and 37 of the Arbitration rules, First Schedule to ACA 2004.
652. Section 25 ACA 2004 and Art. 34 of the Arbitration rules, First Schedule ACA 2004.

Idornigie is of the view such orders are not awards *stricto sensu* but just procedural orders.[653] I totally agree with this view but state that it is classified as a type of award only to depict that it is one of the pronouncements an arbitral tribunal can make.

(6) Partial award:
A partial award is one given with respect to a part of a monetary or other type of issues submitted to an arbitral panel leaving the rest to be decided on subsequently.

(7) Default award:
This is an award given in the absence of participation of one of the parties in an arbitral proceeding. Except the parties had otherwise agreed, where the respondent fails to state his defence without showing sufficient cause, the tribunal may continue the proceedings and make an award. Again, where any of the parties fail to appear at a hearing or fail to produce documentary evidence as requested by the tribunal, the proceedings may continue and an award is made.[654] The award given in any of these circumstances is a default award.

Content of an Arbitral Award

658. An arbitral award shall contain the following:[655]

(a) The reasons on which the award is made. However, if the parties agree that no reasons should be given or the award is a consent one, then it shall not contain reasons.
(b) The date it was made.
(c) The place of the arbitral proceedings as agreed by the parties or as chosen by the arbitral tribunal whichever applies. The place of the arbitral proceedings is deemed to be the place of the award.

A copy of the award shall be delivered to the parties. An arbitral proceeding terminate at the given of a final award by the tribunal.[656] However, the arbitral proceeding can also be terminated when the tribunal issues an order of termination of proceeding. This can happen in the following circumstances:[657]

(1) When the claimant withdraws his claim. This will however, not lead to the issuance of an order of termination of proceedings if the respondent objects to the withdrawal and the tribunal finds a legitimate interest on the part of the respondent to see to the final settlement of the dispute.

653. P.O. Idornigie, 'The Making of Arbitral Awards', in *Alternative Dispute Resolution and Some Contemporary Issues: Legal Essays in Honour of Hon. Justice I.T. Muhammad* 291 (A.A. Ibrahim ed., M.O. Press & Publishers Ltd 2010).
654. Section 21 ACA 2004.
655. Section 26 ACA *ibid.*
656. Section 27(1) *ibid.*
657. Section 27(2) *ibid.*

(2) When the parties agree that the proceedings be terminated.
(3) When the tribunal finds that continuation of the proceedings has become unnecessary or impossible.

659. Generally, when an arbitral proceeding is terminated, the tribunal becomes functus officio with respect to its mandate. However, the law allows the tribunal even after termination of the proceedings by the giving of an award to correct in the award, any errors in computation, clerical and typographical errors or errors of a similar nature. It can also give an interpretation of a specific point or part of the award. In addition, the tribunal can make an additional award as to the claims presented in the arbitral proceedings but which were omitted from the award. A party, who wants the tribunal to take any of the above actions with respect to the award it has given, must make such request to the tribunal within thirty days of the receipt of the award (unless another period has been agreed upon by the parties) and put the other party on notice. Where the tribunal considers the request justified, it shall within thirty days of the receipt of the request (for a request of an additional award, the tribunal shall within sixty days from the receipt of the request make the additional award) make the correction or give the interpretation and such shall become part of the award. The tribunal may where necessary extend the time limit within which it may correct errors, give an interpretation or make an additional award. It should be noted that the tribunal can *suo motu* within thirty days from the date of making an award correct any errors of computation, clerical, or typographic and errors of similar nature.

Chapter 7. Recourse Against Arbitral Award

660. A party to an arbitral proceeding who is aggrieved with an award made by the arbitral tribunal may apply to the HC to set aside the award. This the party may do within three months of the making of the award. The circumstances where the court may set aside arbitral awards are:[658]

(a) If the party applying to set aside the arbitral award furnishes proof with regard to any of the following:
   - that a party to the arbitration agreement was under some incapacity;
   - that the arbitration agreement is not valid under the laws that the parties have indicated should be applied or it is not valid under Nigerian laws;
   - that the party applying to set aside the award was not given proper notice of the appointment of an arbitrator or of the arbitral proceedings or was not able to present his case; or
   - that the award concerns a dispute that is not contemplated and outside the ones submitted for arbitration; or
   - that the award contains decisions on matters not submitted for arbitration and decisions on those submitted, and as such where these decisions can be separated, the ones on matters not submitted for arbitration should be set aside; or
   - that the composition of the arbitral tribunal or the procedure adopted was not in line with the agreement of the parties. It must be noted however that for the court to rely on this fact to set aside an arbitral award, the agreement of the parties in this regard must not conflict with the provisions of the ACA 2004 for which no derogation is allowed. Where there was no agreement between the parties, the court may aside the arbitral award where the applicant proves that the composition of the tribunal and the procedure adopted by it was not in accordance with the provisions of the ACA 2004.

(b) The court may set aside an arbitral award on the application of a party where an arbitrator has misconducted himself or where the arbitral proceedings or award has been improperly procured. The court may also on the application of a party remove an arbitrator who has misconducted himself.

(c) The court may set aside an arbitral award if the court finds any of the following facts correct with regard to the arbitral proceedings:
   - The subject matter of the dispute is not one that can be settled by arbitration under Nigerian laws.
   - The award is against public policy of Nigeria.

661. The court have held that from the combined reading of sections 29, 30, 48 and 52 of ACA 2004 the following are the grounds for setting aside an arbitral award:[659]

---

658. Sections 29 and 48 ACA 2004.
659. *Adamen Publishers (Nig) Ltd v. Abhulimen supra.*

(a) The arbitrator is guilty of misconduct.
(b) The arbitral proceeding or award was procured improperly.
(c) A party to the arbitration agreement is not valid under the laws which the parties have indicated should be applied or under the law of the country where the award was made.
(d) There is failure to give proper notice to a party of the appointment of an arbitrator or of the arbitral proceedings or a party was otherwise unable to present their case.
(e) The award deals with a dispute not contemplated by or not falling within the terms of the arbitration agreement.
(f) The award contains decisions on matters beyond the scope of the arbitration agreement.
(g) The composition of the arbitral tribunal or the adopted procedure was not in accordance with the agreement of the parties or with the law of the country where the arbitration took place.
(h) The subject matter of the dispute is not capable of settlement by arbitration under the laws of Nigeria.
(i) The recognition or enforcement of the award is against public policy.

Misconduct by an Arbitrator

662. That an arbitrator has misconducted himself is a ground for setting aside an arbitral award. It becomes necessary then to discuss what constitutes misconduct on the part of an arbitrator. The court has held that misconduct of an arbitrator will occur in the following instances:[660]

(a) where the arbitrator fails to decide all the matters which were referred to him;
(b) where by the award the arbitrator decided matters that were not in fact included in the agreement of reference;
(c) where the award is inconsistent or in ambiguous;
(d) if there has been irregularity in the proceedings; irregularities here include where the arbitrator failed to give the parties notice of the time and place of meeting, where the agreement required the arbitrator to take evidence orally but the arbitrator instead received affidavit evidence, where the arbitrator refused to hear the evidence of a material witness, where the arbitrator failed to have foreign document translated into the agreed language and where the arbitrators (where they are more than one) did not act together;
(e) where the arbitrator failed to act fairly towards both parties; examples of unfair acts include: where the arbitrator hears one party but refuses to hear the other, deciding the matter in default of defence without warning, taking instructions from or talking with one party in the absence of the other, taking evidence in the absence of one party or both parties, not giving one party the opportunity of

660. *Atoju v. Triumph Bank Plc* (2016) 5 NWLR (Pt 1505) 252 (CA).

considering the other party's evidence, making the award without calling witnesses when he had promised to do so, deciding the case on a point not put to the parties, and so forth;
(f) if the arbitrator refuses to make a case stated or allow an opportunity of applying to the court for an order directing the statement of a special case;
(g) if the arbitrator delegates any part of his authority to a stranger, one of the parties or a co-arbitrator;
(h) if the arbitrator accepted the hospitality of one of the parties being done for the purposes of influencing the arbitrator's decision;
(i) if the arbitrator acquires an interest in the subject matter of the arbitration or is otherwise interested;
(j) if the arbitrator took a bribe from either of the parties.

663. When the HC sits over an application to set aside an arbitral award, the court sits in its original jurisdiction in a supervisory capacity. Its role in this instance is not that of an appellate court, as it cannot delve into the merit of the case. Rather, its role is the same as when it is exercising its jurisdiction to hear an application for judicial review. The court is to simply look at the award and decide whether based on the applicable law as understood by the arbitrator and shown on the face of the award, the arbitrator had complied with the law as perceived by him whether rightly or wrongly. The court has to put itself in the same position as the arbitrator and not above him. Upon hearing an application to set aside an arbitral award, the court either sets aside the award, upholds it or remits it back to the arbitrators to reconsider a particular aspect. The court's jurisdiction to interfere with the award of an arbitrator is limited to setting outside the award or sending it back to the arbitration for reconsideration of specific issues. This was the position held by the SC in *MTN (Nig) Communication Ltd v. Etuk Hanson* in its interpretation of sections 29, 30 and 48 of the ACA.[661]

664. The decision of the HC setting aside an arbitral award or refusing an application to set aside an arbitral award is a final decision of the HC and can be appealed against as of right. The issue of whether or not an appellant aggrieved with the decision of an HC on an application to set aside an arbitral award can appeal from the decision as of right came up in *MTN (Nig) Communication Ltd v. Etuk Hanson*,[662] and the court held that by section 241(1)(a) of the 1999 Nigerian Constn the appeal is as of right.

661. (2017) 18 NWLR (Pt 1598) 394 (SC).
662. *Ibid.*

Chapter 8. Recognition and Enforcement of Awards

665. An arbitral award irrespective of the country where it is made is binding and enforceable. Any of the parties can apply for the recognition and enforcement of an arbitral award. A party applying for the enforcement of an arbitral award must exhibit the following documents to his application:[663]

(a) the duly authenticated original award or a duly certified copy of it;
(b) the original arbitration agreement or a duly certified copy of it;
(c) where the award or arbitration agreement was not made in English, a duly certified translation of them into English.

666. The application for recognition and enforcement of an arbitral award should be made after the expiration of three months of the making of the award. This is because, the law allows any of the parties, within three months of the making of the award apply, to set it aside. So it is until after this period has expired and any of the parties did not utilize the window of applying to set it aside that application for its recognition and enforcement can be made. The court in *Atoju v. Triumph Bank Plc.*[664] held that the right to apply to the court for the recognition and enforcement of an arbitral award could only arise after the expiration of three months allowed for a party to apply for it to be set aside.

667. Any of the parties to an arbitration agreement can request the court to refuse recognition or enforcement of an arbitral award. The conditions that must be present for the court to refuse to recognize or enforce an arbitral award are substantially the same as the conditions for the setting aside of an arbitral award which have already been discussed in paragraph 660.

668. Section 52(2) ACA 2004 provides that the court where recognition or enforcement of an award is sought or where application for refusal or enforcement is brought may irrespective of the country in which the award is made refuse to recognize or enforce the award if the party against whom it is invoked furnishes the court with proof that he was not giving proper notice of the appointment of the arbitrator or of the arbitral proceedings or that he was not able to present his case. This provision was upheld by the Court of Appeal of Nigeria in *Continental Sales Ltd v. R. Shipping Inc.*[665]

663. Section 51 ACA LFN 2004.
664. *Supra.*
665. (2013) 4 NWLR (Pt 1343) 67 at 88 (CA).

Part XI. Mediation

Chapter 1. Legislation and Definitions

669. Mediation is a dispute resolution mechanism that entails a neutral third party helping the disputing parties to resolve their dispute. Mediation can be defined as a facilitative process whereby disputing parties consent to a third party guiding them towards the resolution of their dispute. Usually, mediators cannot impose a decision on the parties, but their roles are limited to assisting the parties in resolving their dispute using mediation techniques and skills and to guide the parties into a resolution of the dispute. These techniques and skills include ability to open up the channel of communication between the parties, promoting understanding in the parties of the issues involved in the dispute thereby helping the parties understand themselves better, channelling the parties' focus towards their interest and the ways to resolve the issues between them. It is a voluntary process that parties must agree to. However, the state in order to promote the use of ADR methods in general and mediation in particular has established structures such as the multi-door courthouse (which is a court-connected ADR centre) and the Court of Appeal of Nigeria Mediation Programme respectively. As a result, the use of these structures has been incorporated into the rules/laws of the courts.[666]

Similar to the characteristic of any ADR mechanism, mediation has many features and advantages over and above litigation. The following are some of the basic characteristics of mediation:

(a) It is party controlled.

The disputing parties have full control of the mediation process unlike litigation where the parties take a back seat. The mediation is only in the process to guide the parties and cannot impose his views or decision on the parties. As an expert in the process, the job of the mediation is to avail the parties of his knowledge and experience in resolving and then take a back seat and allow the parties to make the decision on how to resolve their dispute. This power of control of the process is a chief point for ADR processes apart from arbitration and in the long run is an important factor that puts an obligation on the parties to execute whatever decision they arrive out.

666. The HCCPR of the various jurisdictions enjoins the court to encourage parties to settle their dispute through alternative dispute resolution mechanism such as mediation. For examples, Order 19 HCCPR Abuja and Order 28 HCCPR Lagos. Also the Court of Appeals Rules 2016 provide for the Court of Appeal Mediation Programme in Order 16 of the Rules.

(b) It is voluntary.

The party of their own volition chooses the process. They may have been advised that mediation is an appropriate means of resolving their dispute, but ultimately it was their decision to opt for mediation. The issue of voluntariness pops up at every stage of the mediation process. This ranges from choosing the process as a means to resolving their dispute to the choice of mediator, to the decision to participate in the process and then the choice to reach an amicable settlement or not.

(c) The process is flexible.

The parties have a wide leverage to choose their mediator, the venue for the mediation sessions, the time for carrying out an agreed settlement and so on.

(d) Confidentiality.

A mediation process enjoys confidentiality. The parties choose who they want to be present at the mediation sessions, and the mediator is under an obligation not to disclose any information received by reason of the mediator's position. In addition, whatever information divulged by any of the parties cannot be used in any court proceeding as they are made without prejudice to any action the parties may take in the future.

670. In Nigeria, there is no substantive legislation on mediation. It is simply regulated by the agreement of the parties. Having said that, it is pertinent to state that where the mediation is done at a multi-door courthouse in Nigeria (several jurisdictions in Nigeria have a multi-door courthouse annexed to the HC. For example, Lagos, Abuja and Port Harcourt) or the Court of Appeal of Nigeria Mediation Programme, the process will be guided by the mediation rules of the multi-door courthouse which is incorporated into the multi-door courthouse Practice Direction made by the Chief Judge of the state. For example the Practice Direction on Mediation Procedure for the Administration of Mediation Matters at the LMDC 2008 and the AMDC Practice Direction 2003 made by the Chief Judge of the Federal Capital Territory, Abuja. There is also the Negotiation and Conflict Management Group's code of conduct for mediators. However the general trend in private mediation has been to have a flexible mediation process without any specific rules. Also, there are Mediation Centres established by the government, where parties in dispute can request for mediators as well as conduct mediation proceedings. An example is the Citizens' Mediation Centre Lagos, which provides a non-adversarial forum for the mediation and settlement of disputes between parties who voluntarily agree to mediation.

Chapter 2. Rights That Can Be Subject to Mediation

671. It is not all disputes that are suitable for mediation. There are some factors that determine whether mediation is a suitable means of resolving a dispute. These include where there is need to preserve pre-existing relationship between the parties, the nature of the dispute, psychological considerations and so on. As such matrimonial causes, child custody, parental actions, inheritance, chieftaincy or personal actions in tort, disputes arising from employment, contractual disputes, commercial disputes, etc. are disputes suitable for mediation.

Chapter 3. Mediation Agreement

672. Parties may by agreement in a contract stipulate that in the event of a dispute arising from their contract, the disputes should be submitted to a mediation process. This constitutes the mediation agreement. Where there is the existence of such a clause in an agreement entered into by parties, then the parties have to result to it first before embarking on any other means of resolving their dispute. Where a matter is filed in court without the parties first resorting to mediation, on application by a party, the court will stay proceedings to enable the parties explore the mediation option. However, due to the fact that mediation is voluntary, where one party is unwilling to respect the mediation clause and pursue mediation as a means of resolving their dispute as contained in their agreement, though the other party may seek to enforce the observance of the clause, the process is unlikely to be successful. In addition, parties are free to choose and end the process at any time and sanctions are imposed on a party who refuses to cooperate with the mediation process as agreed in the mediation agreement.

Chapter 4. Persons/Institutions That Can Act as Mediators

673. Generally, anyone can act as a mediator as long as the disputing parties consent. This is particularly so in private mediation. However, in a mediation process that occurs within a structured framework such as the multi-door courthouse, citizens' mediation centre and the Court of Appeal mediation process mediators are selected by the parties from a list of neutrals. The list of neutral consists of recognized professionals in different dispute resolution mechanism as complied by the relevant authorities. This does not however take away the right of disputants to opt for their own choice of mediator though such a person is not on the list of neutrals.

Chapter 5. Mediation Procedure

674. Since there are statutory regulations for mediation in Nigeria, it is mainly the mediation rules of the multi-door courthouse that provide a guide for the mediation programme. These rules are also not mandatory as parties are free to adopt whatever procedure suits them. In practice, the procedure for resolving a dispute through mediation is divided into stages and there are basically five stages in a mediation process.

§1. Stages of Mediation

I. The Preparation Stage

675. In this stage, all the preliminary issues to be considered before a mediation process takes off is considered. Issues such as a mediation agreement, appointment of mediator, fees for the mediator and how it is to be paid, date and venue for the mediation, approach to be adopted are all considered and agreed upon. The parties will at this stage get to meet the chosen mediator, and they have to meet the mediator together to avoid suspicion or likely bias of any kind. The mediator should in the first meeting with the parties enquire as to the parties' experience with mediation processes and if there is a pending suit in court and what the parties have done or intend to do about such pending litigation in the wake of the mediation process.

II. The Opening Stage

676. In this stage, all that will be required by the parties is laid out. Where the parties have not met with the mediator before, introduction of the mediator to the parties will take place. Where there will be other persons in attendance in the mediation sessions such as witnesses for the parties, they will also be introduced. At this stage, the mediator makes what is usually called the opening statement. In the statement, the mediator intimates the parties of the ground rules regulating the process, the confidentiality of the process and the role of the mediator as an impartial and neutral facilitator of the process. Where the parties have written statements of their issues, the mediator can at this stage make a summary of them. Where otherwise, the parties may be allowed to make their opening statement outlining the issues as perceived by them.

III. The Discovery Stage

677. In this stage, the mediator would have heard the parties state the issues, as each perceives it and would have discovered the real issues in controversy between the parties. Many a time, it may be different from what the parties had earlier stated. At this point, the mediator helps the parties identify and focus on their interest with regard to disputes rather than their rights. The mediator could resort to meeting the parties in caucuses or jointly to achieve this goal.

IV. The Negotiation Stage

678. Having identified the interest of the parties, the mediator in this stage steers the parties towards bargaining an amicable settlement of the dispute. The mediator may suggest to the parties possible solutions with regard to each issue between them but cannot impose such suggestions on the parties. The parties are at liberty at all times to decide how they wish to resolve the dispute.

V. The Settlement Stage

679. Here they parties have reached an agreement, and the mediator has a clear picture of the areas of agreement. For avoidance of doubt, the mediator should read out the agreed terms of settlement between the parties to them for their confirmation. Where the parties are able to amicably settle the dispute, the settlement is reduced into writing and signed by the parties. When the parties have signed the written settlement agreement, it becomes binding on them.

Chapter 6. Settlement Agreement

680. Where a mediation session is successful, it will usually result in the parties coming to some form of agreement with regard to the disputes between them. The agreement is reduced into writing signed by all the parties as the settlement agreement. Where the parties are a pending court action with regard to the dispute and had undertaken mediation as an alternative means of resolving the dispute either on their own or as induced by the court, the settlement agreement is filed in court. The parties will request that the filed settlement agreement be made the judgment of the court. Where the court makes the settlement agreement its judgment, it is referred to as consent judgment. This can happen whether the mediation took place informally or at the court connected multi-door courthouse.

681. The settlement agreement can be filed in court if there was a pending suit in court or where there was no pending suit, a suit could be filed in court making the settlement agreement the subject matter of the suit. Mediation settlement agreements reached by parties at the LMDC are enforceable under the LMDC Law 2007. By section 19 of the LMDC Law, any settlement agreement duly signed by parties shall be enforceable as a contract by the parties and when such agreement is further endorsed by an ADR Judge or any other person as directed by the Chief Judge, it shall be deemed to be enforceable as a consent judgment of the HC of Lagos State. In addition, under Order 28 Rule 4(1) HCCPR Lagos, a decision reached at the LMDC may by leave of a judge be enforced in the same manner as a judgment or an order of the court. In Abuja, where a matter was referred to the AMDC by a judge before whom the matter is pending, the court or judge shall on the application of the parties enrol terms of settlement reached at the AMDC as consent judgment, and it shall have the same force and effect as a judgment. Where there was no pending case in court, the parties who had approached the AMDC may apply to an ADR Judge by a motion on notice for an order to enrol the decision or terms of settlement reached at the AMDC as consent judgment.

Chapter 7. Setting Aside a Settlement Agreement

682. Where a mediation agreement was filed in court by the parties and consequently made as the judgment of the court, it is a final judgment of the court, which can only be set aside on appeal. A party seeking to appeal against such a judgment is required to seek the leave of the court that gave it.[667]

667. *See* s. 241(2) of the 1999 Nigerian Constn.

Chapter 8. International Mediation

683. Where there is a cross-border dispute that requires mediation to resolve it, the law that will regulate the process will be the one chosen by the parties. This is because there is no legislation on mediation in Nigeria, but pockets of rules which are not binding on parties as mediation is essentially a private process and ultimately whatever rules the parties decide should regulate the process and will be applicable as long as it is not contrary to Nigeria's public policy.

Selected Bibliography

Adegoke, O.A., R.E. Badejogbin & M.E. Onoriode. *Law in Practice: Professional Responsibilities and Lawyering Skills in Nigeria*. Jos: Jos University Press Ltd, 2014.

Efevwerhan, D.I. *Principle of Civil Procedure in Nigeria*. 3rd ed. Enugu: Snaap Press Ltd, 2018.

Ibrahim, A.A. (ed.). *Alternative Dispute Resolution and Some Contemporary Issues: Legal Essays in Honour of Hon. Justice I.T. Muhammad CON*. Kaduna: M.O. Press & Publishers Ltd, 2010.

Obi Okoye, A. *Law in Practice in Nigeria (Professional Ethics and Skills)*. 2nd ed. Enugu: Snaap Press Ltd, 2015.

Stanley-Idum, M. & J. Agaba. *Civil Litigation in Nigeria*. 2nd ed. Lagos: Renaissance Law Publishers, 2018.

Selected Bibliography

Index

The numbers here refer to paragraph numbers.

www.ingramcontent.com/pod-product-compliance
Ingram Content Group UK Ltd.
Pitfield, Milton Keynes, MK11 3LW, UK
UKHW020136290926
15471UKWH00003B/522

9 789403 546216